Events in the City

Cities are staging more events than ever. Within this macro-trend, there is another less acknowledged trend: more events are being staged in public spaces. Some events have always been staged in parks, streets and squares, but in recent years events have been taken out of traditional venues and staged in prominent urban spaces. This is favoured by organisers seeking more memorable and more spectacular events, but also by authorities who want to animate urban space and make it more visible.

This book explains these trends and outlines the implications for public spaces. Events play a positive role in our cities, but turning public spaces into venues is often controversial. Events can denigrate as well as animate city space; they are part of the commercialisation, privatisation and securitisation of public space noted by commentators in recent years. The book focuses on examples from London in particular, but it also covers a range of other cities from the developed world. Events of different scales are addressed and, there is dedicated coverage of sports events and cultural events.

This topical and timely volume provides valuable material for higher level students, researchers and academics from event studies, urban studies and development studies.

Andrew Smith is a Reader in the Faculty of Architecture and the Built Environment at the University of Westminster, UK. Andrew is an urban geographer who specialises in tourism and events research. His first book *Events and Urban Regeneration* was published by Routledge in 2012.

Routledge advances in event research series
Edited by Warwick Frost and Jennifer Laing
Department of Marketing, Tourism and Hospitality,
La Trobe University, Australia

Events, Society and Sustainability
Edited by Tomas Pernecky and
Michael Lück

Exploring the Social Impacts of Events
Edited by Greg Richards, Maria deBrito and Linda Wilks

Commemorative Events
Warwick Frost and Jennifer Laing

Power, Politics and International Events
Edited by Udo Merkel

Event Audiences and Expectations
Jo Mackellar

Event Portfolio Planning and Management
A holistic approach
Vassilios Ziakas

Conferences and Conventions
A research perspective
Judith Mair

Fashion, Design and Events
Edited by Kim M. Williams, Jennifer Laing and Warwick Frost

Food and Wine Events in Europe
Edited by Alessio Cavicchi and Cristina Santini

Event Volunteering
Edited by Karen Smith, Leonie Lockstone-Binney, Kirsten Holmes and Tom Baum

The Arts and Events
Hilary du Cros and Lee Jolliffe

Sports Events, Society and Culture
Edited by Katherine Dashper, Thomas Fletcher and Nicola McCullough

The Future of Events and Festivals
Edited by Ian Yeoman, Martin Robertson, Una McMahon-Beattie, Elisa Backer and Karen A. Smith

Exploring Community Events and Festivals
Edited by Allan Jepson and Alan Clarke

Event Design
Social perspectives and practices
Edited by Greg Richards, Lénia Marques and Karen Mein

Rituals and Traditional Events in the Modern World
Edited by Warwick Frost and Jennifer Laing

Battlefield Events
Landscape, commemoration and heritage
Edited by Keir Reeves, Geoffrey Bird, Laura James, Birger Stichelbaut and Jean Bourgeois

Events in the City
Using public spaces as event venues
Andrew Smith

Forthcoming:

Event Mobilities
The politics of place and performance
Edited by Kevin Hannam, Mary Mostafanezhad and Jillian Rickly

Approaches and Methods in Events Studies
Tomas Pernecky

Visitor Attractions and Events
Locations and linkages
Edited by Adi Weidenfeld, Richard Butler and Allan Williams

Critical Event Studies
Karl Spracklen and Ian Lamond

Events in the City
Using public spaces as event venues

Andrew Smith

Routledge
Taylor & Francis Group

LONDON AND NEW YORK

First published 2016
by Routledge
2 Park Square, Milton Park, Abingdon, Oxon OX14 4RN

and by Routledge
711 Third Avenue, New York, NY 10017

Routledge is an imprint of the Taylor & Francis Group, an informa business

British Library Cataloguing in Publication Data
A catalogue record for this book is available from the British Library

Library of Congress Cataloging in Publication Data
A catalogue record for this book has been requested.

ISBN: 978-1-138-78885-5 (hbk)
ISBN: 978-1-315-76512-9 (ebk)

Typeset in Times New Roman
by Swales & Willis Ltd, Exeter, Devon, UK

MIX
Paper from
responsible sources
FSC
www.fsc.org   FSC® C013604

Printed and bound by CPI Group (UK) Ltd, Croydon, CR0 4YY

'City administered play has spilled beyond the spatial boundaries of the pitch, arena, concert hall and theatre to inhabit the wider public spaces of the street and city centre.'

(Hughes, 1999: 124)

'Instead of cultural organisations running programmes across a limited range of traditional venues such as concert halls, theatres, galleries and arts centres, a very large number of organisations . . . have become involved in staging events in many different spaces across the city.'

(Richards and Palmer, 2010: 27)

Contents

Figures

Boxes

Preface

The controversy surrounding the use of Greenwich Park for the London 2012 Olympic and Paralympic Games provided the inspiration for this book. This prolonged dispute got me thinking about the relationship between major events and public spaces. Living in London exposed me to a series of other examples – many of which feature here. My institutional situation has also been influential: I am a geographer interested in events located within a Faculty of Architecture and the Built Environment. This has helped me to address one of the key objectives of the book: to apply ideas from the established fields of urban design and urban studies to the emerging field of event studies.

Andrew Smith, June 2015

Acknowledgements

I would like to thank several people for helping me to research, edit and publish this book. I have worked with two academics on some of the research that is published here and both deserve credit. I have spent many enjoyable hours discussing public spaces and their commercialisation with Guy Osborn and some of the ideas and examples in this book have emerged from these conversations. I would also like to thank Graham Brown with whom I collaborated to collect survey data in Greenwich Park. Jo Thornhill helped me to edit the final draft of the text and Mason Edwards produced the two maps. Thank you to both. Finally, I would like to thank Emma Travis and Pippa Mullins from Routledge and the Advances in Events Research series editors who have supported this project since I first suggested it back in 2013.

Figures 6.1 and 7.1 were produced by Mason Edwards.

All the other figures were produced by the author.

Acronyms and abbreviations

AEG	Anschutz Entertainment Group
BBC	British Broadcasting Corporation
BEF	British Equestrian Federation
CBC	Canadian Broadcasting Corporation
CCTV	Closed Circuit Television
DCLG	Department for Communities and Local Government
DCMS	Department for Culture, Media and Sport
EAC	European Athletics Championships
EU	European Union
FIFA	Fédération Internationale de Football Association
GB	Great Britain
GLA	Greater London Authority
IAAF	International Amateur Athletics Federation
IMG	International Management Group
IOC	International Olympic Committee
JWP	Joint Working Party
LOCOG	London Organising Committee for the Olympic and Paralympic Games
NBA	National Basketball League
NFL	National Football League
NHL	National Hockey League
NIMBY	Not In My Back Yard
NOGOE	No to Greenwich Olympic Events
ODA	Olympic Delivery Authority
RBKC	Royal Borough of Kensington and Chelsea
SEL	Sports and Entertainment Limited
UEFA	Union of European Football Associations
UK	United Kingdom
US	United States

1   Introduction

The established geography of events is shifting. More organised events are being staged in public spaces: in our parks, streets and squares. Public spaces in cities have always been used for events, but they are increasingly being used as venues for commercial and ticketed occasions. Events that were once confined to purpose built arenas are now being staged in public spaces. These trends provide the focus for this book.

The main aim of this book is to explore the use of public spaces as event venues. The book will explain this trend, explore the debates that surround it and, perhaps most importantly, it will examine the outcomes for public spaces. Parks, streets and squares change when they are used for events; they are reconfigured temporarily and in more enduring ways. In the urban design literature events are often regarded as valuable tools to animate cities: to revive them and make them feel more alive. Others argue that events are part of wider processes that are undermining our public spaces. For example, Spracklen et al. (2013: 167) worry about 'blind obedience to the belief in events as transformative' – something that ignores the way some events contribute to more problematic processes: of commercialisation, privatisation and securitisation. These contrasting interpretations are introduced and explained in this book.

From the city as stage, to the city as staged

In a book about using urban spaces as event venues, it is impossible to ignore the idea of *the city as a stage*. This is a very established notion and one that is commonly used without referring directly to the role of cities as event venues. For example, Atkinson and Laurier (1998: 200) cite the idea that our increasingly sanitised, historicised cities are 'three dimensional stage sets for tourism'. Every stage needs actors and analysing city users as performers on a stage is an increasingly common perspective within urban studies. Other theatrical metaphors are also used to understand the production and consumption of urban experiences. This book illustrates that, rather than merely an apt metaphor or analogy, the idea of our cities as stages is now a reality. Urban parks, squares and streets are used as stages for a variety of commercially-, community- and politically-oriented events. As Richards and Palmer (2010: 27) state, cities have become 'a stage across which a succession of events is paraded'. References to stages suggest cities are merely platforms or backdrops for events, but this underestimates the role of the city in urban events. When these events are staged in public spaces, the city is as important as any other content. Public space is 'performed' (Thörn, 2006; Merx, 2011) and the contemporary city is not just a stage; it is *staged* (Colomb, 2012).

In this book the process through which events affect the urban spaces they occupy is referred to using the term 'eventisation'. It is worth emphasising that city space is not the only phenomenon that has been 'eventised'. There has been a more fundamental eventisation of society (Žižek, 2014) and an associated eventisation of history – with times past reduced to a series of supposedly pivotal events. As Pine and Gilmore (1999) emphasise, there has also been an eventisation of our economy. To add value in contemporary capitalism, products are now staged – rather than merely manufactured or promoted. These complex processes provide the context for this book. However, the intention is not to explore them in depth. Instead, the aim is to explore the way urban public spaces have been eventised by staging official events in them.

The focus of this book

Events come in various forms. The focus in this book is official events that are pre-planned and sanctioned by urban authorities. Belghazi (2006: 105) suggests these 'rigorously planned events' provide entertainment, but are designed to achieve important objectives – hence they represent 'serious fun'. Unplanned events and those which are work oriented (conferences, meeting etc.) are not addressed directly in this book. This focus on planned, leisure events does not mean other types of events are deemed to be less important. The critical urban studies literature is already replete with texts that address unofficial, radical, spontaneous events. Events that challenge the status quo and established interests are particularly associated with the situationists (Pløger, 2010). Protest events are not addressed directly in this book, but are covered by other texts (e.g. see Lamond and Spracklen, 2015).

There are certain advantages of the purposeful focus on official events. Focusing on pre-planned, sanctioned events helps to explore the way recent trends are driven by official urban policy and event management objectives. It also helps to avoid a drift into a more general analysis of urban activities and trends. In any case, having official events as the focus does not mean looser, unsanctioned events are completely ignored. As several authors point out, official events provide the framework or inspiration for unofficial happenings (Stevens and Shin, 2014), something that is discussed further in Chapter 4. And just because events are 'official' does not mean they are experienced in the manner intended: authorised meanings are negotiated and resisted in ways not necessarily envisaged by organisers (see Chapter 8).

Focusing on official events doesn't entirely resolve definitional problems as it is difficult to define what we really mean by an event. Events are themed occasions which are ultimately defined by their limited time frame and their spatial focus. Urban events are defined by their contrast to the everyday – they are deliberately designed to be different from the normal functioning of a city. The implicit objective is to create a differentiated space and time: a time 'out of sync' with clock time and an 'out of place' space. How well this is achieved determines the event experience. Planned events are perhaps best defined by Jakob (2013: 448) who deems them to be the: 'deliberate organisation of a heightened emotional and aesthetic experience at a designated time and space'. Despite these specifications, it is still sometimes difficult to distinguish between events and other time limited phenomena. For example, it seems artificial to separate events from public art, street markets or pop-up installations.

To examine the urbanisation of events, this book addresses events staged in public spaces that might have previously been confined to more conventional arenas or non-urban locations. Good examples include sport events and music festivals. Unlike other key texts on events and cities (Richards and Palmer, 2010), this book addresses both cultural events and sport events. This is important because sport events are increasingly being staged in urban public spaces and these events are neglected in the existing literature which is skewed towards cultural festivals. This book examines a wide range of events both in terms of their theme and in terms of their scale – from small-scale events to mega-events.

Alongside clarifying the types of events covered by this book, it is also worth emphasising the types of spaces addressed. The focus is events staged in urban public spaces: but public space is a complex and contested concept. Chapter 2 examines different interpretations and explains how the term is defined and used in the rest of the text. This book not only examines urban public space in general, but centrally located urban public spaces in particular. Indeed, one of the main themes addressed in Chapter 3 is the way events have relocated to city centres in recent years. This is part of a wider trend in which the modern project to establish separate reservations for leisure and play in cities has been undermined (Stevens, 2007).

In addition to the spatial focus, there is also a focus on certain types of places. The text examines large cities in developed countries particularly those in the UK, US, Australia and Canada. There is a specific emphasis on capital cities (Berlin, Canberra, Edinburgh, Helsinki, London, Paris, New York, Singapore, Valletta) as these are very good examples with which to illustrate some of the difficulties reconciling global (external) objectives and local (internal) priorities. Other global cities in Canada and Australia also feature: Melbourne, Montreal, Toronto, Sydney and Vancouver. Inevitably there is a UK focus and several large British cities are covered: Belfast, Birmingham, Bristol, Edinburgh, Glasgow, Leeds, Manchester and Newcastle. At the site level, various examples of streets, squares and parks are cited, including some which will be familiar to many readers; the Champs-Elysées (Paris), Trafalgar Square (London), and Central Park (New York).

For various reasons, the book focuses particularly on London. The author lives and works in London and this is where much of his events research has been conducted. There are more objective reasons for this spatial focus too. London is one of the world's great events cities. Many events staged here have a long history, but the authorities have made specific efforts in recent years to bring new events to London and to use events strategically. Since 2005, events strategy has been dominated by attempts to optimise the legacies of the 2012 Olympic Games. During this period there has also been a concerted attempt to use London's public spaces as event venues. The city's parks, squares and streets have always been used for events, but this practice has intensified in recent years. Since 2000, London has elected a Mayor with executive powers in various public policy domains which govern how events are staged in public spaces: e.g. tourism, city marketing, policing, transport and emergency services. Accordingly, various organisations linked to the Mayor's Office have led efforts to use events more strategically. Famous public spaces like Trafalgar Square, Hyde Park and Regent Street have been programmed as venues, but this approach has also been adopted in lesser known spaces: for example, in Gillett Square, Finsbury Park and Berwick Street. This provides a fascinating context within which to study the use of public spaces as events venues.

Staging events in urban public spaces: a brief history

This book examines recent trends – in particular the increasing use of public spaces as event venues. However, it is important to note that centrally located, public spaces in cities have always acted as venues for events. Indeed, some parks, streets and squares were specifically conceived as arenas. In other instances, events were always intended as one function that influenced the design of public spaces (Foley et al., 2012). Historians have noted the way some urban spaces were developed for mass rituals (Hobsbawn, 1983), with Red Square in Moscow cited by Roche (2000) as a good example. Therefore, to provide context – and to allow an evaluation of whether we are seeing anything genuinely new – a brief review of the history of staging events in public spaces is included below. This review also provides an opportunity to introduce some of the themes addressed in the rest of the book.

Carnivals and fairs

Many participatory events such as carnival are essentially street events which have long inhabited the public realm of our cities. Although there are clear parallels with Saturnalia (a Roman festival), carnival was inadvertently created in the eleventh century via the insistence by religious authorities that worship should be more formal and less exuberant. This pushed religious festivity into the streets (Ehrenreich, 2007). Other religious occasions provide historical examples of the close connection between events and public spaces. Many city squares originated as extensions of churches – these were places for people to gather before and after worship, but also sites for religious ceremonies when churches could not accommodate everyone (Giddings et al., 2011). St. Peters Square in Rome remains the best example of where a city square still performs this function.

During the seventeenth, eighteenth and nineteenth centuries, civic elites were fearful of carnival events because of the likelihood of disorder and disobedience. In Northern Europe, the rise of Protestantism and industrialisation meant carnival became unpalatable for ruling authorities (Ehrenreich, 2007). Accordingly, events were shut down or shifted to the edges of towns and cities. Interestingly, some of these discontinued events have been revived in recent years and the Venice Carnival is a very good example. This hedonistic event reached its peak in the 1600s when people travelled long distances to engage in a debauched and elongated celebration that featured various illicit activities permitted for carnival (e.g. masking, gambling and prostitution) alongside more formal entertainment that was invented for the event (e.g. opera). The Venice Carnival fitted awkwardly with the new political landscape of the eighteenth century and disappeared when the Republic of Venice fell in 1797. Hopes of a revival dissolved when the event was banned during the Austrian occupation in the nineteenth century (Davis and Marvin, 2004).

Like many other cultural events the Venice Carnival was re-established in the latter part of the twentieth century. The event was revived in 1979 and twenty five years later it was attracting over 100,000 visitors a day (Davis and Marvin, 2004). However, Davis and Marvin (2004) suggest that corporate involvement means Venice's event is now a 'privatised carnival'. This reflects more general concerns discussed later in this book about the privatisation and commercialisation associated with contemporary events (see Chapter 5). One of the problems with the revived Carnival, apart from its over-commercialisation, is the unsuitability of Venice's public realm for large public events: Davis and Marvin (2004) suggest the complex topography is unsuited to grand processions. Nevertheless, the Venice Carnival provides a good example of the way in which urban street events flourished in pre-modern societies and then disappeared, before being revived in the post-modern era.

In the UK, the fair and the fairground perhaps represent the most significant events staged in urban public spaces during the seventeenth, eighteenth and nineteenth centuries. These events were staged in the public realm: on a city's streets, squares or common land. Fairs were originally staged to coincide with Saints days, but they evolved into something removed from religious celebrations. It is hard to represent their diversity in the small amount of space available here, but they usually involved a wide variety of attractions including music, plays, processions, jousting, archery, wrestling, cock fighting, duck hunting, juggling, tumbling, fire-eating, pole climbing and dancing (Harcup, 2000). Fairs were raucous events, but it would be a mistake to see them as unregulated festivity: men at arms were present in case things got out of control (Harcup, 2000). This is sometimes ignored by commentators who tend to eulogise about the liberating qualities of historical fairs and bemoan the securitised nature of contemporary events.

The Nottingham Goose Fair is regarded as the UK's oldest surviving example of a Fair. Its long history is illustrated by the fact it already existed before it was awarded a Royal Charter in 1284. Charters were granted to ensure that the Crown benefitted from the revenues earned; highlighting that there has always been a financial imperative for staging events in public spaces. This links to the discussion in Chapter 3 that explores why contemporary urban governments want to hire their spaces to event organisers. Nottingham's Goose Fair was staged in the city's Market Square, but like many other fairs it was eventually moved from its central location to the edge of the city (in 1929). The Goose Fair has since grown in size; and is still staged every year, albeit for a shorter period of time.

By the mid-nineteenth century fairs were much tamer affairs than they had once been. Industrial bosses were keen to end the culture of extended revelry as these events interrupted the work patterns of mill and factory workers. It is well known that many UK fairs were ended by the Fairs Act 1871 which sought to close down events deemed to be corrupting and dangerous. It is perhaps less well known that, at the same time, other fairs were actually established to promote moral values. Newcastle's Town Moor Fair was established in 1882 as a Temperance Festival to encourage people not to drink or gamble. There is a nice contrast here with the supposed attractions of the Venice Carnival in that the inaugural edition of Newcastle's event was judged a success because there 'were no card sharpers, no gambling booths and few people under the influence of drink' (National Fairground Archive, 2015). Newcastle's Fair involved a mix of different events, including a traditional fair, but it was also fused with more modern elements: sports, competitions, brass band concerts and military displays. There was a dispute in the early part of the century because of the condition of the site at the end of the Fair (National Fairground Archive, 2015). This argument is often voiced by opponents of contemporary events staged in public spaces (see Chapters 5 and 6 of this book). Tellingly, in both Nottingham and Newcastle, attempts to move or discontinue these Fairs have always been resisted by the respective local authorities who have always benefited financially from the rents paid by organisers.

Just as several carnivals have been reinstated to many urban public spaces in the past thirty years, there have also been attempts to reinstate fairs. Contemporary fairs usually take the form of funfairs (a mix of rides, amusements and stalls; see Figure 1.1), making them less interesting than their more diverse antecedents. For example, in 1992, Leeds introduced an annual St Valentines Fair into its central streets and the event soon became the biggest street fair in Europe (Harcup, 2000). In line with the ideas discussed in Chapter 4 about the ways events reconfigure urban space, this funfair temporarily transformed the centre of Leeds into a place of play. The local authority used the event to promote the streets of Leeds city centre as 'a theatre of unscripted spectacle' (Harcup, 2000). Ultimately, the event became a victim of its own success. The Fair became too big and noisy for the streets on which it was staged (The Headrow, Cookridge Street and Portland Way) and in 2001 the event was moved to land adjacent to Elland Road, the city's football stadium, just outside the city centre. This case highlights that attempts to restore festivity to a city's streets are complicated and controversial – something discussed further in Chapters 5 and 6 of this book.

Fairs staged in the seventeenth and eighteenth centuries also helped to conceive circus acts and circuses in general – events that still appear in our parks and open spaces. Early circuses also inhabited the public realm more widely – when they entered a town performers would often parade around the streets to promote the impending events. The earliest versions were dominated by equestrian acts, and the name circus is derived from the circular performance area used by pioneers of these events. There is a nice parallel here with the equestrian case studies addressed in Chapters 6 and 8 of this book. There is also a link to the public realm in that many of London's most famous street intersections are known as circuses because of their shape. By the early nineteenth century circuses were touring all over Europe and America using temporary structures: or tenting as it became known (The Victoria and Albert Museum, 2015).

Modern events

Alongside carnivals, fairs and circuses, sport events also have a long history of being staged in urban public spaces. The earliest forms of football were played in the streets of UK towns and cities. As Giulianotti (2011: 3298) points out, early football games were 'often part of public carnivals during festive periods'. However, by the late 1800s sport had become a more regulated and spatially constrained practice. Boundaries were implemented to create specialised fields of play. However, there were still events staged in street settings. For example, at the turn of the twentieth century, running events like the Olympic marathon (re-est. 1896) and cycling events such as the Tour de France (est. 1903) were staged in the public realm. Soon after the invention of the automobile, motorsport races were staged on public streets, for example The Isle of Man TT Motorcycle Races (est. 1911) and the Monaco Grand Prix (est.1929).

By 1900 public parks had been opened in many cities, but these were usually conceived as formal spaces for promenading and the passive consumption of

Figure 1.1 A funfair on Blackheath Common, London.

landscapes. Bandstands were erected and events were staged but parks were not used for festive occasions. As Brewer (1997: 65) states, British public parks were genteel gardens where entrepreneurs 'hired musicians, opened places to sit and eat, and commissioned sculptors and artists to shape pleasing but edifying environments'. Raucous events did not feature; and it was some time before organised sport was accepted as a normal function of a public park. Pioneering examples such as Peoples' Park (Halifax, UK) 'forbade games altogether' (Taylor, 1995: 215). However, parks established later in the nineteenth century (e.g. Wolverhampton, Altrincham) did include provision for active recreation (e.g. cricket, football) in their design (Taylor, 1995). Festivity and more spectacular forms of entertainment tended to be staged in 'pleasure gardens', a slightly different type of venue where people had to pay to enter. Pleasure gardens hosted dancing, fireworks, fetes and spectaculars (Taylor, 1995) and in recent years there have been efforts to restore these event spaces. For example, Vauxhall Pleasure Gardens (1661–1859) in London has recently been regenerated and reopened to the public.

Perhaps the most famous temporary use of a park for an event in the early modern era was the 1851 Great Exhibition staged in Hyde Park, London. The Crystal Palace was constructed to stage the Exhibition and, although this structure was removed afterwards, the event left some important legacies for Hyde Park and for public spaces. The Great Exhibition helped to democratise Hyde Park both symbolically and legally. Millions of people from all over the country came to see 'the world for a shilling' and this was the first time many attendees had mingled in public with people from other social classes. The event was linked to the Crown Lands Act (1851) which transferred the management of London's Royal Parks from the monarch to the government. Subsequently, Hyde Park became not only a place for elitist conspicuous consumption, but a renowned site for protests and demonstrations by the working classes (Roberts, 2001). Since the infamous Rolling Stones concert in 1969 (see Figure 1.2), Hyde Park has also become a commercial events venue. This case study and the ways political sites are being re-semanticised as event spaces are discussed in Chapter 5 of this book.

With the onset of the modern era (circa 1851) sport and culture were increasingly formalised and institutionalised. As the city became larger and denser there was less space to host events. So in the industrialised city leisure was confined to particular zones, rather than comprising an integrated part of a city's function and activity. Modernisation often meant creating specialised structures and spaces in which to stage more regulated events. The urbanisation of events noted in this book partly counters this trend, although as shall be seen, this doesn't necessarily make events more accessible, or less regulated (see Chapter 5). The contemporary city is still regarded as a highly zoned entity and some authors such as Spracklen et al. (2013) feel that public spaces for free leisure (or politics) remain spatially marginalised, i.e. restricted to the city margins.

The idea of an urban festival as a festival of the arts was also conceived during the late nineteenth and early twentieth centuries. Events in Bayreuth (est. 1876) and Salzburg (est. 1920) were early examples, with other cities less affected by Second World War (e.g. Edinburgh, est. 1947) taking the lead in the post-war period. Pioneering festivals often emerged in cities away from established urban

Figure 1.2 A water fountain commemorating concerts staged in Hyde Park, London. This is a strange choice of monument given the restrictions on taking water and other items into the events staged here. The fence erected every summer to secure the events site can be seen in the background.

centres, allowing them freedom from dominant cultural institutions (Quinn, 2005). This explains the rise of the Avignon Festival (est. 1947). These festivals pushed boundaries in a metaphorical sense in that they brought cutting edge art to cities, but they also pushed spatial boundaries. Urban arts festivals were instrumental in bringing elite arts out of concert halls and into public streets and squares. This was best exemplified in the fringe events that developed alongside more formal arts festivals, for example the Edinburgh Fringe (est. 1958). Pioneering examples of these festivals challenged the social and political order (Johansson and Kociatkiewicz, 2011). However, as the century progressed, they became more commercialised: they became more market oriented and their positive place based associations meant they were integrated into neoliberal place marketing agendas. This is illustrated well by Edinburgh's explicit branding as 'City of Festivals' (Jamieson, 2004) and complaints about the formalisation and commercialisation of the Fringe Festival (Lee, 2012). Edinburgh's commercial agenda can be linked directly to the way festival events are staged in central, public spaces. According to Quinn (2005) this spatial arrangement privileges tourists and excludes residents. The commercialisation of festivals reflected a wider trend in the late twentieth century – a period when official events became predominantly economic, rather than social phenomena.

Madden (2010) notes that in the US during the 1960s and 1970s, various financial, economic and social problems meant that a lot of public places – particularly parks – fell into disrepair. Dereliction meant that urban public spaces became unattractive to some users, often because they were associated with crime and activities deemed anti-social or undesirable (e.g. drug-use, prostitution, gambling, violence). This was also true in the UK. Boffey (2014: 19) suggests that in the 1970s and 1980s 'some parks deteriorated into wastelands with high rates of crime'. In this context, events were seen by urban authorities as a way to civilise these spaces, to bring back the more affluent and privileged classes who were deterred by the presence of 'undesirables'. The attitude of influential people like Whyte (1988: 158) was that 'the best way to handle the problem of undesirables is to make the place attractive to everyone else'. Zukin (1995) and Madden (2010) describe how fashion shows, circuses, movie screenings and cultural performances were introduced into Bryant Park in New York City to try and reclaim this space. The idea was to bring in middle class professionals who would spend money (on tickets and refreshments), but who would also police the park by acting as 'watchers', making the park feel safer. Their presence would also entice other members of the consuming classes into this public park. These initiatives are the direct precursors of the trends that are the focus of this book. They reinforce the dominant theme of this introductory chapter: although urban public spaces may now be used more intensively as events venues for different types of events, there is nothing new about staging events in urban public spaces.

Foundations, approach and structure

Before the contents of this book are outlined, it is perhaps worth explaining how the text fits into and builds on existing literature. There is already a vast literature on the way culture and entertainment have risen to prominence in urban policy (Harvey, 1989; Zukin, 1995). Events feature in these more general analyses, although they are not usually given dedicated attention. The complex social, political and economic reasons for this shift are also addressed very well in the existing literature. With this in mind, this book does not devote too much space re-reviewing these ideas. Instead it aims to provide a more focused analysis which builds on these important foundations. Rather than addressing the rise of events within urban policy generally, the aim is to focus on events staged in public spaces.

Using public spaces as event venues has already received some attention from academics. Mark Lowes' (2002) book *Indy Dreams and Urban Nightmares* addresses efforts to stage a motor race in a public park and the ways this was (successfully) opposed. This text is cited extensively here. Other works which have provided a useful foundation for this book include papers on the public space dimensions of football mega-events – for example, those by Anke Hagemann and Francisco Klauser. Recent papers published in European Urban and Regional Studies journal (Jakob, 2013; Johansson and Kociatkiewicz, 2011) have also influenced the book. In the urban design field, the work of Quentin Stevens (and his co-authors) has been influential, particularly his general work on urban space (Franck and Stevens, 2007) but also more specialised texts on events (Stevens and Shin, 2014) and urban play (Stevens, 2007).

The approach adopted here is guided by the notion that the most useful aspects of academic books are often the contextual chapters rather than the specific cases. Therefore, this book tries to place more emphasis on the general context and overview (Chapters 2–5), and give detailed case studies less prominence (Chapters 6–8). Favouring the general over the specific hopefully means the text is relevant and useful to more people. One of the other key aims of this book is to synthesise the event and urban literatures. Events are addressed within the urban studies and urban design literatures, and one objective of this work is to bring these ideas and cases to the attention of the scholars within the emerging field of event studies. There are already some good texts on events and cities written by scholars inside the events field (e.g. Richards and Palmer, 2010; Foley et al., 2012). However, unlike these books, this text focuses not so much on events and their organisation, but on the city spaces that are used to stage them. Books about urban space tend to be unhelpfully impenetrable. The writing style and terminology used can be off putting, especially to those unfamiliar this academic field of study. This book tries to adopt a clearer style. Some urban theorists may regard the arguments as over-simplified, but in a choice between obscure complexity and clear simplicity, the latter seems preferable.

The research presented here is derived from an amalgamation of work conducted over an extended period of time (2006–2015), rather than one concentrated project. Alongside detailed consideration of academic texts, this book is based on scrutiny of policy papers, planning applications and legal documents. Instances were also recorded where the use of public spaces as event venues was debated in the public sphere: material was gathered at public meetings, from blogs/internet forums and media articles/letters to newspapers. Formal and informal observations were also undertaken at relevant sites: notes were made and photographs were taken – pictures which are used to illustrate this book.

Structure of the book

This introductory chapter has explained the focus and purpose of the book. It has also provided some historical context and highlighted that events have always inhabited our urban public spaces. Chapter 2 provides a conceptual foundation for subsequent sections. The purpose of this chapter is to explain what public space is, how it is produced and what makes good public space. Some of the processes that undermine the public-ness of public spaces – privatisation, securitisation and commercialisation – are also introduced here. Chapter 3 focuses on the relationship between events and the city, in particular the way events have been urbanised in recent years. This part of the book explains the context in which this has happened (urban festivalisation) but it also provides a more specific examination of how and why the urbanisation of events has occurred. Chapters 4 and 5 need to be read as a pair as they artificially separate processes that are linked and that happen simultaneously. Chapter 4 focuses on the eventalisation of space – how public space is both animated and produced by staging events. Chapter 5 focuses on the eventification of space – the way in which events contribute to the commercialisation, securitisation and privatisation of public space. In simple terms, Chapter 4 explains how events make urban spaces more public and Chapter 5 focuses on how events make urban spaces less public.

These generally focused chapters are then accompanied by a series of case study chapters. The first (Chapter 6) focuses on one event staged in one particular site: it examines how using Greenwich Park for Olympic equestrian events was advocated and resisted. This leads to a wider analysis of the Royal Borough of Greenwich in Chapter 7. This London Borough hosted a series of events in the run up to, and aftermath of, the 2012 Games and Chapter 7 examines how a variety of public spaces were used for a range of events across a whole urban district. The objective of Chapter 8 is to assess the potential of measures that can be taken to address some of the problems noted in previous chapters. This chapter focuses on the possibilities offered by different forms of regulation and resistance. Two cases where events were prevented from happening are given special attention. The book culminates in a concluding chapter (9) which summarises and synthesises the main arguments.

2   Urban public space

Introduction

This chapter introduces and analyses the idea of urban public space. The discussion provides the foundations for subsequent chapters which discuss the ways events can help create and erode such space. The aim is to provide a conceptual foundation for the rest of the book. This means outlining what public space is, but also identifying some of the ways that contemporary public spaces are threatened by processes such as privatisation, commercialisation and securitisation. By drawing heavily on the notion of loose space (Franck and Stevens, 2007), this chapter aims to address a very difficult question; what is good urban public space? The chapter also explores the complex ways in which public space is produced – by planners but also by users. This is important, as this perspective is adopted throughout the rest of the book. The final section emphasises the links between events and the emerging literature on temporary uses of urban space.

Urban space

Before we can understand events staged in urban public spaces, we first need to consider what we mean by public space but also what we mean by urban space. Urban space is a term that is used very specifically by some authors, but more generally by others. The word implies the absence of something, but within urban studies space is not necessarily indicative of emptiness. At a specific, technical, level urban space is deemed to be the spaces that are created via the imposition of buildings and other material structures. These structures are not inserted into space: spaces are created and configured by the structures that frame them. This interpretation is often used by urban designers and architects who are interested in the way indoor and outdoor spaces are created by the introduction and modification of built form.

Within urban studies (and related disciplines), the notion of urban space is now referred to as a much more general phenomenon – it is the name given to the three dimensional region in which matter exists (Cowan, 2005). Use of the term is normally accompanied by recognition that space comprises more than the inevitable outcome of built structures. Space is not just a physical container: it is a social and cultural phenomenon. Work by behavioural geographers and environmental psychologists means the need to analyse human perceptions of space is now widely acknowledged, but urban space is conceived and imagined, as well as perceived (Lefebvre, 1991). It is also lived. Recognising the lived dimension of space is important because it highlights that the users of cities help to create the spaces they inhabit. And the people who use urban spaces may imagine them and perceive them very differently than those who conceived them. Nevertheless, how a space is conceived can affect the way in which spaces are lived, perceived and imagined by users, so when analysing space, especially public space, it is important to acknowledge that these spaces are produced via a combination of processes: perception, conception and imagination. Despite recent emphasis on the imagined and conceived city, physical form and material 'things' remain important.

The discussion above highlights that any perspective on urban space requires addressing fundamental (and somewhat pretentious) questions such as: what is a city?; what is the nature of existence in cities?; and how do material and subjective entities correspond to produce urban space? Cities are partly physical and partly human entities and any analysis of them needs to find a way of acknowledging both these dimensions and the fuzzy region that exists in between. Rhythm, atmosphere, memory and feel are examples of important phenomena that exist between the physical and the imagined and they are as important in the production of an urban space as material structures and pre-conceived designs. This is a particularly relevant perspective in a book dedicated to the way transient events change the spaces they inhabit. As Montgomery (1995: 104) argues, 'attention to the soft infrastructure of events programmes and activities is as important for successful urban revitalisation as building works and street design'.

One of the main themes in recent urban analyses is the notion that urban space can be seen as a liquid, dynamic phenomena, something that is 'always in the process of being made: it is never finished' (Massey, 2005: 9). Amin and Thrift (2002) argue this means placing emphasis on the process and potential of urban space, rather than any fixed, pre-determined reality. The modernist conception of urban public space is 'pre-occupied with safety and stasis' and this can encourage the design of fixed, single purpose spaces (Pugalis, 2009: 224). A good example is the modernist tendency to discuss the planning of roads for cars, rather than the design of streets for people (Montgomery, 1995). Ultimately, seeing it as fixed neglects the fact that 'space is eventful' (Pugalis, 2009: 224). This kind of perspective is important to help our general understanding of cities and urban space, but it is very appropriate for this book which explores how events change spaces. With or without organised events, spaces are always changing. This is why many authors assert that urban space can only be understood by recognising its temporality (Massey, 2005). Space is inherently unstable – it is created in the moment it is experienced.

Public space

> Public urban space has a mixed character as a concrete abstraction, as a
> product and as a producer.
>
> (Lehtovuori, 2010: 151)

Truly public spaces don't really exist; and they probably never did. Many authors are unconvinced that there has ever been 'democratic places where a diversity of people and activities are embraced and tolerated' (Low and Smith, 2006: vii). The idea of urban space that is owned by the people and managed democratically for the use of everyone is an idealistic vision rather than any discernible reality. However, that does not mean that the concept of public space is rendered obsolete. Indeed, it is important to have high expectations of our urban spaces. Moreover, the commonly accepted credentials of public space can be used as criteria with which to assess the public-ness of space. These are analysed further below.

Accessibility

One key characteristic that is often used to define public space is accessibility. Back in the 1970s, Lynch (1972) questioned how open our public spaces really are: 'are they accessible physically as well as psychologically?' This is still a concern. For Ercan (2010), space is public only if it is accessible – physically and socially. Physical accessibility refers to the presence of physical barriers; e.g. fences, walls, and other structures that restrict entry. For obvious reasons Flusty (1997) calls urban spaces which are surrounded by walls or check points 'crusty space'. Enclosing a site and charging an entry fee is also a barrier that restricts access – although this imposes a financial, as well as a physical, obstacle. Social accessibility means how attractive the space is to different social groups and how comfortable they feel in these spaces. For example, Carmona (2010) notes that some spaces contain subtle visual cues that only certain people are welcome.

Nominating accessibility as a defining aspect of public space is fraught with various complications. Public parks are often seen as the epitome of urban public space, but they are often gated, with access restricted to certain times of the day. Enclosure is seen as a negative trait; but it can be positive too: by protecting spaces and users (Reeve and Simmonds, 2001). In terms of social access, as Carmona (2010) notes, we live in a divided society; and therefore any attempt to provide equal access to a 'mythical general public' is doomed to fail. Urban spaces that are attractive to some will deter other groups, so universal access is an ambitious objective – perhaps an impossible one. Exclusion can also result from the design of an atmosphere or sense scape (Degen, 2003) that encourages some and discourages others. Therefore, whilst some commentators bemoan the restricted accessibility of our contemporary public spaces, this has always been the case. This book examines whether events contribute to physical, social and symbolic exclusion, and the ways in which they might increase accessibility.

Ownership

It is widely believed that spaces have to be owned by the public to qualify as public spaces. This idealistic and tenuous view is hampered by several inconvenient truths. Many privately owned spaces are accessible to the public whereas many publically owned ones are not. A low and diminishing proportion of urban space is owned by public authorities and, even when space is publically owned, there isn't necessarily any guarantee that universal access will be provided. There are plenty of government owned sites which are inaccessible to the public: try and gain entry to military, political or judicial sites if you don't believe this. Many of the most important city spaces in the twenty-first century (e.g. shopping malls) are privately owned, but are generally perceived to be public spaces. The people who use these spaces don't really care who owns them, they just want to be feel safe, welcome and comfortable. This highlights that public space can be defined by use, rather than by ownership.

It is also important to note that the boundaries between private and public ownership are increasingly blurred. For example, there is extensive public regulation of private space and an increasing amount of private management of publically owned space. Palmer and Whelan (2007) highlight the growth of 'mass private property' which is privately owned but open to the public. In this type of space, access is a privilege and not a right (Banerjee, 2001). It is now common to see signs on streets, squares and gardens reminding the public that, although they are allowed to use the space, the right to access has been granted by the private owners (see Figure 2.1). This leads to the argument that we are now seeing a new kind of urban space: one which is described by Palmer and Whelan (2007) as 'newly constituted communal space' and by Banarjee (2001) as pseudo-public space.

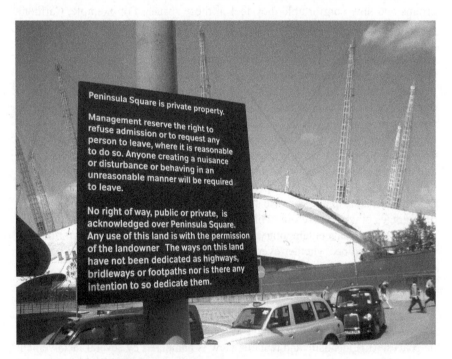

Figure 2.1 Private public space. Peninsula Square outside The O² Arena, London.

Ownership is not always a helpful criterion for assessing what is and what isn't public space. Some think of public spaces as those which are *controlled* by public actors (to serve the public interest) rather than necessarily confining the definition to those spaces that are *owned* by the public. However, distinguishing between publically controlled space and other types of urban space can be awkward too because, ultimately, most spaces – including private dwellings – are controlled by governments via planning restrictions and property laws. Both ownership and control are fluid rather than fixed phenomena: land can be sold, but it can also be rented, hired or appropriated. This is particularly relevant to events where sites are temporarily owned by event organisers.

Management

A final dimension that often appears in definitions of public space is the issue of management. In some accounts this is combined with ownership/control via reference to the idea of stewardship. Space is deemed to be public if it is managed in a way that is conducive to public use and public benefits. In over-simplistic accounts, it is often presumed that regulation and management are the antithesis of public space and that these spaces should be free from the petty rules that restrict freedom. However, there is increasing acknowledgement that public use is something that requires careful regulation. Without it, spaces may be affected negatively by anti-social behaviour or conflicting uses. As Carmona (2010) argues, spaces that are left alone and 'under-managed' may enter a spiral of decline, something that will reduce their appeal and limit their potential use. However, space which is managed in a very heavy handed fashion will also deter certain groups, reducing the diversity of uses and users.

Thörn (2011) discusses this issue with reference to Gothenburg in Sweden, and her work highlights the essential dilemma. Thörn (2011) notes that there has been a public space renaissance here in recent years, with the new meeting spaces highly valued. However, to maintain their security and safety, Gothenburg's public spaces have become highly controlled and regulated. This illustrates why there is disagreement about whether there has been a renaissance or a decline in the availability of urban public space. New spaces have been provided and there is more awareness of the need for public areas, but some people worry that new spaces are not public enough because they are so tightly secured. Accordingly, when considering recent trends in public space provision, some feel the difference between renaissance and revanchism has become increasingly blurred (Pugalis, 2009).

What is public space?

The discussion above highlights that there are various complications in defining what we mean by public space. Spaces that are owned by the public, managed by the public and that are universally accessible are very rare. Very few spaces reach the threshold of being genuinely public, and so it is important to use a definition of public space in this book that is more realistic and more representative, whilst bearing in mind the commendable goal of genuinely public space. In this book, public space is regarded as urban space that is available for use by any person at no cost. This reflects Cowan's (2005: 312) definition, where public space is regarded as the parts of a city 'that are available, without charge, for everyone to see, use and enjoy, including streets, squares and parks'. As this definition confirms, streets, squares and parks are fundamental examples of public spaces and, accordingly, they are addressed at length in this book.

Treating streets, squares and parks as inherently public spaces is a little misleading in some ways. For example, many parks are not accessible 24 hours a day and in this sense they share similarities with many indoor sites. These represent a second tier of public space which includes railway stations, shopping malls, (free) museums, and festival marketplaces. Sites such as these are typical of what several authors refer to as 'third spaces' – communal, social spaces that are neither users' homes nor their places of work. This second tier may be gradually gaining significance: indeed, Boyer (1992) feels that in the late capitalist city the street mall replaced the boulevard in the urban imaginary. Many streets, particularly in North America, have been covered over to create malls and lots of squares have been converted into atriums. This interiorisation of public space even extends to parks: the revival of winter gardens has (re)created indoor park space. Because this book focuses on events, indoor 'public' spaces aren't dealt with in detail here. However, it would be hypocritical not to recognise that many of these spaces also match our more limited definition of public spaces.

Sites which require some form of membership or payment are not regarded as public spaces even though they may share some of the characteristics of the 1st and 2nd tier public spaces described above. Spaces requiring payment or membership are dubbed semi- public spaces by Conway (1991) who puts pleasure gardens, zoos, botanic gardens and golf courses into this category. Semi-public spaces might also include university campuses, libraries, paid for visitor attractions (e.g. historic buildings and their grounds), school playgrounds and various types of sports grounds. These facilities offer open space and do stage events, but are not considered here because they are not normally available for use by any person without charge.

The most important public spaces in cities are streets, squares and parks and these are the spaces addressed in this book. A city's streets, squares and parks are not merely places where people can socialise; they are also channels of communication and arenas for political activism (Pugalis, 2009). John Ruskin (1819–1900) famously stated that a city's greatness could be measured by the quality of its squares and parks. In the contemporary era when cities are more desperate than ever to promote themselves, the symbolic function of public space is vitally important. Public spaces symbolise (synecdochically) the cities in which they are located, but they can also communicate key values, and some public spaces have come to symbolise democracy itself. Following this logic, there is a link between public space and the public sphere. These two ideas are different entities although they are sometimes confused, especially in the digital age where 'space' is regarded by some as encompassing the virtual world too. Despite the confusion, there is still a link between the public sphere and conventional public spaces. This is highlighted in Amin and Thrift's (2002: 135) observation that 'the erosion of public spaces is seen to threaten the public sphere'. Public spaces are the physical manifestation of the public sphere (Inroy, 2000), allowing politics and democracy to become less abstract. Indeed, Franck and Stevens (2007) think that without the material spaces in which it is enacted, society remains a meaningless abstraction.

In times of political insecurity or turbulence, people gather in prominent squares to demonstrate. When they want to protest or demand political action people march down central streets or gather for rallies in public parks. These events – sometimes planned, sometimes spontaneous – are perhaps the most important city events that are staged in public spaces. The hugely significant events that took place in North Africa during 2011 illustrate this point well. Public spaces are important sites of protest and celebration, but they are also the sites for the everyday aspects of life that underpin an open society: discussions and mingling with different people from outside your own social group. Amin and Thrift (2001: 137) are sceptical about whether contemporary public spaces can reach beyond this function and be politicised spaces: 'at best public spaces can be seen as spaces of tolerance and sociability . . . they are not the formative spaces of hybrid identities and politics'.

In some instances, the symbolic function of public spaces overrides their eponymous function. Lloyd and Auld (2003) see 'ceremonial spaces' not as sites for (and of) the public, but as vehicles through which the cultures and values of a city are communicated and exhibited. Inevitably these cultures and values tend to be those of civic elites. As Lowes (2002: 113) recognises, urban public spaces are ideological tools as they 'provide sites for civic elites to articulate a particular set of ideas, values and assumptions about the way a city is and how it ought to be organised spatially and socially'. Jacobs (1961: 229) reminds us that 'meanings associated with the built environment are not innate, but rather authored by certain social groups and interests'. To communicate the intended meanings requires spaces to be controlled. Streets, squares and parks have always been orchestrated spaces which, despite their appearance as open and accessible, are normally heavily regulated. Although 'controlled spontancity' is encouraged on urban streets, elites seek to replicate historical precedents where there was 'hegemony of aesthetics regarding who and what should and should not be seen' (Coleman, 2003: 32). Squares and parks are controlled for similar reasons. City squares are often designed to accentuate the symbolic impact of adjacent buildings: hence they are also part of the way that ruling elites communicate their values. Urban parks usually exhibit the aesthetics of order (Nevarez, 2007) and there are strict rules governing behaviour. These examples highlight that urban public space is often designed to control behaviour – not to host unfettered interaction. This is the 'hard reality of administered space' (Inroy, 2000). Such control assists the management of citizens, but it also ensure the right images and messages are communicated to external audiences. Whether consumed in person or remotely, many public spaces are framed for 'passive perception', rather than being spaces that encourage lived action and participation. This is something reaffirmed by Nevarez's comment (2007: 157) that the aesthetics of order 'distances users'. Ultimately, many prominent public spaces function not as spaces for the public, but as symbols of the regimes that govern cities. As subsequent chapters of the book demonstrate, this symbolic power also makes public spaces attractive to event organisers.

Threats to urban public space

Recent analyses suggest urban public space provision is being eroded by the triple threats of privatisation, commercialisation and securitisation. These threaten the three key tenets of (idealised) public space outlined above: public ownership, accessibility and management. The summative effects of these processes are encapsulated in Van Deusen's (2002) observation that public space has shifted from being 'somewhat open', to 'somewhat closed'. A key objective of this book is to assess whether events help to counter these threats or, conversely, whether they heighten them. Before more event-focused analysis is provided in later chapters, some (critical) analysis of these supposed threats is provided.

Privatisation

The idea that public space is being privatised is a big theme in urban studies research. This threat is related to the wider privatisation of public assets: a common policy adopted by governments aligned to a neoliberal philosophy. According to Banerjee (2001: 9) 'we are experiencing a steady withering of the public realm, a trend exacerbated by a worldwide campaign for market liberalism and downsizing governments'. Parks, streets and squares were traditionally owned and managed by local councils, but they are increasingly managed (or part-managed) by private organisations or companies. This supposedly allows for more efficient management, and is linked to the need for public amenities to be made more self-sufficient financially. Parks, streets and squares are expensive to secure, maintain and upgrade; and in a climate of government cutbacks, local authorities are keen to delegate management to specialised organisations who are better positioned to raise the necessary funds to pay for them. As Zukin (1995: 29) notes 'a major reason for the privatisation of some public parks is that city governments cannot pay for taking care of them'. Zukin (1995) famously analysed the 'aggressive' privatisation of Bryant Park, New York which was reclaimed from 'undesirable' users and placed in the hands of corporate members of the local Business Improvement District. This fascinating case is discussed several times during this book.

Unsurprisingly, there are various problems associated with private management arrangements – both from an ideological and practical perspective. If our public spaces exemplify public culture, then 'handing such spaces over to corporate executives and private investors means giving them carte blanche to remake public culture' (Zukin, 1995: 32). Private management (further) distances the electorate from decision making. It also means that more stringent and more discriminatory regulations governing use and behaviours might be introduced. In more extreme cases, rather than merely being managed by private organisations, public spaces have been sold to private companies. This represents a more permanent and more fundamental form of privatisation that is difficult to reverse.

Commercialisation

The private management of public spaces is inherently linked to the commercialisation of spaces – another complex issue and another perceived threat to public space provision. Urban public spaces are vulnerable to market forces, something that can squeeze out their use-value in favour of their exchange value. In other words, how these spaces are used is becoming less important than their revenue generating potential. For example, public spaces' contribution to surrounding real estate values is now pivotal – something that affects the way they are managed (Van Deusen, 2002). Public spaces are also 'valued' because of their contribution to local trade and tourism (Pugalis, 2009), and these commercial objectives are sometimes prioritised over social and public functions. In qualifying these concerns it should be noted that there is research that demonstrates that use value and exchange value are 'mutually constitutive' (Pugalis, 2009). In other words, use value helps to create exchange value – and vice versa. It should also be noted that, beyond their use and exchange values, urban public spaces have *symbolic* value. Urban public spaces are part of the symbolic economy, something that Zukin (cited in Richards and Palmer, 2010: 1) defines as 'the process through which wealth is created from cultural activities including art, music, dance, crafts, museums, exhibitions, sports and creative design in various fields'. According to Marling et al., (2009) urban public spaces also need to be analysed with respect to something they call 'experience value': their value in the experience economy, where value is created by staging products and services rather than merely making and promoting them (Pine and Gilmore, 1999). The symbolic and experiential aspects of public space are particularly important in explaining why they are increasingly used for major events.

A related issue is the amount of advertising and corporate sponsorship visible in public spaces. For example, Coca-Cola and Snyder's have bought the rights to be the official drink and snack providers in Cleveland's Metro Park (Garvin, 2011). Whilst this may bring in much needed revenue, it is thought by some to be demeaning, particularly in prestigious spaces perceived to have high symbolic value. As Garvin (2011: 183) states, in seeking commercial revenue authorities 'may go too far, detracting from a park's responsibility to serve the general interest'. Some people wish to see public amenities such as parks and squares protected from the commercial reality that dominates the rest of the city, but this is increasingly hard to realise. According to Mitchell (2015), corporate interests already have already infiltrated every aspect of the public landscape: 'so we've missed our chance for that debate' (see Figure 2.2).

Banerjee's (2001) contention that parks are the only exception to the otherwise privatised world of city building is an example of the rather naïve attitude that public spaces somehow transcend the world of commercial and property interests.

Figure 2.2 Yonge-Dundas Square, Toronto. This heavily commercialised space is used
to stage many events.

In London, Regents Park may seem like a tranquil escape from the city's relentless commercialism, but this masks its origins: 'Regents Park was designed in
conjunction with the housing in and around it – for the profitability of the development was as important as beauty, health and convenience' (Conway, 1991: 12).

In many instances commercialisation of public space is not an unfortunate
side effect of our increasingly commercial world but a deliberate strategy. Urban
governments attract commercial activity to streets, squares and parks – to help
animate them, but also to help generate the revenue required to maintain these
amenities. There has 'always been a strong link between commerce and urban
public space' (Carmona, 2010: 145) and this undermines many complaints about
creeping commercialisation. A good example of the potential dilemmas involved
here is the rise of cafés and 'cappuccino culture' in many UK streets and squares.
This is an attempt to emulate the lifestyle and culture of Mediterranean urban public spaces. Outdoor seating has been encouraged by local councils and the trend
has been welcomed by urban populations. However, this trend is also responsible
for the commercialisation and standardisation of public space.

The introduction of more commercial activities to public spaces is linked to the
commodification of these spaces – these spaces are increasingly treated as products which perhaps means they are more likely to feel detached from the places in
which they are situated (Carmona, 2010). Several authors note that public space

is now treated as a commodity, rather than as an exception to the commercial city. As Lloyd and Auld (2003: 345) suggest 'the production and design of most public leisure space is driven by the need to support economic outcomes'. For example, new public space is often provided not as an amenity in itself, but as an effective as a way of selling or justifying new real estate developments. We shouldn't be too pessimistic about this trend, especially given the propensity for people to imagine and use space in creative and unintended ways. Lehtovuori (2010: 136) provides a good example: he identifies that Exchange Square in Manchester has been developed as an extension of the surrounding shopping centres, but asserts that this space 'has the potential to become more actively and politically used'. Eldon Square in Newcastle is another insightful example: this space is dominated by the Eldon Square Shopping Centre which now surrounds it on three sides. However, it is regularly used as a meeting point for counter-cultural groups: every Saturday, in amongst the hordes of shoppers, local goths congregate here.

Securitisation

Securitisation represents a third threat to public spaces. The securitisation of public space is linked to a wider trend in which we have seen cities reconfigured to produce less open, more defensible space (Newman, 1996). It is also linked to the idea of 'splintering urbanism' (Graham and Marvin, 2001), a term which describes the increasing fragmentation of the urban environment into sanitised zones (Klauser, 2013). This highlights the spatial logic underpinning urban securitisation: enclosing and fixing spaces make them easier to control. A range of hard and soft measures are now used to manage public spaces and these represent a threat to civil liberties. Urban public spaces are often highly securitised: with a mix of punitive design features, extensive public and private policing, video surveillance, and regulations used to deter undesirable uses or users.

Although securitisation seems like an exclusively negative trend, some users welcome tighter security measures. Most people prioritise safety over liberty so any lack of security is likely to have a detrimental effect on the diversity of uses and users. Although many urban spaces are unfairly labelled as dangerous, fear of crime is one way that some users are symbolically excluded from public spaces. Security measures are one way to make people feel safer. However, the difference between under- and over-secured spaces is a fine one, highlighting the difficulties faced by those responsible for managing urban space. Whilst there are no simple answers to these dilemmas, one valuable option is ensuring that more people are present in parks, streets and squares throughout the day and night. The presence of people can act as a security measure and make people feel safer. Therefore, the of-cited need for animation in public spaces is not merely linked to fun and enjoyment, but to more fundamental objectives too.

For some authors (e.g. Banerjee, 2001) the threats discussed above are gradually reducing the amount of public space that is available in our cities. This is contested by others who argue that, as we lose some public spaces, other public spaces are being created (Carmona, 2010). The argument that we are losing public space also relies on the dubious notion that lost spaces were once genuinely public and unhindered by private involvement, commercial activity or overzealous security measures. The reality is that public spaces have long been infiltrated by these characteristics. The idea that we are losing public space is also undermined by recognition that space is constantly changing. We are not necessarily losing public space; instead new types of public space are being created. Rather than bemoaning the loss of public space; this book seeks merely to analyse how public spaces are changing. One objective is to assess if and how events activity can be linked to the processes of privatisation, commercialisation and securitisation discussed above.

What makes good public space?

To understand how events may contribute to, or detract from, urban public spaces it is important to first consider what might be considered to be 'good' public space. The discussion above has already provided some pointers: good public spaces are those which come close to the idealistic definition of public space: publically owned (or controlled), publically accessible and managed in a way that is conducive to public use. However, in trying to think about what good public space is, it is perhaps useful to avoid too much emphasis on the term public – especially if we accept Carmona's (2010) argument that there is no such thing as 'the general public'. With this is mind, the notion of inclusivity is an important idea (and ideal). Good public space can be thought of as inclusive space: that which invites a diversity of uses and a diversity of users. Several authors provide useful conceptual ideas to help us to understand what inclusive space is like, such as Lloyd and Auld's (2003) identification of multi-public spaces, those which support difference rather than benefiting a homogenous community (community space), or which are open to all but where some users are discouraged (liberal space). Carmona (2010) discusses similar concepts in his identification of open versus closed space, with the former exhibiting the positive traits of weakly defined boundaries and social mixing.

The idea of inclusive space that is open enough to be accessible to all, yet secured enough to avoid concerns about safety, seems like a difficult thing to achieve. There are some examples of public spaces that supposedly realise this balance. Chatterton and Unsworth (2004) describe Millennium Square in Leeds thus: 'it exists in a difficult intersection between controlled/secure and open/spontaneous; it does not have a fixed meaning as it is used by various social groups and interests'. The undetermined meaning and diverse range of users suggest this might be an example of good public space. However, Spracklen et al.'s (2013: 171) research found that the same Square 'was not a space that was attractive or welcoming to our respondents'. This highlights the inherent subjectivity involved in assessments of public space. It also reaffirms the pessimism of authors such as Van Deusen (2002), who argue that public space is always exclusionary, because certain people or behaviours are tolerated whilst others are not. This type of thinking helps to explain why many authors see public spaces as inherently constituting spaces of *conflict* (Koch and Latham, 2011).

Inclusiveness (openness and diversity) is also linked to the oft cited notion that good public spaces should encourage social activity and casual contact between strangers, perhaps leading to a more tolerant, more civil and less individualised society (Sennett, 1978). The notion of the stranger is very relevant to urban public spaces because these are often considered as places in which one can be anonymous, something that can be liberating because there are fewer constraints on behaviour (Franck and Stevens, 2007). Pugalis (2009: 222) sees the city marketplace as the ideal 'theatre' in which people can meet and co-mingle with strangers and feels that these interactions mean that 'markets are the prime example of the dynamic and heterogeneous nature of urban public space'. However, street markets are temporary installations, and intense activity concentrated at a certain times can make the spaces feel 'dead and boring' on non-market days. Organised events cause these temporal variations in activity, and one aim of this book is to examine whether temporary changes lead to more permanent changes in the way spaces are conceived, perceived and lived.

Just because people are sharing the same space does not necessarily mean they are interacting. Without interactions between strangers, urban public space is merely a platform for co-presence, rather than a forum for sociability (Rowe and Baker, 2012). To encourage interaction, urban designers use the principle of triangulation – where external stimuli are arranged in ways that encourage people to begin talking (Stevens, 2007). One innovative form of triangulation increasingly favoured by urban planners is the food kiosk; placing these in public spaces can *slow* people down and encourage both activity and interaction (Montgomery, 2013). Nevertheless, some argue these represent unnecessary commercialisation. In our increasingly commercialised world, spaces are often designed to maximise contact between individuals and goods (Reeve and Simmonds, 2001). This highlights that public spaces are increasingly places of individualised consumption, rather than of casual socialising.

The failure of public space design to encourage sociability is not just a product of the commercial orientation of many new public spaces; it is also something caused by risk-averse organisations who fear the unpredictable and who are keen to displace those they see as undesirable. In one sense this is a purposeful failure. To avoid the threat of 'undesirable' people inhabiting them, new public spaces are deliberately designed as anti-social spaces, ones where mingling, dwelling and assembling are actively discouraged. Flusty (1997) calls spaces that are difficult and uncomfortable to occupy 'prickly space'; the public are allowed to pass through these spaces but not use them. Montgomery (2013) feels this is a principle that has infused the design and management of many plazas in Downtown Manhattan. Companies are sometimes required to provide public space in order to get planning permission for new buildings or extensions to existing buildings. These companies don't want to provide public spaces – they have to – leading to rather mean-spirited manifestations.

A recent example in The City of London (perhaps the area most equivalent to Downtown Manhattan) illustrates this well. Permission was granted for a very bulky building at 20 Fenchurch Street with the condition that a large public space was provided at the top. This was meant to be a publicly accessible park: an indoor space with incredible views over the City and beyond. When the 'Sky Garden' opened in 2015, Londoners and the local planning authority were surprised to learn that gaining entry required both advanced booking and photographic identification. This contravened the idea of accessible public space. The Sky Garden feels more like a corporate atrium, or a hotel lobby, than a park: the expensive restaurants and bars mean this is essentially a commercial space. The disappointing scale and underwhelming landscaping meant critics dubbed it the Sky Rockery (Wainwright, 2015). This example highlights the problems with treating public space as compensation for private development, rather than as something in its own right. Why would resident corporations or their landlords want to encourage people to hang around outside their buildings or, in this case, on top of their buildings? Following this selfish logic, the temptation is to create something that meets planning obligations but that restricts the chances of the space being used by diverse groups.

When new urban spaces are constructed, there are various stakeholders involved: the owner of the site, public authorities and potential users, but also the architects and designers who have been commissioned to design the spaces. Whereas architects and urban designers may have once been driven by utopian visions and new social relations, they now seem less interested in the social context of their sites and more interested in aesthetics (Van Deusen, 2002). This is illustrated nicely in Pugalis's (2009) research into public spaces in the north east of England which found that there was a large discrepancy between the attitudes of designers and the attitudes of users. The designers were obsessed with materials and aesthetics, whereas the users of the spaces stressed the importance of social encounters and cultural experiences. This reaffirms the traditional idea that designers make *spaces*, but people make *places* (Cowan, 2005). Pugalis's (2009) research suggests that urban designers are not producing sociable places because they are not prioritising sociability in their designs. The obvious response to this problem is to ensure that users are involved in the design of spaces: not just consulted, but actively involved. In an era of co-production, where companies benefit from the input of consumers into the redesign of products, it is not unreasonable to expect urban planners and designers to involve potential users in their work. Of course, this is already happening in many enlightened examples. But adopting this practice more generally would help respond to Jane Jacobs' (1961: 238) famous call: 'cities have the capability of providing something for everybody, only because, and only when, they are created by everybody'.

Social mingling requires not just appropriately designed spaces, but the will to do it. This raises the question: is the decline of public life in our cities caused by the poor provision of public spaces, or is the poor state of urban public spaces caused by the lack of public life? Charles Montgomery (2013: 160) has faith in the role of good urban design: 'can we build – or rebuild – city spaces that enable easy connections and more trust among both families and strangers? The answer is a resounding yes'. However, his namesake, John Montgomery (1995: 108) is much more sceptical: arguing that there is 'mistaken belief that large public spaces will produce an outbreak of public sociability'. Ultimately, the decline of civic life has caused the decline of civic space, rather than vice versa. Richards and Palmer (2010) feel that there has been a conscious withdrawal of people from public space, citing Goffman's idea of defensive destimulation to help explain this process. People now surround themselves with people they know, rather than those they don't, undermining efforts to encourage mingling with strangers.

In trying to work out whether it is anti-social people or anti-social spaces that are responsible for the decline of urban public spaces, is it worth reminding ourselves of what urban space is. Space is both a product of social relations and a producer of those relations. This suggests the process works both ways: good public space can encourage sociability, but urban public space can also be produced by social interactions. Indeed, Massey (2005: 9) reminds us that space is 'the product of interrelations, as constituted through interactions'. It is not only urban planners and urban designers that create public space: users do too. As Van Deusen states (2002: 151), 'public spaces emerge from the practices of people . . . as well as from the designers who create them'. This type of thinking is employed later in this book (see Chapter 4), where it is noted that events can help to produce informal urban public space where it would not normally exist.

Good public space is not just about accessibility and sociability. According to the Project for Public Spaces (2007, cited in Richards and Palmer, 2010), 'activities' and 'comfort' are also required if an urban public space is to be successful. If we want people to linger in public spaces, rather than just pass through, then they need to be comfortable and/or have something to do. Comfort usually means providing appropriate seating, shade and shelter. As Gehl (1987) emphasises, people like spaces where they can sit and watch other people. Activities are more complicated to introduce, especially as many of the things that people like to do in public spaces (such as skateboarding, playing football, drinking alcohol, protesting) may not be welcomed by other users, or by the managers of those spaces. For example, Inroy (2000) describes a fascinating struggle in Glasgow between the council who wanted a new park as a city marketing tool and young people who wanted to play football in it. The difficulties reconciling the use and symbolic values of public spaces help to explain why opportunities to consume food/drink, and to watch organised performances (either live or via big screens), are increasingly being made available. These are relatively safe, uncontroversial activities that can be enjoyed by a wide variety of people.

In the quest to find good examples of public space to emulate, it is tempting to turn to cities of the past. There are various examples from Mediterranean history that are often cited as being the ultimate examples of public space. Earlier in this chapter, the qualities of marketplaces were explained, and the classical Greek iteration of the city market – the agora – is often regarded as the epitome of public space and the one to which contemporary cities should aspire. This is perhaps a rather rose-tinted view of the past: people often ignore the fact that access to the agora was quite restricted (Smith and Low, 2006). A more imaginative Greek example is offered by Papastergiadis et al. (2013) who advocates the Stoa as an example of a public space prototype. The Stoa was a shelter, although not a closed room. It was a transitional space, nether inside nor outside; one in which people could dwell, mingle, eavesdrop and move on (Papastergiadias et al., 2013). In this sense, perhaps like the hotel lobby, the hospital reception or the corporate atrium in the twenty-first century city, the stoa was 'the pivot point at which the public and private spheres interact' (Papastergiadias et al., 2013: 338). The other example often used to illustrate the ideal public space is the Italian piazza, most famously Siena's Piazza del Campo; a wide semi-circular promenade. The key qualities of 'the Campo' include the way the space 'functions as a stage across which the entire city parades', a trait which is enhanced by the 'tremendous' sight lines (Montgomery, 2013: 151). According to Montgomery (2013), this space is successful because it draws people together, and because it slows them down. Interestingly, given the focus of this book, this 'stage' is one designed and used for events.

Loose space

In their exploration of 'Loose Space' Franck and Stevens (2007) also deal with the idea of inclusive public space. Loose space is that which can be used by a range of people in different ways. Indeed, Franck and Stevens (2007) define loose space as that which does not have a prescribed use: the lack of a committed, determined function encourages greater potential for a diversity of occupants and activities. Their work has similarities with Lefebvre's in that they share the view that when space is determined and demarcated 'space necessarily embraces some things and excludes others' (Lefebvre, 1991: 99). This perspective is also evident in Koch and Latham's (2011: 522) work on public space: 'we need to think more carefully about how they [inhabitations] are woven together and how the presence of certain practices offers accordances for certain kinds of inhabitation and not for others'. One explanation for the way in which different users and uses integrate successfully in some public spaces is Goffman's 'cohesion code'. Goffman notes how there is often a tacit social contract between people occupying a social place, which basically involves the premise that people allow each other to play their public roles, on the understanding that they are able to perform theirs (Reeve and Simmonds, 2001). This reflects Franck and Stevens' (2007: 4) definition of loose spaces which allow people to carry out their 'desired actions while recognising the presence and rights of others'.

Loose space is a really important idea for this book, as it provides a useful framework within which to understand how spaces may be made more/less accessible, and therefore more/less inclusive. With this in mind, it is worth exploring the notion further. Franck and Stevens (2007: 16) see loose space as dynamic space – static tends to mean tight. Loose space can become tight space and vice versa due to changes in the 'form, regulation and use' of a given space. Some kinds of layouts encourage more freedom, such as porous designs where one can move through and between spaces easily. But Franck and Stevens (2007: 15) see loose space as something principally generated by people's actions – 'people create looseness' – and through the lack of rigid controls, rather than by changes to the materiality of a space. According to Franck and Stevens, the 'activities that make space loose may be impromptu or planned in advance. They may occur only once or they may take place on a regular schedule' (2007: 2) and 'are different from the primary, intended ones' (2007: 4). These observations highlight the potential value of using loose space to assess the effects of staging events.

Franck and Stevens' (2007) account also helps us to understand loose space by explaining what it is not. According to the authors, 'loose space is a space apart from the aesthetically and behaviourally controlled and homogenous themed environments of leisure and consumption where nothing unpredictable must occur' (2007: 2). The splintered urbanism of shopping malls and business improvement districts is seen as tight space. However, the authors feel that in these spaces, there are still opportunities to create loose space, even if this is just a temporary phenomenon. The opposite of loose space (tight space) is defined by its 'certainty, homogeneity and order'. The antithesis of this is how Stevens (2007) thinks we should define open space – not as those spaces that are free of buildings and development, but those which do not have prescribed uses/users.

There are strong links between Franck and Stevens' (2007) ideas, and the qualities admired by other urban design academics. Montgomery's (1995: 108) statement that places are successful 'because they exhibit a fair degree of disorder' suggests he shares a belief in the value of loose spaces. Following in the tradition of Jacobs (1961), Montgomery (1995) thinks this is best achieved through an active street life. The privatisation, commercialisation and securitisation discussed above are threats to this kind of space, but Franck and Stevens (2007) are confident that loose space not been eradicated in the contemporary city. One of the aims of this book is to examine how events loosen or tighten space. Whilst the rather anarchic qualities admired by Franck and Stevens (2007) are sometimes a little unrealistic and unconvincing, this book follows their principle that loose public space is good public space: because it is more inclusive and because it facilitates a range of possibilities and potentialities.

Koch and Latham's (2011) description of the successful transformation of an urban space in London provides a useful account of how loose space can be realised. These authors avoid claiming that the space has become more public, but highlight that it is now a better space as 'it is used by a greater range of people, affords a greater range of possibilities for use and offers a more effective way of dealing with conflicting demands on the space' (Koch and Latham, 2011: 526). These three outcomes: a diversity of users; a diversity of uses; and, perhaps most difficult of all, the successful management of all this diversity; are useful criteria with which to judge urban public spaces.

The idea of loose space contradicts some of the traditional tenets of urban planning and urban design. Pløger (2010) regards urban planning as something that orchestrates urban life, and urban design as a practice that tries to discipline or tame space. These descriptions emphasise the idea of planning and design as exercises in control, rather than as tools for liberating urban space. Zoning different activities or uses into different spaces, and the preoccupation with visual order (Montgomery, 1995), seem difficult to reconcile with the principle of loose space.

Pugalis (2009) sees conceived spaces – planned/designed spaces – as something that reduces the liveliness of spaces, because they are inherently detached from the lived city. However, more creative and less traditional approaches to planning and design may be able to assist the provision of loose space. The challenge for professionals involved in these fields is to try and design in flexibility and looseness; and to avoid determining exactly what spaces are for. One notable example is New York's High Line: a linear park suspended above the city on a former railtrack. This park is designed as a planned wilderness in keeping with the notion of 'terrain vague' – space which is not overly contrived or programmed (Kamvasinou, 2006).

Analysing loose and tight spaces has clear links with some well-known ideas within urban studies and critical urban theory. For example it is possible to link loose space to the notions of territories and territorialisation. Following the work of Sack (1986), we normally think of territoriality as an attempt to control a geographical area. However, Sack's interpretation is not shared by other urban commentators who think territories are created through relationships and less deliberate efforts. Authors such as Brighenti (2010) and Raffestin (2012) have significantly enhanced our understanding of how space becomes territory and these accounts take our understanding further. Following ideas about the wider notion of space (see above), territories are now usually thought of as processes, rather than objects: because they are constantly produced and re-produced. This is why authors identify different types of territorialisation: 'de-territorialisation' – the opening of space; and 're-territorialisation' – the closure of space. Identifying the way space is opened and closed has clear links to the notions of loose and tight space discussed above and these ideas will be employed explicitly in later sections of this book.

Closing or tightening urban space is also sometimes referred to using terminology derived from Deleuze and Guattari (1987). These authors, and those inspired by their work, often discuss attempts to 'fix' urban space (Frew and McGillivray, 2014). Deleuze and Guattari (1987) regard space as comprising a combination of striated and smooth space, with the former 'state-oriented and static', and the latter 'nomadic and dynamic' (Frew and McGillivray, 2014). As with tight space, striated space is associated with more determined relations, and following the same logic as theories of territorialisation, various forces 'fix' smooth spaces; so this space is constantly in danger of being subsumed within striated space. However, by identifying the possibility of resistance and 'lines of flight', Deleuze and Guattari (1987) suggest that alternative spaces can be realised within striated space. This has similarities to the idea discussed previously which asserts that more inclusive/loose spaces can be created out of tight, semi-public ones. Striated space has similarities to the qualities of tight space in that it has a stabilised identity, rather than one that is in a state of becoming. The word striated derives from the Latin word stringere – to draw tight (Dovey and Polakit, 2007). Similarly, the idea of smooth space shares qualities with the notion of loose space: especially as the interpretation of smooth by Deleuze and Guattari (1987) is one that implies seamlessness and movement, space freed from boundaries.

There are obvious parallels between tight/loose space and striated/smooth space, but it is important to point out some differences too. In Deleuze and Guattari's (1987) work, striated and smooth spaces are very complex and interlinked entities that are folded together. They are not separate types of space, but rather ways of thinking about space (Dovey and Polakit, 2007). The ideas of loose and tight space are more straightforward ideas. Loose space is presented by Franck and Stevens (2007) as an 'ideal' type of urban space and this makes it a more useful concept, especially for the purposes of this book. At present the ideas of Deleuze and Guattari (1987) are very much in vogue, and there are plenty of accounts which use and apply their ideas. This book uses Franck and Stevens (2007) concepts of loose and tight space, providing a fresh and more pragmatic perspective. However, it would be foolish not to acknowledge the fundamental influence of previous work regarding territorialisation and smooth / striated space on these ideas.

Temporary urbanism

Alongside analysing various ideas and concepts that help us understand urban space, in a book about events it is also important to address ideas concerning *time*. Unlike space (and scale), time has been neglected in urban studies (Tonkiss, 2013). In recent years – perhaps because of the global financial crisis that stalled development in many cities – there has been increased interest in temporary urbanism. There are other possible reasons why the temporary has risen to prominence: for instance new technology and new spatial configurations in a 'liquid' form of modernity (Bauman, 2000). A simpler explanation is that people like temporary structures. In their book *The Temporary City* Bishop and Williams (2012: 3) suggest there is some evidence of 'a cachet associated with time-limited exclusivity that has consumer appeal'. This helps to explain why major brands are keen to establish pop-up stores.

By definition events are time limited phenomena, so temporal ideas and concepts are particularly important when considering the effects of city events in (and on) urban spaces. In urban planning and urban design there is an 'overwhelming obsession with permanence' (Bishop and Williams, 2012) which means the value and influence of temporary urbanism tends to be neglected. Even in the literature that does exist, temporary uses of space tend to be referred to as interim, meanwhile or stop-gap uses, terms which Bishop and Williams (2012) feel are quite dismissive. The emerging literature on temporary urbanism tend to focus on 'pop-up' structures and radical appropriation of space (e.g. guerrilla gardening), but organised events are one of the most important and prevalent examples of temporary uses of urban space. The literature on events has mushroomed in recent years, but very few texts analyse events using ideas from temporary urbanism as the conceptual foundation. This book aims to addresses this.

Acknowledging the role of temporary uses is important because these uses can have significant effects in the short, medium and long term. They can provide more efficient uses of space, but they can also provide the foundation for more creative and more participatory forms of urbanism. One of the lesser known benefits of the new focus on temporary urbanism is the way it helps to break down the assumed division between the makers and users of urban space. This fits well with the philosophy adopted in this book: the idea that people produce urban public space. The new interest in temporary uses of urban space is very noticeable in the academic literature, but also in professional practice. For example, temporary uses have become part of Mayoral policy in London (Tonkiss, 2013). The adoption of 'phased packages of smaller, often temporary initiatives' in urban development and regeneration provides a nice a nice link to the notion of 'loose space' in that plans that accommodate temporary urbanism are looser spatial strategies than traditional land zoning (Bishop and Williams, 2013: 3). In these cases, the spaces conceived by planners and developers which are normally seen as the antithesis of loose space may even contribute to its provision. However, as with other concepts, there is also a danger that planners and developers adopt the idea (in rather diluted form) to serve their interests, and to maintain the status quo, rather than to radically alter the way the built environment is produced. Tonkiss (2013) fears that the idea of temporary uses has already been hijacked by boosterist mayors and architectural style magazines.

Summary

This chapter provides an important foundation for the rest of this book. The preceding sections explain how the term urban public space is used and what good urban public space is. Put succinctly, urban public space is a normative idea. However, a realistic and workable definition is identified: city spaces which anyone can use freely. Good public space is inclusive, loose space that invites a diversity of users and uses. The chapter also addresses how public space is produced. One of the key ideas is that public space is both the outcome of interactions between people and a vehicle that facilitates such interactions: because public spaces are social and physical phenomena, they are both product and producer. Such thinking is used later in the book to explain how events commercialise public space and socialise commercial space. Chapter 4 explains some of the positive aspects of events; how events may also help to loosen public spaces (making them more accessible and more inclusive); and how they help to create urban public spaces. Chapter 5 of this book will explain how events contribute to the processes of commercialisation, privatisation and securitisation. However, before these issues are discussed it is important to provide a more detailed discussion about the key trend discussed in this book – the urbanisation of events.

3 The urbanisation of events

Introduction

Official events are increasingly staged in central, public spaces such as parks, streets and squares. This trend is referred to here as the 'urbanisation of events'. It is important to illustrate this trend and to explore why it has occurred and these are the main objectives of this chapter. To contextualise the discussion, the wider 'festivalisation' of cities is discussed too. Urban festivalisation is regarded as the overarching process within which the urbanisation of events is taking place. The chapter also introduces a more specific conceptual framework that is used to structure subsequent chapters – one which helps us to understand the effects of 'urbanising' events'. The latter sections of the chapter are dedicated to explaining how and why events have been urbanised, with specific attention dedicated to the potential benefits for key stakeholders.

The eventisation of urban space

Staging leisure events in city centres, in prominent public spaces, is a trend that was predicted by some commentators. For example, Lefebvre (1991) anticipated the way that spaces of consumption (specialised leisure zones, where leisure is consumed) would give way to the consumption of space – where the city itself becomes the focus on the consumption experience. This reaffirms the frequently cited notion that the city has moved from being the container of consumption, to the content of the 'playful consuming experience' (McKinnie, 2007). These ideas are particularly relevant to city events. Following the same logic, the city is no longer merely the backdrop for urban events; the city has become a key component of event consumption (Richards and Palmer, 2010). This process is often linked to the notion of urban festivalisation; a term which is explored further below.

Urban festivalisation

Festivalisation is a term used differently by different authors. However, it is most commonly treated as a general process and one which characterises urban and cultural policy since the late 1970s. Festivalisation involves using cultural phenomena to achieve economic restructuring and urban competitiveness in a post-industrial and symbolic economy. Culture is used to generate economic activity, but also to frame cities (Zukin, 1995) and recently there has been a 'shift towards a wider conceptualisation of culture, to include popular culture and events programming' (Tallon et al., 2006: 353). In this context festivalisation involves the use of festivals, events and entertainment to generate economic and symbolic capital. Staging events in general, and big events in particular, is fundamental to this process. As Jenkins (2012) suggests, we are witnessing a new economy of big events – what he and Zimbalist (2015) refer to as circus economics – which fuels demand for ever more grandiose occasions. Events have become central to the urban economy, and central to the various professional activities that urban authorities use to support and regulate it. As the leader of Manchester City Council has recently stated, the 'clustering' of events in cities like Manchester is 'not, of course, a coincidence' nor an expression of the city's history or creativity: instead 'it's a direct acknowledgement of the catalyst that culture can be for economic growth' (Leese, 2015). The rationale here is clear - post-industrial cities need to stimulate consumer spending and economic activity. As Jakob (2013: 468) suggests, festivalisation involves the 'introduction of festivals into city planning . . . to advance local urban and economic development, consumer experiences and city images'.

In her detailed analysis of Berlin post-1989, Colomb (2012) identifies a more extreme example of urban festivalisation. Rather than merely using festival and events strategically in urban policy, the city is 'staged': in other words, the city as a whole is offered as an event. This involves turning various parts of the city into a theatrical stage for spectacular events and dramatising urban phenomena which wouldn't normally be regarded as events. Colomb (2012) suggests this characterised the approach adopted by Berlin in the 1990s after the reunification of Germany. The events staged in the 1980s such as the city's 750th anniversary (1987) and the European City of Culture event (1988) provided the original foundations for this strategy. Later efforts were more intensive; not only staging big events (The 2006 FIFA World Cup, The 2009 World Athletics Championships) and intensive promotion of regular events (e.g. Carnival of Cultures, Film Festival, Love Parade), but also packaging a series of non-events into a big event (Colomb, 2012).

Colomb (2012) sees urban festivalisation as very closely aligned to urban tourism objectives. This reflects other accounts. Johansson and Kociatkiewicz (2011) identify three different aspects of urban festivalisation: building a tourist-friendly image; the sanitised translation of a city's past; and creating distinctive festivalised spaces. Importantly, all three dimensions show 'festivals as bounded events clearly separated from the quotidian experience of the city' (Johansson and Kociatkiewicz, 2011: 402). Hence, events are defined as an antithesis of the everyday. The intentions of festivalisation are to present urban spaces as 'eventscapes', something which promotes a rather restricted and sanitised version of the city 'rather than life in its complexity and multiplicity' (Johansson and Kociatkiewicz, 2011: 403). This highlights the links between the notion of the festival city and the idea of the concept city, a term used by De Certeau to explain how the multiplicities of city life are simplified to convey an appealing unified vision (Jamieson, 2004). Festival, events and culture more generally are used to frame the contemporary city, highlighting that festivalisation is not just an instrumental process involving new economic modes, but one which involves the wider reframing of the city as a site of play and consumption.

In German literature, particularly in the field of urban sociology, festivalisation is interpreted in a slightly different way. Here, the emphasis is less on the festivalisation of space and culture, and more on the festivalisation of politics. Indeed, in many texts, most notably those by Hausserman, the term refers to a form of urban boosterism – attempts by public-private coalitions to promote their place-based interests. One translation of festivalisation in this context is as 'politics through big events' (Roth and Franck, 2000). Festivalisation is seen as a process used to gain political and economic capital for civic elites and to deter resistance to their control. As this type of boosterism is usually implemented by public-private partnerships or newly created private organisations (e.g. Business Improvement Districts, see Zukin, 1995), the term is used critically to refer to urban policy that lacks democratic legitimacy (Roth and Franck, 2000). From this interpretation it is easy to see why the festivalisation of urban politics is often equated with theories such as the 'society of the spectacle' (Debord, 1984), which postulate how citizens are pacified – with real problems hidden behind a 'carnival mask' (Harvey, 1989). This interpretation is inherent in Jakob's assertion that:

at a time when city governments hold fewer and fewer regulatory instruments and resources to influence housing, employment, education and the welfare of their citizens, experience planning in the form of festivals not only hides these weaknesses but also becomes a sort of propaganda.

(Jakob, 2013: 456)

Festivalisation is also a form of temporalisation. Events help to make cities more meaningful by emphasising specific times. Temporalising space changes its meaning (Lefebvre, 1991). As Hughes (1999: 132) states, in recent years, cities have used time and 'time imagery', to recuperate spaces using 'carnivalesque images of celebration and conviviality'. However, the idea of temporalisation is more confused in an era where festivity is promoted as a perpetual feature of cities. Richards and Palmer's (2010) interpretation of urban festivalisation – as the attempt to turn the city into a continuous festival – illustrates this. They cite Avignon's attempt to position itself as a 'permanent show' to help illustrate this phenomenon. The idea of a city being in a permanent state of festivity comprises an ambitious communications strategy rather than one which represents any discernible reality. However, in a world dominated by media and social media, the image of the city and the material city are increasingly hard to separate. Rather than promoting a specific event at a specific time, cities are increasingly marketing themselves as places in which events are always happening. For example, Manchester has recently been promoted as an events destination using the slogan 'always something happening' and inviting visitors to take 'an eventful short break' (Observer, 29th June 2014). Another UK example also helps to illustrate this. In Edinburgh's events strategy, one of the key objectives is 'to make the city lively all year round' (The City of Edinburgh Council, 2007: 8). Again, this implies a deliberate attempt to communicate year round festivity.

Perpetual festivalisation is also linked to the de-differentiation of leisure. Festivals and events are not necessarily distinct activities that happen at stipulated times every year, they are now phenomena that merge into consumer activities more generally. As urban festivalisation progresses, consumption and entertainment become indistinguishable (Richards and Palmer, 2010). This aforementioned case of Berlin provides a good example. During the 2000s, 'when there was no high profile event to promote, small events and the normal cultural, retail and entertainment amenities of the city were re-packaged into thematic or seasonal happenings and branded to entice flows of visitors throughout the year' (Colomb, 2012: 236). This is not something unique to the German capital: if you look at the event calendars of most cities they are supplemented with a range of regular experiences that are not conventional events: markets, shopping and entertainment. The idea of festivalisation as de-differentiation of leisure is also illustrated via the rise of the 'shopping festival' as an urban event (Richards and Palmer, 2010). For example, Anwar and Sohail (2004) discuss the rise of the Dubai Shopping Festival. The way in which shopping and festivals are explicitly connected is perhaps most evident in the festival marketplace. These public-private spaces are discussed at length within the urban studies literature and Kuala Lumpur, Malaysia, provides a good example. In this Asian city the 'Festival City' is a shopping mall: one aptly promoted using the strapline 'every day is a celebration'.

Ultimately, festivalisation refers to a broad process which represents how and why urban culture, urban space and urban politics have changed in recent decades. The term provides a useful context and overarching frame for this discussion in this book. This text focuses particularly on the festivalisation of space, rather than the festivalisation of culture, or politics. However, these domains are clearly linked. Festivalisation is best understood as a broad city wide process where events are used in combination with each other and with other forms of consumption, entertainment and leisure. This text is more focused on how individual events affect specific public spaces and so it is more valid to use a narrower concept, or set of concepts than festivalisation. Following Jakob's (2013) lead, we need terminology that illustrates processes that operate at a smaller scale and in shorter timeframe than urban festivalisation. Therefore, the term eventisation is used. This term seems more relevant to a book that covers sport events and entertainment events as well as cultural festivals. Eventisation also involves different processes and outcomes. For this reason, this book identifies and uses the subsidiary terms *eventalisation* and *eventification* as ways of understanding the diverse but related effects of staging events in urban public spaces. These processes should not be seen as distinct from one another: most events involve both the eventalisation and eventification of space. However, to allow the processes involved to be understood better, they are discussed separately. Eventalisation and eventification are both awkward words and their similarity means they might be easily confused, so the following section provides a clear explanation of their derivation, and their meaning.

Eventalisation

The term eventalisation refers to the process through which urban space is produced via the staging of events. A good way to remember the meaning of the term is to think of it as a combination of events and revitalisation (event-alisation). As Chapter 4 illustrates, events can be effective ways of animating spaces, inviting new users, encouraging new uses, and, ultimately, changing the identity of urban spaces. They can bring people, sociality, activity and atmosphere – all things noted as being qualities of good urban space. This activity can even make spaces feel more secure. Many urban public spaces are 'dead' – they lack vitality, conviviality and stimulation – and events can act as ways to address this situation on a temporary or more permanent basis. However, the term eventalisation is also used to refer to occasions in which urban public spaces are created in parts of the city where they don't normally exist or where they have been lost. This has similarities with the way situationists try to create informal spaces out of formal ones using events (Pløger, 2010).

In defining this term, it is acknowledged that the notion of eventalisation is used by other social theorists in a more general, slightly different, way. Pyyhtinen (2007) uses eventalisation as the English translation of Simmel's notion that society is now best understood as an event, rather than something more substantial. This is also a key theme in more recent philosophical analysis – most obviously in Žižek's (2014) work. Society has been eventalised: so to understand it we have to grasp it in the act of its becoming. Like an event, society is never wholly present in an instant (Pyyhtinen, 2007). This wider interpretation of events and eventalising is also reflected in Batty's (2002) urban research in which he interprets the city not as a thing, but as 'a cluster of spatial events'. Whilst this represents a slightly different meaning than the one used in this book, there are parallels with the approach to urban space adopted here. Analyses of dynamic relations, processes and potentialities are deemed to be more helpful ways of understanding the city than analysing substances, things or static phenomena.

Eventification

It is always dangerous to divide processes into dichotomous categories: especially when they are aligned to ideas that are supposedly positive/negative. However, to help understand event spaces better the term eventification is used in this book to refer to instances where urban public spaces are altered detrimentally by events. A good way to remember the meaning of this term, and to distinguish it from eventalisation, is to think of it as a combination of events and commodification (event-ification). Hence, eventification essentially represents the way events can tighten urban public spaces through creeping commodification and the related processes of commercialisation, privatisation and securitisation. Many events are ticketed, and even if they are not, they can deter and exclude people because they introduce certain practices and associations. When we think of events we often associate them with feelings of freedom. But some events result in the introduction of more stringent rules governing access/behaviour and events can splinter urban spaces, as well as liberate them.

It is important to point out that the word eventification has also been used previously by other researchers too. The term is used by Jakob (2013) in research concerning the use of cultural events by urban growth coalitions. Jakob focuses primarily on the eventification of cultural forms, sharing Chatterton and Unsworth's (2004: 377) concern that 'without real commitment, culture usually drifts into the service of place marketing and attracting tourists'. In this book, as the focus is public space, the term is used to refer to the commercialisation of space, rather than the commercialisation of culture. However, when discussing spaces such as parks, squares and streets, and given that space is (partly) culturally produced, space and culture are hard to separate.

Variants of the term are also apparent in recent literature. Spracklen et al. (2013) uses the term 'eventization' to refer to similar processes. According to Spracklen et al. (2013: 167) eventization is 'the transformation of (free or cheap) communicative leisure activities into (expensive) corporatised spectacles and privatised spaces'. According to the authors, this process of commodification turns spaces of belonging into spaces of exclusion. This book also covers the way in which events can privatise and monetise urban spaces; and exclude certain people from them. The work of Spracklen et al. (2013: 1673) is important because they emphasise that there is often 'blind obedience' to the notion that events have positive effects when they are staged in urban spaces. This assumption is misguided, and Chapter 5 explains how events can contribute to the production of exclusive, splintered space, and how they can inhibit the use of these spaces. It should also be noted that, although the eventification of space is, by definition, a detrimental process, it can be negotiated and resisted (see Chapter 8).

The urbanisation of events

There is now widespread recognition of the festivalisation of space, culture and politics, and some appreciation of the more specific processes of eventisation, eventification, and eventalisation. However, there is less written about the urbanisation of events – the way in which the geography of city events is changing. This process involves impetus and co-operation from various event stakeholders including organisers, rights holders, promoters, venues, property interests and public authorities. The next section of the book aims to redress this imbalance of attention. In her analysis of football events, Hagemann (2010: 724) has pointed to the importance of analysing the 'urbanisation of events' alongside the 'eventisation' of host cities. Urbanisation in this context means the way events are increasingly staged in central, urban and public spaces, rather than in peripheral, rural or purpose built venues. The urbanisation of events is a process that occurs in various different ways and these are discussed further below.

Relocation

One obvious way that events are being urbanised is via the relocation of existing events. Events that were previously staged in purpose built urban arenas – outdoor stadiums, indoor arenas, theatres and concert halls – have been moved into city centres (Richards and Palmer, 2010). This relocation can involve the entire event being moved or merely part of it. There are examples of this trend in both the sport and cultural sectors, although it is perhaps more common in the sports sector. For example, whilst running races may be an established feature of our streets, other track and field events are now being staged in the public realm for the first time. In the UK; London, Manchester and Newcastle have all staged 'track' events in city centres. After the 2015 edition of the annual 'City Games' staged on Manchester's streets, Lord Coe (Vice President of the International Amateur Athletics Federation) said that this format was needed 'for athletics to attract a new and growing fan base' (Cited in Ingle, 2015). This rationale for urbanising events is explored further in later sections of the chapter.

More extreme examples of even urbanisation include the relocation of motor races out of purpose built ovals or circuits into central streets. Singapore and Valencia now have Formula One Grand Prix street circuits, with annual races staged on public roads in and around waterfront areas. These events represent thinly veiled attempts to emulate the success of world's best known motor race the Monaco Grand Prix, which has been staged on the streets of this densely urbanised principality since 1929. Other cities have also staged city centre motor races, including Vancouver, Adelaide, Toronto, Detroit, Edmonton, Baltimore and Birmingham (UK), which staged an annual 'Super Prix' race through the city's streets in the 1980s (Smith, 2002). These events are sometimes staged on roads within urban parks – which means very disruptive road closures can be avoided. For example, in June 2015 a Formula E motor race was staged in Battersea Park, London for the first time.

The relocation of events from conventional arenas into public spaces is happening within the cultural events sector too. Large companies that stage concerts in indoor arenas have sought licenses to stage events in public spaces. One of the most significant event companies in the world is AEG Ltd. This US company owns and/or operates a series of high profile indoor arenas (including Wembley Arena and the O^2 Arena in London), but it also stages events in public spaces. For example, in 2013 the live entertainment arm of the company (AEG Live) announced a five year partnership with The Royal Parks: the agency responsible for managing London's most prestigious public parks. Under this agreement AEG Live will stage six summer concerts per year, meaning a large part of Hyde Park becomes an AEG venue during the summer. Indeed, whereas the O^2 and Wembley Arenas may be AEG's flagship venues in the winter months, in the summer their main venue is Hyde Park (see Figure 3.1). Jenkins (2013a) bemoans this situation, arguing that London's Royal Parks should be competing with the English countryside, not commercial events venues. Another major US events company 'Live Nation' have also been awarded licenses to stage major music festivals in

Figure 3.1 People arriving at one of AEG Live's 'British Summer Time' music events in
Hyde Park, London.

London's urban parks: for example the Calling Festival on Clapham Common and
the Wireless Festival in Finsbury Park.

The trend described above has made the competition between venues for big
events even more intense because traditional arenas now have to compete with
other conventional arenas *and* outdoor public spaces. An additional factor is that
high demand for urban land means that some indoor venues have been closed (e.g.
London's Earls Court closed in 2014), something that contributes further to the trend
identified here. In many densely populated cities, the value of land means that centrally located arenas are worth more as residential developments than as venues. This
emphasises that market forces and real estate values are also key factors to consider
when explaining why commercial events are being pushed into public spaces. Just
because it might not make financial sense to maintain a venue in a city that has
high property prices does not mean there is insufficient demand for these facilities.
According to John Reid, European President of Live Nation, the recent surge of
interest in live music has put pressure on major cities (Blackhurst, 2015). Rather
than electronic and social media replacing demand for live events, these technologies
seem to be fuelling interest in them (Jenkins, 2012). One result is there isn't enough
capacity to stage major music events. Reid feels London does not have enough suitable covered venues: 'we urgently need another venue' (Blackhurst, 2015: 44).

Other events traditionally staged in indoor arenas such as exhibitions and trade shows are also beginning to appear in our public spaces. Although air shows used to be confined to aerodromes and airfields, many cities now host Air Races – where aeroplanes are raced round a circuit in the sky. This introduces a vertical and air-borne dimension of events staged in public space. Other shows and exhibitions are also appearing in more conventional public spaces. Regent Street in central London now hosts an annual motor show every November, where approximately 300 vehicles are exhibited on this famous thoroughfare. Similarly, in nearby Regents Park, an art exhibition and a food & drink exposition are now held regularly in temporary venues. Taking these events out of exhibition halls into public spaces not only makes them more visible and accessible, it can also mean a shift in their meaning and content. In Melbourne, Weller (2013: 2854) describes how the city's fashion festival is increasingly staged in urban public spaces; 'incursions' that blur the distinction between this trade event and 'the celebratory ethos of local festivals'. This case is explored in more detail in Chapter 5.

Venue extensions

A related (second) sub-trend is the way that traditional event venues are being extended into the public spaces that surround them. Events staged in traditional arenas are constrained in time and space, so one way to enhance the event experience of spectators is by extending the event into these spaces. In this scenario, although the core activity remains in a traditional venue, the event is augmented by various activities and subsidiary events that are programmed in adjoining streets, squares and open spaces. These are often referred to as 'activations' by the professional involved. This trend is something identified by Cairns (2014) who argues that venues traditionally used for one or two hour-long events are being expanded into wider leisure destinations – places in which people might spend the whole day.

The USA's National Football League (NFL) is a well-known proponent of this type of approach. NFL football games become the centre of an 'eventscape' which covers a much larger area than just the stadium. The NFL now stages several regular season games in London every year and it is interesting to see how these events are extended into areas around the host venue – Wembley Stadium. In 2014 organisers created a 'Games Day Fan Plaza' on Olympic Way, the famous avenue that connects Wembley Park underground station to the Stadium. Their use of the word Plaza implies that organisers want to communicate the public-ness of the events by recreating the spatial feel of urban public space. Alongside the usual mix of street dressing, corporate hospitality, sponsor exhibits, concessions and merchandise stands, this Plaza hosted performances, inflatable games, museum exhibits and a version of the famous 'tailgate' parties for which the NFL are famed. These are the pre- and post-game communal gatherings where people park and open their vehicles to share food and drink. In 2014 the Wembley tailgate party (promoted as the biggest ever) started seven hours before the American Football action commenced, highlighting that the NFL's Game Day Fan Plaza represented a temporal, as well as a spatial, extension of the main event.

The type of venue extension described above is a fan park or 'fan zone' (see Figure 3.2). These 'events' are staged in conjunction with large events and they allow fans to engage with the event even if they don't have a ticket. Fan zones are also provided as an added attraction for spectators who do have tickets, but want to extend their event experience. They are generally something provided in conjunction with sport events, rather than cultural events. Pioneering examples were conceived for the 2002 FIFA Football World Cup in Japan and South Korea (Hagemann, 2010), although the subsequent edition of this mega-event staged in Germany (2006) became famed for developing the concept. German organisers staged a series of official 'Fan Fests' including a Fan Mile in Berlin which stretched from the Brandenburg Gate into the Tiergarten (the city's large central park). This fanzone attracted one million visitors per day when matches involving the host nation were played, and the country's Fan Fest hosted 18 million visitors in total during the tournament. Ironically, because fan zones are more accessible to ordinary fans, the atmosphere is usually better than in the venue. For example, with respect to football events, Hagemann (2010) feels that fan zones have a more dynamic atmosphere than the staid atmosphere of actual stadia. Hence, TV producers now cut to footage of the fan zone at key moments (e.g. when a goal is scored), rather than the fans in the stadium.

Although normally associated with football tournaments, fan zones are also now used in conjunction with other events too. Over the past few years, London

Figure 3.2 Fans at the NFL Fan Rally in Trafalgar Square, London.

has hosted central them in conjunction with triathlon, basketball, cycling and American Football events. There was even one in Vienna during the 2015 edition of the Eurovision Song Contest. Sometimes these fan zones are hosted directly outside event venues. In this sense they represent a literal 'enlargement' of a venue (Hagemann, 2010). For example, there is a fan zone directly outside the Air Canada Centre when the Toronto Maple Leafs (National Hockey League [NHL] team) and the Toronto Raptors (National Basketball Association [NBA] team) play their home games. This space normally functions as an access road, but on match days the road is closed to traffic providing a space for fans to watch a large screen attached to the outside of the main arena (see Figure 3.3). The cost of NHL/NBA tickets and the difficulties getting hold of them means that this fan zone centred around a big screen has become a key way that fans engage with their team's fixtures. This is emphasised by a large illuminated sign that hangs nearby which announces: 'We believe that watching the game on a two storey high HD TV is a sports fan's given right'.

Fan zones are often arranged in a very formal manner, with tickets and pre-booking required. However, they can also comprise loose concentrations of event related activities. In the pioneering German examples, eight cities charged admission fees (e.g. Cologne, Munich), but the others, including the Berlin Fan Mile, were free to enter (Eick, 2010). During the London 2012 Olympic and Paralympic Games there was a mix of very tightly organised and more loosely organised fan

Figure 3.3 Venue extension. The fan zone site outside the Air Canada Centre, Toronto.

zones. Some were open access and relatively informal. In other instances – such as the official 'Live Site' in Hyde Park – access was highly controlled using a combination of physical barriers, security checks, conditions of entry and queuing systems. The advantage of this arrangement for event organisers is that the fan zone acts as a security and crowd control system (see Chapter 5), something that was pivotal to the rationale for pioneering examples. Fan zones attract event enthusiasts who do not have tickets to inhabit certain spaces in the city - allowing them to co-mingle with other fans. This is why some authors see fan zones as something that democratises mega-events. But the spatial concentration of fans also makes it easier for urban authorities to control them. This is a key theme in Frew and McGillivray's work. These authors describe FIFA Fan Fests as 'an attempt to diffuse potential deviant activities and cultivate largely passive forms of behaviour' (Frew and McGillivray, 2008: 191). Other critical analysis of fan zones identifies their role in supporting commercial objectives. For example, Kolamo and Vuolteenaho (2013) see them as something that helps draw attention to official sponsors.

Several cities have taken the idea of venue extensions a stage further. Rather than merely extending an event into the areas immediately around a traditional venue, some cities have tried to extend events into central spaces too. The best example is Gothenburg in Sweden. Gothenburg's compactness and the arrangement of the main venues means organisers of major events can use the whole central district as a venue (Thörn, 2006; Smith, 2012). Here, the city becomes the venue for events, even when they are principally staged in conventional arenas. The best example was the 2006 European Athletics Championships (EAC). During the EAC, key ceremonies (e.g. opening ceremony and medal ceremonies) were staged in urban public spaces. A cultural festival was also staged in conjunction with the event - something that helped to transform Gothenburg's central district into a venue for the time the event was being staged (Smith, 2012). An even more extensive version of this happens during mega-events. During the 2012 Olympic Games: the Greater London Authority (GLA) 'wanted to extend the Games experience from the competition venues to London's landmark destinations such as bridges, parks and other tourist destinations as well as local sites' (Edizel et al., 2014: 28). This included routes between transport nodes and venues and various 'Experience Themed Areas' to extend the event into London's public realm. The GLA provided £50,000 for each Borough to dress their parks, streets and squares – money which was also used to 'purchase content' from the London 2012 Cultural Festival (Edizel et al., 2014).

Urban public spaces are staging more live events but they are also increasingly being used to mediate events that are taking place elsewhere. The 'big screen' has become a regular feature in many public spaces and these also provide examples of venue extensions. In most instances, these screens are temporary installations; they are erected for the event and then removed. But in some cities, the big screen has become a permanent architectural fixture (see Chapter 8). These fixed screens tend to be located in main squares either in city centres or close to event venues. Screenings are events in themselves: sometimes they are loosely configured, and

require no pre-booking, ticket or payment. However, in other instances, organisers charge an entry fee and/or erect barriers to control accessibility.

There are strong links between big screens and major events. The first big
screen – the 'JumboTron' – was famously exhibited for the first time at the 1985
World Expo in Tskuba, Japan (McQuire, 2010). Screens are or often used as the
centrepiece of the fan zones that are discussed above and they are sometimes
retained afterwards. For example, large screens introduced to host fan zones are
sometimes part of the physical legacy of mega-events. In Manchester a major
'public space broadcasting project' involving the BBC emerged from the screens
introduced during the 2002 Commonwealth Games. There are indications that
future event screenings may not merely be shown on purpose built screens, but
projected on to buildings and structures within our cities. In line with this trend,
some of the latest sport stadia are designed so that images can be projected on to
external facades (Cairns, 2014).

Obviously many sport events are now screened in public spaces, but opera and
ballet performances are often shown too. City squares such as Trafalgar Square
in London have hosted performances not just from nearby venues such as the
London Coliseum, but from operatic and theatrical venues all around the world.
Using the same technologies, cinematic events are also staged in public spaces.
In lots of parks there are regular screenings of films during summer months. Luna
Cinema organise open air cinema in several prominent public spaces in London:
including Greenwich Park, Holland Park and Battersea Park. These events are
promoted using the strapline 'classic films in the capital's most incredible settings', highlighting that the allure of these events has more to do with the venue
than the film on offer. In one sense, these events represent a contemporary version
of the drive-thru – the original manifestation of outdoor cinema. But open air cinema is also a good example of the way public spaces are increasingly being used
for events, and a useful illustration of the way that public spaces allow established
leisure activities to be transformed into events.

Rural-urban migration

Jenkins (2012) suggests many events have moved 'from the desert and the countryside, to complex modern cities'. This highlights that, alongside relocations and
venue extensions, a further sub-trend is the urbanisation of events that previously
took place in open spaces in rural locations. Sport events such as cross country
races, equestrian events and triathlons were traditionally staged in rural settings,
but they are increasingly being staged in the centres of major cities. In the UK,
the traditional venues for equestrian events are large country parks like Hickstead,
Badminton and Burleigh. However, the two biggest events staged in recent years
have both been in London: the 2012 Olympic and Paralympic equestrian events
in Greenwich Park and the 2014 Longines Global Champions Tour (staged in
the Olympic Park in 2013 and Horse Guards Parade in 2014). In these examples,
temporary venues were constructed in urban spaces to stage the events. Three
day eventing requires a cross country course, not something you would expect to

see in a city location, but during the past two Olympic Games this event has been staged in an urban park (2012) and on an urban golf course (2008). There is also an established athletic discipline called cross country. This is the epitome of a rural event, but many of the World Championships in recent years have been held in cities. When suitably rural land can't be found, golf courses, parks and horse racing tracks are used.

Triathlons have also become city events. Triathlons require roads to cycle and run on, but also open water for the swimming element. For this reason, you might expect rural or coastal locations to be favoured, but the largest triathlon events are now usually in cities. Indeed, the annual World Triathlon Finals are now staged in and around Hyde Park in London. This is something that troubles Jenkins (2013b) who feels that 'people who want to swim, cycle and run long distances can do it in plenty of places that do not inconvenience thousands of others'. Other rural sport events have been urbanised too, helping to reaffirm this sub-trend. In 2014, for the third year running, a Motocross City Trial was staged in Manchester's Piccadilly Gardens – one of the city's most central and important public spaces. Trialing is a sport which requires motorbike riders to negotiate a series of obstacles; usually involving mud, logs, water and other natural features. The first edition of this event, inevitably sponsored by Red Bull, was reported as one that 'took trials out of the country and into the heart of Manchester' (Red Bull, 2012). The event is a good example of the way some sports have tried to gain credibility and fashionability by being seen as urban: an adjective that refers to a style of music/dance/youth culture. The best way to do this is by staging the sport in city squares, rather than country fields.

For obvious reasons, winter sports are usually staged in mountain regions. But, following the trend discussed here, skiing and snowboarding events have been staged in city centres. For example, in 2010 the US city of Denver staged a 'Big Air' event in which snowboarders navigated a 106 foot high slope erected in a downtown park. This event attracted 14,000 spectators. Helsinki's Senate Square has also staged snowboarding events and Red Bull has taken their 'Crashed Ice' ice skating race to various cities including Belfast, Edmonton and Lausanne. And at a larger scale, the Winter Olympic Games are increasingly 'hosted' by large cities (e.g. Vancouver, Turin) rather than mountain resorts.

The apparent rural-urban migration of events applies to cultural events too: the outdoor music festival is something that used to be intrinsically associated with rural open spaces, facilitating the desire for escape that motivates many of the attendees. Pioneering festivals like Woodstock, Glastonbury and the Isle of Wight Festival were all staged in locations removed from urban conurbations. Many music festivals are still staged in rural settings, but some of the most successful festivals established in recent years are staged in cities, for example Sziget (Budapest) and Sonar (Barcelona). According to John Reid, the European President of Live Nation, 'more and more, we're running inner-city festivals, not all people want to camp' (Blackhurst, 2015: 44). This isn't necessarily understood by some potential festival goers, who assume that music festivals are rural phenomena. Accordingly, on the homepage of Sonar's official UK fansite, organisers are forced to emphasise that:

In contrast to the summer festivals that many people are used to, Sonar does not involve camping or jumping about in a muddy field. It is a city festival. This means that you'll need to find accommodation in and around the city.

(Sonar, 2015)

Explanations for these trends

The analysis above illustrates the trend for event urbanisation and explains *how* events are being urbanised. However, this analysis hasn't explained why these processes have occurred. Why cities are more interested in staging events in general has been discussed at length in other books so the discussion here focuses on why more events are being staged *in public spaces*. To explain this trend, we need to understand the motivation and priorities of some of the different stakeholders involved: including urban authorities, rights holders and venue managers. Accordingly, the following section is divided into different subsections, each of which deals with a different stakeholder group. In each sub-section the purpose of the discussion is to identify what that stakeholder seeks to gain from staging events in public spaces.

Why cities want to stage events in public spaces

Cities are keen to animate public spaces and this is one of the most obvious reasons why more events are being staged in urban public spaces. The animation of cities via events is one of the main subjects discussed in Chapter 4 so it is not discussed at length here. Urban authorities are not merely interested in animation for the sake of making good space: animated space is more commercially productive. This point is made by Pugalis (2009) who feels that cultural vitality helps to produce economic activity. Populating urban spaces can generate income for urban authorities via licenses, rents and other fees. It can also assist the urban economy, directly and indirectly: providing employment and revenue, but also attracting and satisfying city tourists who may return if they feel they have enjoyed being there. Of the 1215 people Tallon et al. (2006) interviewed in Swansea (UK): 47 per cent said outdoor events made the city centre a more attractive place to be; and 55 per cent of a smaller sample of event attendees (n = 224) mentioned they would like to see more outdoor events and live music in the city centre. Citizens seem to appreciate events, but it would be naïve to think that public opinion is directing urban policy.

It's all about the money, money, money . . .

It is costly to maintain public spaces, so in an era when there are demands for lower taxes and because of the budget deficits faced by many governments, urban authorities are keen to find new revenue streams. Staging events in public spaces is seen as one way of generating the funds needed to pay for their upkeep. The sums involved are not inconsiderable. The local council are estimated to have made £260,000 by allowing Finsbury Park in London to be used as a concert venue over two days in 2013 (Haringey Council, 2013). With this type of commercial income in mind, many public spaces are now available to hire as events venues. For example, London's Royal Parks are facing serious cuts to the government grants they have traditionally relied on. They are now required to generate over half of their own income, which means they now have to seek commercial opportunities. Events are seen as a potentially lucrative source of income. In 2012/3 the Royal Parks generated £6.687 million from events, a figure that was up from £4.856 million the previous year (Royal Parks, 2013a). This situation has existed in the US for some time. New York's Central Park was already raising half its revenue by the early 1990s (Zukin, 1995). As Zukin (1995) warns us, this type of funding comes at a cost – it means that private interests begin to direct park policy.

This situation is replicated in several other public spaces in London which are controlled by public authorities. Authorities such as the Greater London Authority (GLA) and relevant Borough Councils are also seeking additional revenue. Accordingly, London's most famous plaza, Trafalgar Square, is now available to hire for 'promotional events and performance based activities' (GLA, 2014). In 2014 the GLA was charging £1000 an hour for the hire of the Square, with a £10,000 fee applicable for the second day and any subsequent days (GLA, 2014). Other public spaces in the UK capital are also available to rent including Potters Fields on the south side of the River Thames next to City Hall (Figure 3.4). The Potters Fields Management Trust – the public-private consortium responsible for this site – invites people to hire the park for 'events, product placements, marketing promotions and filming'. Yet the Trust claims that 'the park is open to the public at all times' (Potters Fields Park Management Trust: undated). Those offended by this wanton commercialism may be relieved to know that the Trust will not consider: 'anything connected with tobacco, any alcoholic product that we deem is targeted at young people, exclusive corporate events, anything of a political or religious nature' (Potters Fields Park Management Trust: undated). Figure 3.4 illustrates the sort of event that is deemed acceptable – an event promoting Rioja wines. This event neatly illustrates the idea that events staged in public spaces are often aimed at the middle classes, people that can civilise these spaces and reclaim them from 'undesirable' uses and users (see Chapter 5).

Some public parks like Potters Fields do not have perimeter walls or railings, which means they are accessible 24 hours a day. Other parks are gated, which allows greater control over who accesses at what time. These latter sites make ideal events venues as these they are easier to close off to the public. One such park is Victoria Embankment Gardens, a public park on the north side of the River Thames close to Charing Cross Station (see Figure 3.5). This site is managed by the City of Westminster, the local Borough Council. As the Council emphasise on their own website, the space provides a welcome retreat from the very busy streets that surround it. However, that does not prevent the Council from seeking to hire it out as an events venue. The space is available all year round for events, with variable rates charged by the Council depending on the time of year (December and the summer months are most expensive), but also on the type of event being staged. In the summer months the rate for private events is £3000 a day (06:00–00:00), whereas for community groups and charities it is £900 (City

Figure 3.4 An event staged on Potters Fields, London. The combination of the event and the cityscape creates the sort of eventscape that cities and event organisers crave.

Figure 3.5 Closed for events. Victoria Embankment Gardens, London.

of Westminster, undated b). An extra £1000 per day fee is charged for large events (over 500 people), so this space has the potential to generate £4000 a day for the Council when it is used at peak times by private organisations for large events. This highlights the revenue generating potential of urban public spaces.

City image: from public spaces to publicity spaces?

One of the other significant reasons why cities are staging more events in prominent public spaces is to generate attractive images that can enhance a city's position in an increasingly symbolic economy. Cities are under pressure to gain new forms of inward investment and a city's image is seen as a key vehicle with which to secure attention and capital from target audiences. Potential sources of investment include new residents, businesses, students, film crews and tourists. Cities such as Edinburgh (Invest in Edinburgh) and London (London and Partners) have established new agencies dedicated to enticing these audiences. Organisations like these aim to generate attractive, memorable images that provide visual city portraits, but they also need to communicate positive meanings and connotations that might resonate with potential investors. This means thinking about visual imagery as well as initiatives that can communicate the values a city wishes to extoll (Smith, 2005). As Carter (2006: 153) states, events 'provide the spectacles that cities require to dramatise their potential as places for investment'. Therefore, the eventisation of space is related to the 'spectacularisation of space' (Bélanger, 2000). By staging events in public spaces, cities draw attention to these spaces at a time when they are most spectacular and dramatic. These events also communicate important messages about the city more generally. This helps to explain why cities want to stage events in public spaces.

Events staged in public spaces can have a profound effect on people who attend but they are also staged to disseminate images to external audiences. In related media coverage it is essential that these events are placed: i.e. that the audience understands that this event is happening in a specific city. Anonymous, ageographic events are useless to city marketers as the success of events as city marketing tools relies on making visible connections between events and destinations. This incentivises cities to stage events with famous landmarks visible and, as Richards and Wilson (2004) argue, events can add value to these landmarks. Using outdoor spaces for events generates media coverage of identifiable cityscapes and it dramatises them, creating eventscapes. The media coverage of the diving competition at the 1992 Barcelona Olympic Games is perhaps the most famous example of this. Barcelona's diving venue is a permanent facility, but the same effect can be created by staging events in temporary venues. Two beach volleyball events provide good illustrations of this trend: the events staged on Bondi Beach, Sydney during the 2000 Olympic Games, and the events staged at Horse Guards Parade, London during the 2012 Olympic Games (see Figure 3.6).

It is perhaps easiest to understand the place marketing logic behind staging events in central, public spaces by looking at the alternative approach. Many events are staged in anonymous arenas on the edge of cities and in these instances

Figure 3.6 The beach volleyball venue for the 2012 Olympic Games at Horse Guards
Parade, London.

there are no guarantees that a host city will be featured extensively in media coverage. Research into the Women's 'Final Four' US basketball event revealed that,
in the 11hrs and 45mins of televised coverage, visuals of the host city appeared
for less than 3.5mins (Green et al., 2003). Similarly disappointing effects were
recorded by researchers who quantified TV coverage of Sheffield generated by the
2002 World Professional Snooker Championships. During 100 hours of coverage,
the city was only mentioned 123 times. Many of these mentions were incidental
and the authors of the research concluded; 'it would be difficult to argue that such
mentions contribute towards positive images' (Shibli and Coleman, 2005: 21).
This has led some commentators to suggest that host destinations should negotiate
a minimum level of coverage with media companies, or include contractual stipulations that would guarantee the use of certain visuals, commentaries or camera
angles (Chalip et al., 2003).

It is logical that if cities are using events as promotional tools, then they might
try to secure control over the extent and direction of messages delivered. This
was something attempted by Australian tourism officials before the 2000 Olympic Games. According to Brown et al. (2002: 177), by working with the media,
the Australian Tourism Commission aimed to 'make the Olympics a two-week
documentary on all aspects of Australian life'. This approach was emulated by
organisers of the London 2012 Games. Cairns suggests that during this event,

in addition to the images of the stadia . . . television viewers were presented with images of the country's principle buildings, its iconic structures and most famous historic monuments: the Olympics was used as a vehicle for the promotion of the UK in general.

(Cairns, 2014: 1)

This type of coverage is very valuable for host locations, especially as it may be perceived by audiences as more credible than traditional paid for advertising (Smith, 2005). However, there are no guarantees of getting it, especially in the case of smaller events. TV companies screening these events might not have the time or appetite to develop extra features on host cities. In these instances the only way to ensure destination coverage is to stage the event in locations which are identifiable as part of the city: i.e. in urban public spaces.

One knock on effect of the recent obsession with the host city visibility is that it increases the value of mobile events that don't need specialised venues. Marathons, triathlons, cycle races, motor races, air races and boat races can be staged using existing public spaces. These events move round, through or over a city allowing television coverage to incorporate a range of urban features. In an era that prioritises the city as the content (not just container) of events, this makes these events particularly valuable. Unsurprisingly many events are routed (or rerouted) around a city's streets in a way that maximises the number of city icons visible to television audiences. In the build up to London's 2012 Games, the marathon was rerouted so that it finished in central London. This was a departure from the convention to stage the finish in the Olympic Stadium. Organisers claimed this change was made was for logistical reasons, but aggrieved local representatives in East London felt it was a decision directed by place marketing objectives and television audiences. There are other examples of this too. In 2014 the Northern Irish Government paid £3 million to allow Belfast to stage the Grande Partenza – the opening stages of the Giro d'Italia – one of cycling's three Grand Tours. The rationale for the route chosen was clear: 'we just wanted to make sure our main tourist locations were shown off' (Ross, cited in Addley, 2014). However, like in London, the routing of the event was highly controversial. East Belfast was well served, but the West of the City was bypassed causing great consternation amongst the Catholic communities who live there. The local Sinn Fein MP communicated his dismay: 'what we will see is all other parts of the city being touched and being seen worldwide except West Belfast and it is just not good enough' (Maskey cited in Addley, 2014).

The case of the Singapore Grand Prix (est. 2008) which is staged on a street circuit in a central part of the city is another insightful case. The event draws attention to the newly developed Marina Bay area and even though the race is staged at night the organisers clearly use the event to draw attention to the city's main attractions (see Figure 3.7). Indeed, the Singapore Tourist Board has urged more buildings located in the vicinity of the event to illuminate their premises to make sure that the brightly lit racetrack doesn't obscure the city (Henderson et al., 2010). Clearly, in the view of the organisers, the motor race shouldn't get in the way of the real reason for staging the event: the promotion of Singapore as a centre for tourism and entertainment. The intervention of the Tourist Board reinforces the fact that city coverage is not guaranteed, even when staging a motor race through the city's streets. After the controversial V8 motor races staged on a street circuit in Canberra, Australia, a letter to the local paper complained that during the TV coverage 'there was next to nothing shown of Canberra' (cited in Tranter and Keefee, 2004). Opponents argued that that locating the race in the city centre 'was not necessary for any showcasing benefits for Canberra, Even if the event had been built on a purpose built circuit on the outskirts of Canberra, scenic shots of Parliament House and other landmarks could have been shown on TV' (Tranter and Keefee, 2004: 176). This argument ignores the fact that city authorities are not just interested in promoting cityscapes, they want to promote cityscapes dramatised by events (eventscapes).

Televised images may only be disseminated at certain times – i.e. just before, during and just after events – but that does not mean that images of events staged in public spaces have a limited life or a temporally constrained impact. Cities use related images and video coverage on their websites long after these events are staged, increasing their temporal reach. When city agencies tasked with generating inward investment make presentations to potential investors, they invariably feature photographs and films featuring spectacular events staged in public spaces. This highlights one of the key motivations for staging these events – to

Figure 3.7 Marina Bay, Singapore at night: these streets are used for the annual Grand Prix.

capture images of public spaces at times when they are most spectacular, so that these images can be recycled, recirculated and represented.

Internal communications

Cities stage events in public spaces to disseminate images to external audiences, but some events are aimed at internal audiences too. In the last few decades, many cities have experienced high levels of immigration and they have become more ethnically diverse. This has posed challenges for urban authorities seeking to achieve social cohesion. To promote tolerance, and to encourage different groups to mingle, they have staged public events. These events are often programmed in public spaces – to emphasise their openness, but also because these spaces are owned by the city. If urban authorities want to stage events to communicate urban policy it makes sense to stage them in symbolic spaces they control. The main square, the central street and the municipal park all symbolise the city and so staging cultural events in these spaces emphasises that they are citywide events for everyone.

A good example of this type of approach is discussed by Foley and McPherson (2007). In 2002/3, Glasgow introduced a Winter Festival to the city centre: a series of events that aimed to provide an out of season tourist attraction and to unite the diverse population of the city. The event involved a fairground in the city centre, but also celebrations marking various cultural festivals: Guy Fawkes (Bonfire Night), Hogmanay (New Year) and the annual religious festivals celebrated by Glasgow's Christian, Muslim, Hindu and Buddhist citizens. The rationale included an attempt to move away from the status quo: Christmas was usually the only festival visible in the city centre at this time of the year. The aim was to spread the festival over time (November–January) and space (across the city centre), but also to extend its reach culturally (Foley and McPherson, 2007). The plan didn't really work. The authors conclude that this initiative was a lost opportunity to celebrate Glaswegian multi-culturalism, as the event morphed into something 'more conducive to income generation, city entrepreneurialism and post-modern spectacle' (Foley and McPherson, 2007: 154). There have also been various examples of this approach in London. For the past few years major events have been staged in Trafalgar Square to celebrate various cultural and religious festivals: for example, Diwali, Chinese New Year and St Patrick's Day (see Chapter 4).

Other reasons . . .

Gibson and Homan (2004) provide a different explanation for why local authorities stage more events in public spaces. In their case study, the council staged approximately 20 events each year including music concerts, community festivals, film and art festivals and ethnic celebrations. Gibson and Homan (2004: 72) suggest these events are partly staged to compensate for 'the loss of live venues' caused by a combination of rising property process and noise legislation. In this instance, the staging of new events in public spaces is not necessarily a voluntary initiative: it is something forced on authorities because of problems within the traditional venue sector. Now that many public authorities are facing budget cuts, it becomes more difficult to justify publicly funded events. Hence one further reason why we are seeing more private events in public spaces is because local councils want to offer events, but can't afford to stage them themselves (see Chapter 7). Encouraging privately organised events in public spaces provide a direct replacement for the events that local authorities want to host, but can't because they lack the resources to do so.

Why event organisers want to stage events in public spaces

For the reasons outlined above, urban authorities are increasingly keen to use public spaces as events venues. However, in most instances the events staged are not organised by urban authorities but by promoters, rights holders and/or other event management companies. Despite the various complications introduced by using unconventional venues, these organisations are highly enthusiastic about staging events in city parks, squares and streets. These locations are perceived to add value to events, by making them more distinctive. It also means they are more likely to be featured in television and other media coverage. Event organisers think that, both for those people attending in person and those consuming the event via media output, events staged in public spaces are more memorable. In an age when messages are increasingly disseminated via social media, anything that encourages people to tweet, post or upload text about or pictures of an event is regarded as a very positive thing. By staging the event in a spectacular or unusual venue, event organisers can encourage this type of mediation.

Placing an event in a public location may be as important to the event as it is to the city. This is particularly true for smaller events, where an event brand may benefit greatly from associations with a powerful place brand, like London or New York. This provides an extra incentive for event organisers to make sure that everyone knows where this event is happening. And staging an event in a famous park, street or square is a very good way of ensuring the audiences know where an event is being staged. Even in the case of mega-events, event brands utilise public spaces to enhance the value of their franchise. Kolamo and Vuolteenaho (2013) use the term 'mediascape' to refer to the way in which event brands are increasingly communicated via staged representations of urban spaces.

To understand which stakeholders are driving the urbanisation of events, it is important to acknowledge the role of sponsors. Many new events staged in public spaces have been established by – or are indelibly connected to – certain companies interested in the benefits of experiential marketing. In the experience economy (Pine and Gilmore, 1999), a key way to add or create value is by *staging* products. Companies like Red Bull have been at the forefront of such practices, creating and staging outlandish events to animate their brand. For example, the City of Lausanne is one of the hosts of the Red Bull 'Crashed Ice' competition. For this event, the organisers build a course in the centre of the city for a downhill speed skating race. This fast paced, spectacular – and extremely dangerous – competition is extremely popular with spectators. However, in this instance and for similar events, the organisers/sponsors gain as much, if not more, from the urban location. It guarantees greater awareness and exposure for the event (and the associated brands) than if the event was staged in a purpose built venue.

According to Bittner (cited in Hagemann, 2010: 733), in our new experience driven society, 'there is an obsession with urban space'. With this in mind, it is unsurprising that various product launches, film premières, public relations stunts and brand installations are increasingly staged in urban public spaces. These types of events are staged to promote certain products. Many cities now hire out prominent public spaces such as central squares to companies wishing to stage promotional events. These companies obviously benefit from the large volumes of people that may visit or pass through these spaces. There are other advantages of 'exteriorising' or 'placing' brands in this way, not least the fact that 'if a corporation is connected with the emotive qualities of a place, customers will identify more strongly with the brand' (Klingmann, 2007: 83). This may have positive effects for brands, but the effects on the urban spaces used are more problematic – something discussed at length in Chapter 5.

Why event venues want to stage events in public spaces

Whilst cities and event organisers may be pushing to stage events in public spaces, one might assume that people who represent conventional venues may be less supportive. This is obviously true in many instances but there are also examples of venues that have helped to push events into urban public spaces. Some examples have already been cited in the discussion above: venues are creating extensions into the public realm. However, there are also instances where venues take their events to public spaces located some distance from their own premises. If venues receive public money they are often required to demonstrate that they are seeking to widen their audiences. This can be achieved by taking events to the public, rather than trying to persuade people to come to established venues. Hence a key explanation for the urbanisation of events is the push to make some events more accessible symbolically and physically. A good example is the Barbican in London: a prestigious venue for a range of cultural forms including dance, film, music, theatre and visual arts. The Barbican is Europe's largest performing arts venue – involving a series of concert halls, exhibition spaces, cinemas and other events venues. The size of the complex means that there is no logistical reason to take events outside their own perimeter. However, in 2013 the Barbican launched 'Beyond Barbican' an outreach initiative which took several Barbican events into the streets, squares and parks of East London. As the Barbican prides itself on pushing artistic boundaries, it made sense for this venue to work beyond their own performance spaces: 'This summer we go beyond our walls with a series of gigs, festivals, performances, family-friendly and free events across east London' (Barbican, 2013). The Barbican is housed in a rather impenetrable Brutalist building in the City of London and is part-funded by The Corporation of London – one of wealthiest local authorities in the world. Therefore, it is important that the venue reaches out to the relatively disadvantaged districts located a short distance to the East – the London Boroughs of Tower Hamlets and Hackney. However, 'Beyond Barbican' is not project pursued for purely altruistic reasons. The idea of brand transfers mentioned previously is also relevant here in trying to explain the rationale for this initiative. The Barbican benefits not only by advertising itself in East London to new audiences, but it also gains credibility at a wider level. Rather than being seen as an elite cultural institution in the City of London, the organisation becomes associated with East London – where London's most fashionable 'edgy' districts are located (Pappalepore et al., 2014).

Counter trends

Events traditionally staged in specialised venues are increasingly being staged in urban public spaces. However there is an interesting counter-trend emerging too. Some events that were traditionally staged in public spaces are being pushed into traditional venues. For carnival events, where there are often concerns about public safety and criminality, urban authorities have tried to push festivities into more formal settings. In recent decades these events have been more regulated, so it is logical that the next phase of regulation is spatial containment and formalisation. London's Notting Hill Carnival provides a good example. For many years, the police have been eager to move this event away from its street setting into a more contained one: either Hyde Park or an enclosed stadium (Manning cited in Belghazi, 2006). Moving the event is opposed strongly by those involved and this debate is one that seems to be happening all over the world. In Brazil, which hosts some of the world's most famous carnivals, many cities are considering formalisation and decentralisation of events to allow them to be managed better. For example, since 2007 parts of the Ouro Preto Carnival in the Minas Gerais region have been decentralised (Flecha et al., 2010). Part of the event is now staged in a dedicated zone outside the town centre which people have to pay to enter. These examples highlight the way traditional street events are being formalised, whilst at the same time events traditionally staged in purpose built venues are being brought into the public realm.

Summary

The preceding discussion highlights how our cities have been eventised and events urbanised. These compatible processes seem to work in the interests of both events and urban authorities. As Johannsson and Kociatkiewicz (2011: 395) contend, 'city space imbues the festival with meaning, but the process is reciprocal because the festival provides new meanings for the city it inhabits'. This chapter introduces the processes though which we can understand the effects of events on public spaces. Eventalisation refers to the way events produce public space by animating existing spaces or by creating new public spaces. This process will be explored in more detail in the next part of this book (Chapter 4). Eventification is the commodification of space via events; a process that is inherently linked to the privatisation, commercialisation and securitisation of space. This process is explained and discussed in Chapter 5. Before these processes are discussed separately, it is important to reinforce the point that single events can produce both eventification and eventalisation: they are not separate processes but two sides of the same coin.

This chapter also introduces the key trend that provides the focus of this book: the urbanisation of events. Events have been urbanised through: the relocation of events from specialised venues; the extension of existing venues; and the migration of events from rural areas. Perhaps more importantly, the chapter also explores why this was happening. The two most significant reasons are (i) the need to generate revenue, and; (ii) the desire to promote the city to external audiences. However, cities are also staging more events in public spaces because they want to animate moribund spaces and because they want to achieve greater sociability in an era when people are withdrawing to more individualised spaces. These latter concerns are addressed in detail in the next chapter.

4　Eventalisation

Events and the production of urban public space

Introduction

Eventalisation is a process which is usually associated with informal, spontaneous or underground events (Pløger, 2010). This chapter demonstrates that it can be applied to official events too. In the context of formal events, the eventalisation of urban public space involves two dimensions: the (co)production of public spaces in areas not usually regarded as public spaces; and making conceived public spaces more public by loosening and animating them. Ideally, events might achieve these effects both on a temporary basis (during events), but also in the longer term (after those events have finished). This chapter begins by assessing which spaces need animating (e.g. squares) and how events help to achieve this. Drawing on the notion of loose space introduced in Chapter 2, it then analyses how events can loosen spaces which are usually very ordered and regulated (e.g. parks). Subsequently, there is consideration of how events can help produce public spaces in sites that are normally dominated by traffic and commerce (e.g. streets). Finally, and perhaps most significantly, the chapter assesses whether these positive effects are merely temporary or whether they can be sustained. Although the discussion mainly outlines the positive effects for urban public spaces, it is important to note that events always result in some problematic effects. Therefore, this chapter should be read in conjunction with next one (Chapter 5) which assesses some of the detrimental aspects of staging events in public spaces.

Animating public space

The need to animate public spaces is one of the most prevalent ideas within the urban design literature. The verb 'to animate' means to give life to, or to inspirit; and, as these definitions suggest, animation is usually regarded as a positive phenomenon when applied in the context of urban public spaces. Indeed, Shaftoe (2008: 25) regards animation 'anything that brings public spaces to life in a positive way'. Animation can be achieved by various means, but events are commonly used to achieve the desired effects. The idea of using events strategically to animate cities dates back to notion of Animation Culturel which emerged in France in the 1970s. To encourage people to visit and linger in urban spaces some cities contracted cultural animateurs who programmed events and festivals

(Montgomery, 1995). The tradition of Animation Culturel lives on in its most literal form through the work of Royal Deluxe, a French company who specialise in spectacular street theatre. This is the company that brought a mechanical Elephant to the streets of London and Giants to the streets of Liverpool.

Many urban designers regard urban space as something comprising form, activity and meaning – the so-called F-A-M model (Montgomery, 1998) and, following this logic, animation is regarded by designers as efforts to increase the amount of human activity in public spaces. This can make spaces more enjoyable to be in, encourage social interaction and make people feel safer. It can also assist economic objectives by increasing footfall for local businesses. However, there is a fine line between lively spaces and crowded ones. Whilst most people like to watch – and engage with – other people, few like being in spaces that are over-populated: this restricts activity and tightens urban space. It is worth remembering that some spaces are enjoyed by people because they represent an exception to crowded, noisy urban environments. Parks and other places for contemplation are enjoyed by some because they offer peacefulness, sanctuary and isolation. Therefore, animation is not something that should be applied to all urban public spaces.

Where animation is desired, events are seen as a good way to achieve it. Events are varied phenomena which exist at different scales. At the micro scale, a street busker is an event that can enliven urban space, but large-scale cultural festivals have also been introduced using the same rationale. Events are seen by urban authorities as something that can be introduced relatively easily; a quick-fix that can be implemented without the need for major capital investment. Indeed, Shaftoe (2008: 120) sees events as a 'low-cost way to bring public spaces back to life'. As we shall see in the next chapter, this prevailing view perhaps underestimates both the direct and the indirect costs of staging events. This simplistic attitude implies that events are inherently a good thing – something that neglects events' contribution to the commercialisation, privatisation and securitisation of space.

Which spaces need animating?

Although animation strategies have been applied to a range of different urban contexts, it is useful to examine where they are most commonly used and where they are most obviously needed. In city centres there are spaces which are lively because they are inhabited by people in their day to day lives. Others are dead and lifeless. This may be due to their location, their accessibility, their design, their meaning or some other reason. People attract other people to spaces, but the opposite is also true – a lack of people deters people which results in neglected, empty and anti-social spaces. It is mistaken to think lifeless spaces only exist in peripheral locations. Some of the most famous and significant squares in cities are often moribund because they have no everyday purpose. These types of spaces may have been constructed as symbolic edifices – monuments to ruling elites past and present – and this means they are not very inviting. For example, in a typically provocative article (entitled Why I hate Trafalgar Square), author Will Self (2012) writes that Trafalgar Square in London is: 'not so much a place to hang out as somewhere you feel constantly in danger of being hung for treason, such is the discourse of power enshrined in its leonine and general-studded plinths and its admiral-spiked column'.

The cold, unattractiveness of these monumental spaces is a problem in many cities, particularly capital cities where national monuments tend to be concentrated. A good example is Helsinki, the Finnish capital. This city has always been regarded as rather boring and cold, a reputation derived from the city's history as one built to represent the power of the Russian and Finnish states (Lehtovuori, 2010). Helsinki's cold and austere image is reinforced by the city's public spaces. Perhaps the most famous public space in Helsinki is Senate Square which is dominated by the city's cathedral. Like many ceremonial spaces, this square is impressive in photographs but it has always been a rather lifeless place. The square functions as an important symbol of the city, but the space itself has traditionally been under-used by its residents.

Public squares in cities have become synonymous with empty space (Giddings et al., 2011) and staging events is a common way of dealing with this problem. Shaftoe (2008: 122) feels that Queens Square, Bristol, 'only really comes alive when special events are held'. Events can reconfigure physical spaces and the social relations between users (Stevens and Shin, 2014). According to Rowe and Baker (2012), events such as public screenings provide opportunities for spontaneous, corporeal, sensory interactions with strangers – encounters that are increasingly rare in contemporary city squares. Restoring the sociability of public space is often part of the rationale for introducing or reviving festivals. Stevens and Shin (2014: 1) feel that these festivals 'support the redefinition, rediscovery and explanation of local social life'.

Trafalgar Square and Senate Square are typical of many capital city spaces where monumental architecture dominates at the expense of more human, user friendly spaces. In both these examples, events have been used to encourage people to use these spaces, but also to adapt their entrenched meanings. Since the Millennium, a whole series of programmed events have been scheduled in Trafalgar Square, including orchestral concerts (see Figure 4.1), cultural festivals, fan zones, opera screenings and official receptions for victorious English/British sports teams. In 2004 the Square was redesigned in a way that makes it easier to stage such events. The road between Trafalgar Square and the National Gallery was closed to traffic, creating a more pedestrian friendly site that feels less like a traffic island. Pedestrianising one side also helps to loosen the Square's 'rectilinear rigidity' (Self, 2012). Events help to loosen the space too – by encouraging more diverse users, uses and meanings.

Staging more informal, participatory events helps to make Trafalgar Square an active space, rather than a passive one. These events turn the Square into one that Londoners use, rather than one limited to tourists taking photographs. A good example is the Big Dance event. This is a biennial event organised by the Mayor of London which involves mass participation as well as more conventional performances. These types of events help to loosen to the rather stiff image of Trafalgar Square. The identity of the space is inextricably intertwined with the British Empire; therefore the rationale for staging Diwali, Chanukah, Eid, Vaisakhi, Chinese New Year, St Patrick's Day and a new African Festival in the

Figure 4.1 A performance by the London Symphony Orchestra in Trafalgar Square.

Square is clear. These are attempts to communicate that Trafalgar Square is for everyone. Staging these festivals in a prominent, public space also provides an opportunity for people who wouldn't normally celebrate these events to engage with them; thus promoting tolerance and understanding of multi-cultural London.

As well as hosting a regular events programme at weekends, Trafalgar Square has been 'eventalised' using the Fourth Plinth programme. This is a rolling series of art installations that are mounted on an empty plinth in the Square. These art works provide a continuous event, one that gives Londoners and visitors a reason to return to the Square. The juxtaposition of art installations and traditional statues loosens the previously 'fixed' identity of Trafalgar Square – an effect that was perhaps best illustrated by Anthony Gormley's installation 'One and Other' that allowed members of the public one hour to do whatever they wanted on the plinth. Over a period of 100 days in 2009, 2400 members of the public 'performed' on the plinth. The artist responsible for the work highlighted the significance of this example of public space animation:

> In the context of Trafalgar Square with its military, valedictory and male historical statues, this elevation of everyday life to the position formerly occupied by monumental art allows us to reflect on the diversity, vulnerability and particularity of the individual in contemporary society. It's about people coming together to do something extraordinary and unpredictable
>
> (Gormley, 2009)

In Self's (2012) view Trafalgar Square needs more of this ongoing animation to allow it to escape its austere formality: 'What's needed are cafes all over the gaff, open-air and serving excellent espresso; top-notch strolling and – unlicensed – buskers. . . ; an open-air market; some good ethnic food stalls. . . '.

Senate Square, Helsinki, faced similar challenges to Trafalgar Square and events have also been used here to generate activity and a new identity for the space. Events were programmed in Senate Square after the end of the cold war to address the lack of life and the relative uselessness and meaninglessness of the space (Lehtovuori, 2010). A rock concert featuring the 'Leningrad Cowboys' was staged in 1993, an event which 'opened' the Square to a wider range of uses and users. Senate Square is now established as an events 'stage'. This new function of the space ascended a new level in 2000, when Helsinki was nominated by the EU as one of the Millennium European Capitals of Culture. Various ceremonies, concerts and festivals have been staged since and the Square has also hosted sport events, such as the Red Bull City Flight – a commercial snowboarding event. Like in Trafalgar Square these events are seen as a way to bring people into this space and to change its meaning. Lehtovuori (2010) identifies other ways that staging events has changed the Square. Events require large installations to be erected and this helps to reduce the scale of the public space by making it feel less intimidating. However, the effects are not entirely positive. Some worry that events, particularly the commercial events that are staged here, have denigrated this national monument. These are legitimate concerns (see Chapter 5), but staging events does not necessarily diminish the symbolic value of the Square – in fact it does the opposite. As Lehtovuori (2010) highlights, these events and the imagery they generate have helped to enhance Helsinki's image by communicating that this it is a welcoming, vibrant city, not a cold, lifeless one.

Few public spaces in cities are dead all the time, most experience fluctuating levels of activity. Often streets and squares may be busy during the daytime, but very quiet at night. Accordingly, some cities have developed events strategies combined with efforts to boost night time activity. There are good economic reasons to stimulate the night-time economy, or the '24 hour city', but the main motivation is to make these places feels safer (Montgomery, 1995). Perhaps the best example is Montreal. Every summer, Montreal's downtown streets are used to host the Francofolies: a series of festivals that run one after another, including the famous Jazz Festival. Although some events require tickets, many free events are also programmed on the city's streets over an extended period. The events are multi-cultural and a wide range of ethnicities and nationalities are represented in the profiles of performers and audiences. Germain and Rose (2000: 157) state that during this festival there are: 'tens of thousands of people at any one time of all ages and cultures, milling around in a few city blocks until midnight in a completely safe environment with very low key security'. The area that hosts these events is now branded 'the Quartier de Spectacles' to reflect its role as a festival site. Critics might argue that this represents a sanitisation of the city, in line with Martin's (2014) view that promoting urban vibrancy is a euphemism for social cleansing. However, encouraging a diverse range of people into the streets at night should be seen as something positive, rather than dismissed as evidence of gentrification. According to Germain and Rose (2000), the festivals reinforce the safe ambience of the city, even in 'seedier margins' of the festival district.

Many other cities have tried to introduce night time events staged in public spaces to achieve a mixture of economic, cultural and security objectives. One notable type of event that is staged in several European cities is the 'White Night' or 'Light Night' concept (known as Nuit Blanche, Notte Bianca in other parts of Europe) where, assisted by creative lighting, events are programmed in the public realm at night. Shops and cultural attractions stay open late and a festive atmosphere is created. Although this event's origins date back to innovative projects in northern European cities (Helsinki and Paris), Valletta (Malta's capital) hosts a particularly successful example. Valletta has struggled to attract people into the city at night since the relocation of many of its bars and restaurants to a neighbouring district in the 1970s. This has contributed to a wider malaise: the city has experienced depopulation and degeneration so a Foundation has been established to try and bring the city back to life. One initiative that has been important in the long term project to encourage night time activity back is Notte Bianca. During this event 'streets and squares become venues for open-air concerts' (Lejlimdawwal, 2014). The significance of the city to the event is highlighted by the Chairman of Malta's Arts Council who describes the event as 'a cacophony of cultural scapes wrapped around the City of Valletta' (Lejlimdawwal, 2014).

Loosening space: events as ways to loosen stiff parks

Events can be used to enliven moribund squares but they can also be used positively in conjunction with parks. Richards and Palmer (2010: 23) identify that animating parks happens 'organically' as 'different publics lay claim to their use at different times for football matches, picnics, skateboarding or music jamming and drumming'. This emphasises that parks don't necessarily need animating. The need for animation is lessened in some parks because they are often valued as peaceful and quiet places. Chiesura's (2004) survey of 467 people in Vondelpark, Amsterdam's most popular park, found that the main motivations for being there were to relax, to be in nature and to escape from the city. But if a park is too quiet and under-visited, it may be perceived as a dangerous place, thus eroding any stress relieving qualities. In these cases, regular events can be used to invite more people in.

Parks may benefit from programmed events in other ways too: for example, they may benefit from the loosening of space that occurs during some events. Many parks were conceived as formal urban spaces for aesthetic consumption. Although they are regarded as essentially public spaces, parks have always been heavily regulated and ordered. Many were conceived in the Victorian era and therefore they still reflect Victorian values: although they 'are no longer the expression of an authoritarian control of one group by another' (Taylor, 1995: 220). But as Watson and Ratna (2011: 73) argue, parks (especially those in the UK) are accompanied by a discourse 'that reflects local authority control of leisure space and that includes an elaborate legacy of byelaws and restrictions on use'. This is best evidenced by the stereotype of the officious park keeper, whose attempts to regulate behaviour and protect the visual qualities of park spaces are assisted by strict rules and related instructions: KEEP OFF THE GRASS. When people can access a park and where they go once they get in are regulated by hard measures (gates and railings) but also by softer techniques – including landscaping, signage and designated routes. For example, marked pathways tend to direct flows. In some parks, order and control is also furthered by areas which require payment to enter. Lowes (2002: 115) describes Vancouver's Hastings Park in a way which contrasts markedly with the idea of public parklands: 'the reality is that much of the park's landscape is paved or fenced and access to it has been rigidly controlled through admission prices'.

Events can help to loosen park spaces by inviting different uses, users, meanings, flows and behaviours. For example, Nevarez (2007) highlights the way running events and musical performances add elements of excitement and adventure to New York's Central Park (Figure 4.2). This park was conceived as a voyeuristic space, not a vibrant one, and it remains a place of passive recreation (Nevarez, 2007). Therefore, some events – particularly small, participatory ones – are useful ways of adding an active dimension to the park. There are other examples in the literature where authors highlight the role of events in changing the identity and feel of formal public parks. Stevens and Shin (2014: 17) suggest that festivals in Glasgow 'transform the normally genteel Botanic Gardens and Kelvingrove Park

Figure 4.2 Central Park, New York.

into dense, active social spaces'. Events are also good ways of adding a social dimension to new parks introduced as part of urban development schemes. These parks are often seen as overly contrived and events can help return these spaces to the people who live around them; allowing them to support and sustain social networks (Lloyd and Auld, 2003).

Producing public spaces

The discussion above focuses on the animation of conceived urban public spaces, especially lifeless squares. This is an important aspect of eventalisation, but it sits awkwardly with the approach outlined in Chapter 2, which regards public space as something that is produced by people, as much as by designers. With this principle in mind, it is important to emphasise that public spaces can be also be created in parts of the city not normally regarded as public space, and this is something that is particularly relevant to events. In simple terms, events produce urban space. As Lehtovuori (2010: 144) suggests, 'urban events are important ways to produce momentary public urban spaces'. Some might argue this space only exists during the limited life of an event, and therefore is less important than 'everyday space'. But if we accept prevailing ideas about the instability, fluidity, liquidity and transience of urban space, it is hard to avoid the conclusion that all urban space is temporary. If all space is temporary then the space produced through programmed events is as significant as that which is produced at other times. Arguably, it is more important, because memorable events can have enduring effects on the way spaces are imagined and lived.

Reclaiming the streets

Festival and events staged in street settings provide some of the best examples of urban public spaces produced by events. The street festival is perhaps the clearest case where events transform urban space into urban public space. As Stevens and Shin (2014) identify, events such as these can create informal, intersubjective spaces where a multiplicity of identities can be expressed. Belghazi (2006: 106) feels that during festivals 'organisers engineer an image of the city as a space of encounter'. This implies festival space is very much conceived space, rather than necessarily that which that is socially produced by citizens. However, there is evidence that planned official events can help to provide a framework in which social interactions are encouraged in the public realm – thus (co)creating public space.

Streets are seen romantically as the epitome of democracy and publicness, but some are privately owned, or privately controlled, and many are highly commercialised – particularly high streets. As Reeve and Simmonds (2001) point out, although high streets are often seen as convivial, sociable spaces they are not entirely public spaces: they are policed and monitored in the same way that shopping malls are. Therefore, in many streets – especially those where commerce dominates – there is a need to create public spaces which wouldn't otherwise exist. Events can play an important role. Jacobs (1961) famously talked of the street as an event – the 'street ballet', a metaphor also used by Bruce Springsteen in his song lyrics (e.g. on Jungleland). Events and the street are synonymous and, whilst this is mainly something linked to everyday events, official events can (re)produce idealised versions of vibrant street life. According to Stevens (2007), large, programmed events such as the New York Marathon and Berlin's Love Parade are 'special pieces of choreography' which can add to the richness of our streetscapes.

When streets are closed to traffic and when regular uses (e.g. commercial functions) give way to event uses, new public space can be created (see Figure 4.3). There are some very obvious examples where this occurs. Every summer, streets in New York and London are closed to traffic, transforming transport routes and commercial zones into sociable and festive spaces. For example, London's Regent Street is closed to traffic every Sunday in July for the 'Summer Streets' event. This event has exactly the same name as a similar event staged in New York on three Saturdays in July (Montgomery, 2013) suggesting policies and practices are being transferred from one city to another. Regent Street also is closed to traffic on other days too, for the Motor Show (see Chapter 3) and for the 'World on Regent Street Day' where people are invited to 'enjoy food and performances from all over the world'. This event has similarities to the events discussed in Trafalgar Square above, although the multicultural theme is motivated more by business objectives than cultural harmony. On Regent Street events are carefully curated to maximise the long term benefits for the global brands and flagship stores that dominate this street.

Figure 4.3 The Royal Mile, Edinburgh, during the annual Fringe Festival.

There are many other examples where events are staged that transform busy streets into public spaces. Bristol stages a Streets Alive event where the city's streets are turned into living rooms for a day (Shaftoe, 2008). It is a fine line between a creative attempt to produce better public space and a PR stunt aimed to generate publicity. In another Bristolian initiative a main street is closed to traffic and turned into a 300ft. long waterslide. A UK company 'Slide the City' now installs temporary slides in other cities too. Transforming urban streets via events often involves trying to turn them from urban to rural ones. Harcup (2000) describes how a terraced street in Leeds was turfed with 800m² of grass to stage a community festival and a film screening (the film was projected on to the gable end of one of the houses). One of the residents involved explained the justification: 'the houses here have no gardens, and the streets are the only public spaces we have. We have to make better use of them. People have got so used to them being streets that we had to do something' (Ward, cited in Harcup, 2000: 227). A local eight year old explained the motivations more simply: 'we want a playground in the street' (Higgs, cited in Harcup, 2000: 226). The event changed the way the space was used: there was more social interaction, and people strolled, sat and stood together – in other words people slowed down. And, although this was only a temporary transformation, 'it gave those people taking part a glimpse of how our relationships to place and to each other could also be transformed' (Harcup, 2000: 227).

London has tried to emulate some of these projects by launching a £2 milllion 'Future Streets Incubator' programme in 2014. This project aimed to temporarily convert London's thoroughfares 'into spaces where people can socialise and interact' (Beard, 2014). The public official who launched the project called for ideas such as 'temporary public plazas and pop-up street sporting activities' (Dedring cited in Beard, 2014). Her boss, The Mayor of London, also explained the wider purpose of the project: 'Streets aren't just for getting around – they also shape our city and how people feel about it . . . London's streets can be improved through a bit of creative thinking' (TFL, 2014). In line with this new policy, London's first 'Open Streets' event was staged on Great Suffolk Street in 2015. For five hours on one Saturday in May this street became a car free space in which people were invited to 'play, walk, bike, run, or just relax and see your city is a whole new way' (see Figure 4.4). This was a well-intentioned event, but the road closed would have been relatively traffic free anyway on a Saturday afternoon. This – plus the relatively poor attendance – limited the transformative effect of the event. Despite these limitations, hopefully Open Streets will be repeated and extended in future years.

A more extreme and increasingly well-known example of closing streets temporarily to create public space is the Ciclovía event in Bogota, Columbia. This event originated in the 1970s and it has now been copied by several other Latin American Cities. Every Sunday, over 60 miles of city roads in Columbia's capital are closed to cars and thus 'opened' to cyclists, walkers and joggers. This is a highly popular initiative: the public like it and for the government it represents a very cost effective way of creating new public space. Indeed, Montgomery (2013) describes this event as an ephemeral stretching of parkland, rather than merely a

Figure 4.4 Cyclists ride past a live band during London's inaugural Open Streets event on Great Suffolk Street.

car free day. This rationale is reinforced by the origins of the initiative – the project aimed to create a version of New York's Central Park. Instead of having to buy land, evict people, demolish acres of existing properties, and invest in expensive capital projects, new space was simply created by temporarily suspending car traffic. There is also some evidence that Ciclovía satisfies some of the criteria used to assess whether the space created really is public. According to one local business owner (admittedly one that has a vested interest in that he owns a bike shop): 'Ciclovía is one of the few places where Colombians of different classes mix' (Power, 2010).

In recent years (since 2013), London has tried to replicate the essence of Ciclovia with its RideLondon initiative. This is an annual event, rather than weekly one, but it allows Londoners a rare opportunity to ride on the city's central streets with no motorised traffic. The event is bundled up in a weekend long celebration which involves elite and children's races, as well as a long distance event for amateur riders. It takes inspiration from the London Marathon, an event which involves an unusual combination of amateur and elite athletes (see Chapter 7). Although these types of events do reconfigure space and create more public space, they involve similar flows that would be seen during a typical day in London. Instead of motor vehicles flowing through streets, bikes or runners flow through them. Whilst this represents a nice change of emphasis, a welcome change of pace and a different aural experience, it doesn't necessarily reconfigure spatial flows in the way that other streets events do.

The Champs-Elysées

Deroy and Clegg (2012) provide a wonderful example of the role of events in creating more public streets in their analysis of one of the world's most famous avenues, the Champs-Elysées in Paris. This street, 1.25 miles long, is visited by 600,000 people every weekend and 100 million people every year (Deroy and Clegg, 2012). The Champs-Elysées has a long established reputation as a fashionable shopping avenue, but in recent years it has been fighting a 'seemingly losing battle' against 'banalisation' and 'de-socialisation' (Deroy and Clegg, 2012: 360). Like Regent Street in London the street has become dominated by 'flagship' stores for global brands, a trend that that has been resisted but not prevented. A private organisation established in 1906 is responsible for regulating the street: The Comite des Champs Elysees. This Comite has responded to concerns about the street's over-commercialisation by introducing a series of programmed events.

Every July, the final day of the Tour de France cycling race and a large celebration on Bastille Day are staged on the Champs-Elysées. At other times in the spring or summer the street is turfed over, allowing people to have picnics and walk barefoot along the avenue. For example, in May 2010 the street was turfed with 8,000 plots of earth and decorated with 150,000 plants for an event organised by French Farmers. Other events are staged too: for example, film festivals and cultural events. In July 2011, a 'Tropical Event' was staged to promote diversity and to encourage people of different ethnicities to visit the street. Events are often very inconvenient and unprofitable for local businesses, but they are seen as important ways in which the former identity and significance of the avenue can be recovered. By staging events The Comite aims to recapture the historic identity of the street as a sociable place in which people lingered, mingled and interacted. This is a romantic and idyllic objective, and perhaps a rather naïve and flawed one. As Rowe and Baker (2012: 402) argue, the struggle for democratic urban space should be an 'activity involving creation and construction, not repair and retrieval'. Despite this sound advice, there is a yearning in the modern metropolis to restore the past, and events are seen as 'time machines' that allow citizens to experience historic conviviality. As Flecha et al. (2010: 137) identify: 'there is a great desire to return to the spirit of old carnivals with the innocence of the carnivalesque songs and the fantasy, recovering the public space taken by the excitement of modern life, traffic and the rush'.

Deroy and Clegg's (2012) piece of detailed, critical analysis emphasises the positive outcomes of events staged in city spaces. Uniform, commercial and banal spaces are transformed into irregular, sociable and meaningful spaces. Events allow spaces that are accused of symbolising nothing (e.g. the globalised high street) to symbolise something: 'during some special events, the symbolic power of the Champs-Elysées reappears' (Deroy and Clegg, 2012: 369). Deroy and Clegg's (2012) account suggests that events here help to create a street that has more in common with the idealised, though seldom realised, notion of public spaces as interactive spaces which exhibit a community sensibility. Indeed, the authors claim that during special events: 'the Champs-Elysées becomes a place where events drive people to express shared values, feelings and emotions once again', adding that '. . . on these special occasions it displays its ability to create symbolic interactions' (Deroy and Clegg, 2012: 369).

Applying Franck and Stevens's (2007) ideas about loose space, the spaces of the Champs-Elysées are seemingly loosened by official events, with fixed meanings and flows de-stabilised. In other words, these spaces are de-territorialised. New 'potentialities' and possibilities are opened, which increases the likelihood that the spaces might not merely return to their normal 'fixed' or 'tight' state after events have finished. Following Johansson and Kociatkiewicz (2011: 396), events become 'blueprints for subsequent sedimentation of spatial practices'. Logically, this is more likely to be achieved if the events are regular events, rather than one-off occasions. Indeed, for Deroy and Clegg (2012) it is this repetitive dimension that allows the reoriented identity of the street to be reaffirmed. However, there is a fine line between helpful repetition and over-familiarity. Lehtovuori (2010) expresses concern that one of the challenges of these events is to avoid them becoming too familiar – so as to retain their experimental character.

The events programmed on the Champs-Elysées create inclusive, public space out of what is normally exclusive, commercial space. Although these initiatives are organised by a very established private institution, they have similarities with the tactics employed by some radical social groups. For example, in Denmark's capital the Openhagen movement has emerged whose philosophy is that events can act as force that liberates an area. Like The Comite, the Openhagen movement wants to reverse streets' commercial, consumerist, speculative aesthetic and reduce the orientation towards tourists and ordered space (Pløger, 2010). They do this by eventalising the space – staging everyday festivals and low-cost events. The two organisations couldn't be more different. Openhagen is a social movement inspired by the situationists, a group who also wanted to transform formal spaces into informal ones using events (Pløger, 2010). The Comite is a conservative organisation seeking to restore an imperial street to its former glory (Deroy and Clegg, 2012). However, it is interesting to see the similarities in the tactics these two organisations employ.

How events help to produce urban public space

It is important to explore the essential mechanisms through which street festivals change urban spaces, potentially turning them from semi-public spaces into genuinely public ones. Four key mechanisms are identified and briefly reviewed in the discussion below.

On most shopping streets, people walk very quickly and there are few opportunities for people to deviate from the relentless pace. Events can change the rhythms of the street. Many authors have bemoaned the declining rhythmic diversity of contemporary street space and events provide opportunities to introduce new rhythms – by encouraging a decelerated pace and a varying tempo of movement. For example, Stevens and Shin (2014) identify how closing roads for street festivals results in 'slower, more relaxed walking'. Referencing Lefebvre's important work on this theme, Johansson and Kociatkiewicz (2011) also discuss how festivals introduce new rhythms. Many festivals involve a lot of hanging around and/ or meandering through a street setting. Normally, lingering in an urban space is seen as a sinister practice that invites suspicion. But when a city stages a festival, lingering is encouraged; allowing people to interact more easily.

A second, related, mechanism through which events produce public space is interactivity. During street events people are more likely to stop and talk to each other. They may sit, or they may stand, but they are more likely to mingle and interact. As Stevens and Shin (2014) suggest, staging festivals on closed roads increases face to face encounters.

A third mechanism is recirculation. Usually the commercial street exhibits very uniform flows of people. However, when events are staged, these flows are disrupted and re-oriented. Instead of people walking in and out of shops, or to and from work, they walk in different directions, something that changes the look and feel of the space.

Finally, events help to change the sort of people that use the space. According to Deroy and Clegg (2012) different and more varied groups visit the Champs-Elysées when events are staged: for example, sports fans and people from minority groups who would not otherwise come. This fits Tallon et al.'s (2006: 36) contention that events staged in city centres are responsible for 'enhancing participation from a wider range of people' and, ultimately, 'reappropriating public space'.

Street events obviously transform the way streets are used – encouraging different activities not normally seen (e.g. people dancing and singing), but they also change the ways a streetscape is used in more subtle ways. People sitting on kerbs is a good example (Stevens and Shin, 2014). Urban space is transformed by the work of the event organisers, who schedule performances and install artefacts but, as Stevens and Shin (2014) emphasise, it is the informal actions of attendees that ultimately transform streets into temporary public spaces. Large, planned events are sometimes seen as passively consumed spectacles that restrict space, but Stevens and Shin's (2014) research suggests that structured events can stimulate a whole series of 'secondary activities', including lots of spontaneous social interactions. It is this secondary level of events that was deemed particularly significant in Morgan's (2008) festival research. Morgan's research analyses a Folk Music Festival that was staged within the town centre and on the seafront of Sidmouth (Devon, UK). Morgan (2008: 92) established what people enjoyed about the festival experience, and his research emphasises 'the importance of creating or permitting the development of fringe events'. This doesn't necessarily just mean formal fringe performances like those we see in Edinburgh every August but more simply 'the provision of places to meet, socialise and wind down before and after the main performances' (Morgan, 2008: 92).

Providing opportunities to socialise helps to make festivals more enjoyable, but they are also key to the production of urban public space during festivals.

Interactions between people – assisted by the closure of roads and the disruption to normal flows, noises and atmospheres – effectively produces public space. Interaction is more likely in an event setting because of the way events involve the spatial and temporal concentration of people. One way of understanding this dynamic and its outcomes is as the 'co-creation' or 'co-production' of space. The interactions between festival-goers don't just happen in urban space, these interactions help to produce the space. Stevens and Shin (2014: 18) suggest that this interactive, co-creation is more intense around the edge of formalised festival sites 'and in the connective tissue between them'. In this way a festival may allow the production of urban public space in an area much larger than the one designated as the official venue.

The research cited above (Morgan, 2008; Stevens and Shin, 2014) also highlights the importance of the 'permeability' of festival space. In many street events, the movement of people is highly constrained – because of safety measures and access restrictions caused by the use of the road for performances. Cycling/running events and street parades are good examples – it is often hard to move around city spaces when these events are being staged. Road crossings are restricted to designated points/times, large crowds prevent free movement, and transit to and from the roadside is often highly constrained by crowd control measures. There is a danger that if flows of people are too rigidly controlled then the public-ness of the space is automatically restricted: people cannot interact as easily and the spaces become less accessible. Concerns about freedom of movement reflect wider ideas about what makes good public space. For example, Pugalis (2009: 228) highlights that 'unrestricted pedestrian movement' is often advocated as a key quality. Lowes (2002) also emphasises the importance of being able to flow freely through public space. A permeable festival staged on closed streets provides an exceptional opportunity to move and linger within cities – public space is created via the different rhythms and atmospheres that this movement creates. People linger on the street without feeling awkward or self-conscious; they meander aimlessly and chat to people who they would normally ignore. Policing is often more relaxed and people are able to do things they would not normally be allowed to do. In short, the event facilitates the production of urban public space.

Material changes

Most of the literature on animating public spaces discusses ways to bring social activity to existing spaces. However, it is clear from several notable examples that some public spaces have been changed materially to facilitate event animation: in other words they have been redesigned to allow them to host events successfully. Therefore, it is a combination of social and material factors that help produce the space. Many city squares are being reconfigured as events venues: so events are not merely temporary uses, but dedicated functions of the space. The Trafalgar Square case discussed previously is a good example, but there are other, lesser known cases too. Koch and Latham (2012) discuss Prince of Wales Junction, a street intersection in West London, where events have been used to help create 'better public space'. The wide range of events staged here (e.g. musical performances, family fun days, cultural festivals) have to be organised by people but they also need an appropriate space in which to happen. The authors identify that 'the material reconfiguration of the site to include not just an enlarged surface, but new paving stones, lighting, water and electricity points, makes it possible to stage such events' (Koch and Latham, 2012: 524). This case demonstrates that programmed events need certain 'things' to be present – it is not possible to stage events regularly in any public space. This reaffirms the argument made in Chapter 2 about the need to consider the tangible and the intangible when assessing the production of urban public space.

Rather than merely including useful details that can help accommodate events, some urban public spaces have been reconfigured with events at the forefront of the (re)designs. Degen's (2003) research into a post-industrial space in central Manchester notes how events staged to animate this site became formalised as the regeneration cycle progressed: this ultimately led to the construction of a mini arena for events. In a less formal way, landscaping, steps and street furniture can be used to create hybrid public/event spaces. These provide spaces where people sit, play, meet and eat on an everyday basis, but they can also be used for regular events. It is now common to see contemporary amphitheatres at various scales included in the design of city squares, waterfront promenades and public parks. For example, the space along London's waterfront south of the river between Tower Bridge and London Bridge is dominated by a large outdoor theatre sunk into the ground. Other prominent public spaces have also been redesigned as event spaces. Giddings et al. (2011) analyse Chamberlain Square in the heart of Birmingham (UK), which was redesigned recently. In a similar way to Siena's Piazza del Campo (discussed in Chapter 2), this Square benefits from a 6m drop in levels, and features an amphitheater design. This means that Chamberlain Square provides 'a stage for a variety of public events' (Giddings et al., 2011: 208).

Some streets in cities were designed as ceremonial event spaces, but in recent years, other streets have also been modified physically to make them more suited to staging events. This is something recommended by Stevens (2007: 206) who identifies that 'streets are not just for efficient circulation, they frequently have a representational function which needs to be considered when making functional modifications to those streets'. The most obvious example of modifying streets to allow them to serve an event function is the way streets have been reconfig-ured to allow them to host motor racing events. For example, the authorities in Singapore widened, adapted and resurfaced roads, (e.g. removed kerbs) and con-structed a new 1.2km section to make the city suitable for a Formula 1 Grand Prix (Henderson et al., 2010). The material changes sometimes cause controversy. For example, London's Battersea Park is scheduled to stage a series of Formula E motor races from 2015 and one local resident responded to an article about the events in the city's evening paper by writing 'my objection to Formula E is not, as you report, the noise and disruption, which is temporary, rather the vandalism to a heritage Victorian park to get it ready for five years of racing' (Cook, 2015).

Just because some public spaces are designed to stage events, there are no guarantees this will make them good event spaces or good spaces more generally.

One of the most extensive examples of event oriented urban design is Toronto's redesigned waterfront: the Harbourfront Centre (see Figure 4.5). A series of outdoor performance venues were prominent in the redesign. However, these haven't ever really become an integral part of Toronto's theatrical scene or of the city more generally (McKinnie, 2007). This is because these are overly conceived event spaces: not ones produced by local stakeholders, but the products of federal planning (McKinnie, 2007). Perhaps such obvious attempts to turn public spaces into event venues should be avoided. The literature on public spaces (reviewed in Chapter 2) recommends that fixed meanings and determined uses of spaces are unhelpful. There is a danger that when public spaces are visibly redesigned as venues, we introduce events as a pre-determined function of these spaces. This means they become the accepted meaning of a space, rather than a way to loosen that meaning (see Chapter 5).

Longer term effects

Events have the potential to transform, temporarily the spaces they occupy but there are also longer lasting spatial implications that emerge from the hosting of events.

(Foley et al, 2012: 23)

The previous sections of this chapter have highlighted the positive effects that events can have on public spaces. During events there seem to be a series of such effects, including the animation of space (e.g. in squares), the loosening of stiff public

Figure 4.5 The Harbourfront Centre, Toronto.

spaces (e.g. in parks) and the creation of public space in areas normally deemed semi-public (e.g. streets). However, to understand the significance of events it is important to consider whether these effects last beyond the duration of an event and what effects (if any) events have on spaces when those events are not taking place.

As Lehtovuori (2010) states, one of the key challenges for those using events to animate urban space is how to retain the character of events. For this reason it is important to think about what happens after an event, or what happens between events (as events are an increasingly significant function for many public spaces). There seem to be a series of possible scenarios. An obvious one is that the space returns to its former state. However there is also the possibility that the identity, meaning and even the use of the space may change due to events that are staged there. These potential outcomes are explored further below.

Events change the way people think about public spaces. Staging events may mean that established functions and meanings are de-stabilised, something that does not necessarily end when programmed events are over. For Koch and Latham (2011), creating uncertainty about what will restabilise in these spaces can be a very positive thing: this is what is meant by creating 'potentialities'. Events draw attention to the potential uses of public spaces, possibilities that might be enacted upon in the future even when programmed events are not scheduled. This is highlighted by Pugalis's (2009) empirical research into public spaces in the North East of England. Pugalis's findings (2009: 223) suggest that events highlighted the potential of sites to users: 'through the programming of more frequent events, aspirations and expectations are subconsciously raised, elucidating their latent potential'. This argument is also made by Pløger (2010: 851) who asserts that events can be used to demonstrate 'different potentials and heterotopic use' in established places. Lehtovuori (2010) identifies a similar process in his analysis of events in Helsinki. He suggests that the 'experimental juxtapositions' and the temporary space created by a street parade helped participants to 'deepen their ideas about urban life'. This event and others staged in the city helped to 'shatter' fixed and taken for granted attitudes towards urban space (Lehtovuori, 2010: 145). Importantly, Lehtovuori (2010) feels this has led to changes in the use of these spaces rather than merely their meaning: there has been a re-appropriation of urban public spaces.

Another way that events can leave positive legacies for the public spaces they temporarily inhabit is via the production of images and memories. Belghazi (2006) has written about the festivalisation of cities using the example of the Festival of World Sacred Music, which is staged in various spaces across Fez (Morocco). Belghazi (2006: 106) notes that 'although the sites stage an ephemeral event, their impact is enduring because people's memories and images of places are shaped by ephemera'. This provides a useful reminder that the city is, ultimately, a social image. The social image of the city as created by temporary events can be as important to the production of the city as any 'permanent' building. It is worth reflecting on what type of imagery, and therefore what type of city, is produced via events staged in public spaces. As discussed in Chapter 3, cities tend to use these events to show off selective spaces of the city they want to publicise. As Belghazi (2006: 106) notes, the 'city presents a selective version of its material counterpart, typically incorporating only the more historic and status enhancing elements of the physical environment'. A very restricted image of the city is (re) produced – something that feeds into the idea that the 'event city' is very much one linked to the 'concept city': one where the complexity of city life is reduced to a unified impression.

It is worth noting that programmed events in public spaces are as much about place marketing as they are about user experiences. This marketing function also has implications for the longevity of event-related transformations. Events staged in public spaces gain a degree of permanence through their constant use in city marketing materials (Harcup, 2000). Images of these spaces are often infused with event imagery and in a symbolic economy dominated by digital media these are as significant as any other reality. Trafalgar Square provides an obvious example. Representations of Trafalgar Square on the Greater London Authority's website are dominated by event imagery, and people can relive the events staged there by accessing the online gallery of recent events. On London's official tourism website (Visitlondon.com) within the pages devoted to Trafalgar Square, 'Events' is the second most prominent section and even the most prominent section (About) tells readers: 'you'll often find cultural events, performances, shows and other special activities going on'. Instructions about how to find the Square are listed under a section tellingly labelled: 'Venue directions'. Even on independent websites, event imagery dominates, with one-off events (such as when Trafalgar Square was turfed in 2007) used to represent the space. Other prominent public spaces in central London are also permanently infused with imagery of temporary events. Because of the relentless recirculation of images of the marathon, various cycle races, music concerts and royal events, overseas tourists visiting The Mall (London's monumental axis connecting Trafalgar Square to Buckingham Palace) might expect it to be permanently full of people waving flags. When they encounter it in its everyday guise – rather windswept and lifeless – they may be a little disappointed.

Another way that events may have longer term positive effects is by drawing attention to public spaces that had been forgotten or neglected. This may mean they are used more extensively even when events are not taking place. In the same way that other 'temporary uses' are known to inspire future activity (Bishop and Williams, 2012), events may provide the key to unlock the potential of hidden or under-used spaces. This 'spotlight' effect is highlighted by Johansson and Kociatkiewicz's (2011: 394) assertion that 'an urban festival often serves to show the city in a new light by uncovering hitherto neglected or hidden features'. Similarly, Lehtovuori (2010: 139) suggests that temporary uses can focus public attention on forgotten public spaces, meaning that events 'literally produce new public space'.

Much of the discussion in this chapter has been optimistic. However it is worth emphasising that there may be some enduring effects of staging events in public spaces that are detrimental. These are discussed at length in the next chapter. It should also be noted that the transformative effects of staging events in public spaces cannot be repeated time after time. Positive effects may diminish once people have got used to the idea that certain spaces can be used as events venues, or once several editions of the same event have been staged. Events may themselves become established and determined uses for certain public spaces. This undermines their transformative effect. As Lehtovuori (2010) states, events often have a dramatic effect when they are used to 'hi-jack' spaces not normally used for events, but it is difficult to hi-jack urban space again and again.

Even if an event is a great success, with spaces animated in an inclusive and liberating manner, there remains the possibility that the overall effects might still be problematic. One likely effect is that moribund spaces animated for events may seem even more lifeless when those events are over. One of Pugalis's (2009: 223) interviewees told him: 'the festival was a great experience . . . the only trouble was it made the space seem dull the rest of the time'. Pugalis's (2009) research also highlighted that some users do not want their public spaces to permanently exhibit the characteristics they assume during events. There is a danger of presuming that events somehow always represent an improvement in the status quo; when in fact many users of public space much prefer the everyday qualities of these spaces. When asked about a public space in the north of England, one interviewee said 'of course, events are held but what I really like is its daily character' (Pugalis, 2009: 223).

Summary

This chapter suggests that staging official events can have positive effects on urban public spaces. Events can help to produce public space where it might not have otherwise existed: for example, in busy, heavily commercialised streets. Although it is the interactions between people that ultimately produce the space, an official event provides a framework within which such interactions can be encouraged. Eventalisation is achieved both through associated changes to the regulation of the urban environment (e.g. closing roads), but also by introducing different behaviours, rhythms, flows and people into the public realm. Events can also help to make conventional public spaces more public. City squares are good example of spaces that are often under-used or afflicted by their austere image, and events can help to animate these spaces. Events can help under-used spaces seem safer, especially when they are staged at night. Squares and parks were often conceived as very controlled, formal and stiff spaces. Events can help to loosen these spaces, so that they seem more accessible: physically, socially and symbolically. Later sections of the chapter highlight that eventalisation is not necessarily limited to the duration of an event. Some events staged in public spaces are just glorified publicity stunts; and these may have few long term effects. However, other events can help to destabilise the established functions and meanings associated with certain spaces. Staging an event can help to de-territorialise urban space and usher in new spatial practices post-event. Accordingly, festivals and events not only leave their imprint on cities, they help to produce urban public space; through the de-territorialisation of the public realm.

5   Eventification

Events and the denigration of urban public space

Introduction

Chapter 4 highlighted how events can have positive effects on the provision of urban public space. The examples cited were mainly smaller, less commercialised events and many were freely accessible both financially and physically. When larger, commercial events are staged in public spaces their effects are often more problematic. The obvious examples are mega-events. These exemplify some of the potentially negative effects of events on urban space. For example, Sánchez and Broudehoux (2013: 133) describe the 2016 Rio Olympic Games as 'state assisted privatisation and commodification of the public realm'. It is unfair to dismiss all large, commercial events staged in public spaces as inherently damaging – many of the positive effects noted in the previous chapter still apply. But large, commercial events are responsible for making urban space less public and these detrimental effects are discussed in this chapter.

Following the conceptual framework introduced in Chapter 3, the term eventification is used to refer to the process through which events denigrate public space. Eventification represents the way events tighten spaces though commodification and the related processes of privatisation, commercialisation, and securitisation. These processes are used to structure the first three sections of this chapter. This discussion needs to be prefaced by the arguments made in Chapter 2 that urban public space is already commercialised, privatised and securitised to a large extent. So the analysis here assesses the contribution of events to these processes, it doesn't examine whether events *cause* commercialisation, privatisation or securitisation. In the final section, other ways that events denigrate public spaces are discussed: including basic impacts such as noise, environmental damage, and the inconvenience for regular users. In line with the structure used in Chapter 4, ways that spaces are altered temporarily are discussed first, followed by explicit consideration of whether events are responsible for more durable effects.

Commercialisation

Major events are increasingly commercial entities. They are often staged by commercial organisations and they are products or brands which are bought and sold. Major events are also vehicles with which to sell other products – many rely heavily on revenue from merchandising, licensing and sponsorship. Despite these traits, some authors retain faith that events remain social entities, a quality which distinguishes them from traditional goods. For example, Sandel (2012) suggests that events such as popular rock concerts represent more than commercial enterprises. He argues that to treat events like commodities diminishes them, and cites other writers to help illustrate his point: 'records are commodities, concerts are social events and in trying to make a commodity out of the live experience you risk spoiling the experience altogether' (Seabrook cited in Sandel, 2012: 38). The discussion here does not explore whether events are commodities or whether they are inappropriately commercialised to sell other commodities. This is something addressed in other texts. The analysis here focuses on how events commodify and commercialise the public spaces they occupy. When events are staged in public spaces, the commercial dimension is something that worries some commentators who feel that parks, streets and squares should be protected from over-commercialisation. However, we need to take into consideration the arguments made in Chapter 2: many of our public spaces are already commercialised. Alongside worries about commercialisation there are related concerns about commodification. The whole idea of using public spaces as event venues to generate funds inherently represents a type of commodification. In a typically provocative article about city events, Jenkins (2013a) makes his positon clear: 'our open spaces aren't commodities – give us them back'.

Public spaces have long been used as event venues, and events will always be staged in these spaces. The question is whether heavily commercialised events – those which exist to serve commercial objectives – should be staged regularly in prominent public spaces. For example, although staging events in Senate Square, Helsinki, has generally been regarded as a positive phenomenon (see Chapter 4), some events have been regarded as inappropriately commercial for such an important place. The Red Bull City Flight – a commercial snowboarding event – is a good example (Lehtovuori, 2010). In these instances events are explicitly used as a vehicle for promoting companies, allowing a kind of outdoor advertising that would not normally be tolerated. The wider social justifications for events (festivity, animation etc.) are often cleverly cited by organisers of commercial events to justify them, but ultimately these events serve private interests rather than public ones. In this way, Sandel's (2012) noble argument that events are social occasions (not just commodities) is cleverly appropriated by companies to justify staging commercial events in public spaces.

Events have become a key function of urban public spaces but events have also become an important vehicle that allows these spaces to be commandeered by commercial interests. According to Lowes (2004: 73) the outcome is that 'public spaces have come to function almost exclusively as promotional vehicles for the commercial interests which dominate them'. Staging events in public spaces undoubtedly provides a valuable platform for commercial event sponsors. Indeed, event sponsors may be more interested in aligning their brands with urban spaces than associations with a specific event because of potential to accrue symbolic capital. Sponsors of events staged in urban spaces become city sponsors and benefit from powerful place meanings. This seduces the public into accepting companies as natural partners for important places and spaces. As Lowes (2004: 73) identifies, 'events staged in public spaces help to naturalise, and therefore legitimise, vested commercial interests'.

The image below of Hyde Park during the 2013 World Triathlon Championship Finals helps to demonstrate this (Figure 5.1). In ordinary circumstances had Oakley approached Hyde Park, or the local planning authority (City of Westminster), for permission to install a large advertising hoarding like this one, they would have been told that this is not appropriate for a Royal Park. But major events provide opportunities for companies to circumvent normal planning restrictions. Established rules seem to change for major events which often come with clear obligations to allow their sponsors certain privileges. This is not merely an issue for sport events, cultural events allow sponsors to access urban spaces too (see Fig 4.2). To get round this wanton commercialism, events are presented as policy tools, fund raisers and/or recreational activities, rather than commercial enterprises. For example, organisers justified the Triathlon Finals in Hyde Park by claiming this was not a commercial event, but one staged: to give British athletes a chance to compete against international triathletes, and to encourage ordinary people to take up the triathlon (Innes et al., 2013). However, the event was organised by a commercial company and involved commercial sponsors, which meant it was essentially a commercial event.

Figure 5.1 An inflatable banner marking the route of the 2013 World Triathlon Finals through Hyde Park, London.

Fan zones installed in public spaces are particularly prone to accusations that they inherently commercialise the spaces they inhabit. Chapter 3 explained the origins and growth of these events. According to Klauser (2012) fan zones exemplify the 'temporary imprint' of major events on urban public space. This type of event is particularly relevant to this part of the book because a key motivation for staging fan zones is to extend the amount of event space available for sponsors to exploit. Rather than sponsorship being confined to traditional venues, fan zones provide a vehicle to allow urban spaces to be sponsored too. Kolamo and Vuolteenaho (2013: 514) suggest that the FIFA Fan Fest branding concept (also introduced in Chapter 3) was created 'first and foremost to draw attention to the World Cup's official brands'. This is not merely a FIFA issue as it applies to other events franchises too. With reference to the European Football Championships, Klauser (2012: 1043) cites a UEFA document that includes the promise: 'Fan Zones will provide certain commercial partners with an additional opportunity to leverage their commercial involvement'.

Fan zones are staged in a high commercial way, but that doesn't necessarily mean that they are inherently a bad thing. Ultimately, they are popular because they allow events to be watched communally on big screens rather than individually on small ones. It is somewhat ironic that screens are now being used to restore communal interaction in cities, when screens are usually cited as a key cause of the decline of social interactions. Nevertheless, we shouldn't be too quick to dismiss fan zones and public screenings. In some ways they democratise major events because they allow fans without tickets to engage with events. McQuire (2010: 572) mounts a partial defence: arguing that 'legitimate concern over the commercial dominance of public space should not become an alibi for the hasty condemnation of public screens'. This is an important point. Fan zones do commercialise public spaces, but there isn't anything necessarily wrong with public screenings. It is the way they are organised that raises concerns.

The rights holders who control sport events sometimes restrict the visibility of sponsorship in sports arenas because this is seen as demeaning to the event. For example, during the Olympic Games, there is very little sponsorship evident inside the venues. But, somewhat gallingly, the same rights holders encourage cities to install event related branding in public spaces during events (see Figure 5.2). For example, in their analysis of Olympic Games, Horne and Whannel (2012: 60) note that 'sponsors do not get their name in the stadium, but the torch relay provides opportunities to link the brand name . . . and the visual background of the host city'. Other event 'activations' installed in public spaces also provide vehicles for sponsors to attach themselves to the host city. During the London 2012 Olympic Games, Hyde Park hosted a large Live Site which was free to access and attracted 800,000 visitors (Royal Parks, 2013a). This Site is best understood as a commercial platform, rather than a benevolent gesture by the Organising Committee (LOCOG). The Live Site hosted installations promoting the major sponsors; for example 'Cadbury House' a 'brand experience' similar to the sorts of 'brand lands' described by Mikunda (2004). A London 2012 Superstore was constructed and other commercial installations were permitted close to the Live Site.

Figure 5.2 Spectators leaving the Olympic Park during the 2012 Olympic Games. They are literally surrounded by outdoor advertising for Coca-Cola and Adidas.

The Superstore was not merely a retail outlet; it also contained 'sponsor event zones' dedicated to Coca Cola, Adidas and Swatch. This meant that, although the Olympic events staged in Hyde Park (long distance swimming, triathlon) weren't overly commercialised, they were accompanied by a range of 'activations' that were. The outcome was a heavily commercialised park. Normally, Hyde Park provides some relief from the intense commerce that surrounds it. But during the 2012 Olympic Games, the Park acted as an extension of this commercial district (Osborn and Smith, 2015).

Most fan zones, especially FIFA Fan Fests, are vehicles for creating spaces where corporate brands can be lived rather than merely consumed. They are ways for cities to activate their status as event hosts, but they are also ways for event sponsors to activate their sponsorship. For example, FIFA Fan Fests are heavily sponsored by Coca-Cola. At the 2010 FIFA World Cup in South Africa the centrepiece of the Johannesburg Fan Fest was an enormous statue made of thousands of Coca-Cola crates. Coca-Cola's domination of Fan Fests continued at the next World Cup in Brazil (2014). One of FIFA's official videos from the Natal Fan Fest features children hugging large Coca-Cola bottles as if they were cuddly toys. This 'deep sponsorship' of prominent public spaces is particularly valuable for companies like Coca-Cola because they are not just associated with the event, they become inextricably linked to the places that are staging them. Places like Brazil have powerful brand images and by giving sponsors the right to create brand experiences in iconic locations such as Copacabana Beach, companies create value derived from place associations. If the sponsors are the main beneficiaries of Fan Fests, then you might expect that these sponsors or FIFA would be paying the bill. But although 'FIFA provides significant financial support in the form of all infrastructural equipment for the event, including a top quality screen, stage, sound and lighting' (FIFA cited in Panja, 2014), other costs have to be paid for by the host cities. This led to Recife (Brazil) threatening to cancel their Fan Fest in advance of the 2014 World Cup because they couldn't afford to pay for the $4.6million it would cost them to stage the event (Panja, 2014).

Major events are used by corporations as vehicles to plaster their brands all over some of the world's most famous parks, squares and streets. Perhaps the most blatant example of this occurred at the 2006 World Cup in Germany where the Brandenburg Gate in Berlin was the fulcrum of the largest Fan Fest. The monument was covered by the brand names of sponsors, something that in any other circumstances would be prohibited (see Figure 5.3). A similar situation occurred in 2008 for the UEFA European Football Championships which were jointly hosted by Austria and Switzerland. One of the host cites was Zurich, a conservative place where there are normally tight restrictions on outdoor advertising (Hagemann, 2010). During the Championships normal rules were circumvented and Zurich was covered in advertising materials. As one of the managers involved in the event put it, these events 'generate a lot of exceptional situations in which many things which normally would be unthinkable are suddenly possible' (cited in Hagemann, 2010). One of the outcomes is a more commercialised cityscape and a worrying precedent to justify further commercial exploitation in the future. Hagemann encapsulates key concerns about fan zones in her damning synopsis of this growing phenomenon:

> a piece of public space is temporarily cut out of the urban context, fenced off and given over to the control of a private event organiser who is then allowed to economically exploit it and regulate the ways in which it us used.
>
> (Hagemann, 2010: 730)

This quote emphasises that fan zones are not merely examples of commercialisation, they are also examples where public spaces are privatised and securitised. These processes are discussed in later sections of this chapter.

Spaces of consumption, for consumers . . .

Staging events in urban public spaces is part of a wider attempt to revive the urban economy and to turn city centres into profitable centres of consumption (see Chapter 3). This means inviting certain people in, but excluding others. As Waitt (2008: 522) argues, 'urban festivals are conceptualised as a mechanism to exclude and include people from certain spaces'. Just like other forms of urban

Figure 5.3 The Brandenburg Gate, Berlin during the 2006 FIFA World Cup.

entrepreneurialism, events strategies are often aimed at attracting the 'right sort of people' – in other words the high spending middle classes. Van Deusen (2002) provides a good example in his analysis of the redevelopment of Clinton Square in the US city of Syracuse (New York). Events were identified as something that the redesigned Square should be used for: encouraging a more active recreational space to overcome the passive character of the old design (Van Deusen, 2002). In other words, the reconfiguration of Clinton Square was undertaken with event functions in mind. However, Van Deusen (2002: 153) quotes people involved in the management of the space who expressed explicitly that they 'have to be very selective' about what kinds of events are staged. A Country and Western Festival which used to be staged in the old version of the Square was deemed inappropriate for the new space because it generated very little economic benefit. People attended the festival but didn't spend money in nearby bars and restaurants. According to Van Deusen's (2002) interviewees, jazz and blues festivals are deemed appropriate events because the attendees spend a lot of money in the downtown area. Degen's (2003: 875) work in Manchester reaffirms this argument. Space managers are quoted as saying that their events were essentially staged to attract the 'middle class' as 'you cannot put on events for people who are not willing to spend'. These examples highlight the inherently exclusionary nature of events. There are very few, if any, events that appeal to everyone. Each event has a dedicated audience and staging events (and not staging them) automatically privileges some social groups and neglects others. Organised events staged in central public spaces are purposefully designed to attract the consuming classes. This challenges the notion introduced in the previous chapter that events somehow democratise urban spaces, or make them more inclusive.

Further evidence of this exclusionary trait is provided by Atkinson and Laurier's (1998) synopsis of a ticketed festival staged in Bristol's public spaces. The authors juxtapose the event with the traditional notion of a street carnival – where established hierarchies are eroded and greater social equality is (temporarily) attained. The authors state:

> far from resembling an inclusive, carnivalesque inversion of the dominant order, Bristol's Festival of the Sea legitimated the exclusion of certain groups from their homes, lest the sight of them mar the urban spectacle and the city's new image, or affronted the tourist gaze.
>
> (Atkinson and Laurier, 1998: 200)

Waitt's (2008: 522) observation that festivals are inherently linked to the 'neoliberal ethics of consumer citizenship' fits neatly with this interpretation. This prevailing ideology deems that certain groups do not belong in public spaces: 'the poor, the homeless, street level sex workers, yobs and political campaigners' (Waitt, 2008: 522). Wood and Abe (2011: 3252) provide further evidence of this trend: during preparations for the 2007 IAAF World Athletics Championships, the government in Osaka (Japan) 'tightened its policing and surveillance policy so that it would clean up the public space where "impure" homeless people were living'. This 'sanitisation' of public space in association with city events is worryingly common.

The exclusionary nature of some events is even more pronounced during mega-events. Boykoff and Fussey (2014: 260) suggest that 'mega-events such as the Olympics catalyse a range of urban processes that facilitate the invitation and easy passage of wealthy visitors while rendering globalisation's losers immobile and controlled'. The authors link this to Bauman's (1998) notion that in contemporary society people are treated either as 'tourist or vagabonds', with those unable or unwilling to join the consuming classes deliberately excluded and disadvantaged. In this sense, events are typical of the way that public spaces are being reconfigured as spaces for consumers rather than for a more generous or democratic vision of the 'public'. This is by nature exclusionary as not everyone is willing or able to consume. When ticketed events are staged, who belongs in public spaces is determined by 'ability to pay' (Owen, 2002).

Ticketed events are consumer products in themselves and they are also associated with the consumption of other products; food, drink and merchandise. This type of event driven consumption has been encouraged in many parks, for example Bryant Park, in mid-town Manhattan (Zukin, 1995). New York guide books highlight the 'dizzying schedule' of events staged in this Park every summer (Time-Out, 2005). In his restrained analysis of Bryant Park, Madden (2010), stops short of the oft cited idea that this urban space has been militarised or rendered private or inauthentic through such changes. However, Madden (2010: 200) does feel that

Bryant Park has been reconfigured in the service of commerce and consumption, with events used to 're-politicise' the Park as 'the home of a public of consumers'. For Madden (2010), this is evidence of publicness without democracy – the park is accessible but only for certain types of people doing certain types of things.

Other commentators have also highlighted the way events change key public spaces from political sites into consumer sites. In a more famous New York park a few blocks uptown, Nevarez (2007) notes the hypocrisy involved in Central Park's events policy. Concerts and movies are sanctioned on the Park's Great Lawn but political demonstrations are often prohibited via the justification that they might damage the space. Potential damage to the Great Lawn didn't seem to be a major consideration when the decision was made that Disney could stage the Premiere of Pocahontas there (Garvin, 2011). In a similar vein, Jenkins (2013a) cynically suggests that an easy way for authorities to prevent sites from being used for demonstrations is to 'sell' spaces to private event companies and declare them closed. Hyde Park is one the most famous political sites in the UK, famous for Speakers Corner and various political rallies that have been held there. During the 2003 Anti-War March, the government prevented demonstrators from entering the Park, citing spurious health and safety concerns (Jenkins, 2013a). Subsequently, Jenkins thinks the establishment have 'seized it' by turning it into an events venue. Similarly, whilst Trafalgar Square has always been a venue for political demonstrations, Jenkins (2013a) thinks that the range of worthy festivals and events staged there means it has been de-politicised – as the space is now used to demonstrate political correctness rather than for political demonstrations. Using Foley et al.'s (2012) terminology, the space is disciplined – a highly symbolic (loose) space is turned into a (tight) functional one.

Chapter 3 introduced the notion that events are being increasingly urbanised, i.e. they are being taken out of traditional venues and staged in urban public spaces. When commercial/trade events are staged in public spaces – rather than indoor venues – there is obviously a danger that those public spaces are inherently commercialised. One of the best case studies available on this subject is the study of the L'Oreal Melbourne Fashion Festival by Weller (2013). This event is organised by a growth coalition dedicated to the growth of the local fashion industry; and recently the organisers have taken the event into Melbourne's streets. Making connections with Melbourne's cityscape in general makes sense for the fashion industry – the city has a cosmopolitan image and it is replete with values the fashion industry wants to be associated with. Connections with 'the street' are even more valuable: this is where fashion trends emerge so by visibly connecting their wares to the street, fashion companies and their products attain authenticity. In line with the notion of the experience economy (Pine and Gilmore, 1999), garments gain value by being staged in public space. By placing fashion events in street spaces, the organisers are also tapping into the 'celebratory ethos' indelibly associated with local festivals. A commercial fashion event is represented as a type of street festival allowing it to accrue some of the positive connotations attached to such events (Weller, 2013).

Ultimately, in this case, public space is used to create value for the fashion industry. This outcome may be positive for the festival and for the industry, but the outcomes for Melbourne's public spaces are less positive (Weller, 2013). The 'incursion' or 'invasion' of the festival into the public realm has produced new 'industry spaces' dedicated to this particular sector of the economy (Weller, 2013). As Weller (2013: 2862) identifies, the event effectively 'facilitates the extension of retailing into the public spaces of the city'. The event commercialises Melbourne's public realm but the effects are more complicated than that because Melbourne's street spaces are already commercialised to a large extent. With this in mind, the real losers in the process seem to be other non-fashion oriented businesses who normally occupy the spaces 'invaded' by the festival. This conclusion is in line with Deroy and Clegg's (200) observations about events on the Champs Elysees – events can animate city spaces but they are not necessarily helpful for incumbent businesses.

Privatisation

When major events are staged in public spaces, this does not merely represent a commercialisation of space; it also represents a form of privatisation. For ticketed events, people are asked for payment to use spaces that are normally freely accessible. Barriers are erected; security measures installed and event organisers assume responsibility for streets, squares and parks. This is obviously problematic when, as in many cases, the event organiser is a private company or coalition of private interests whose objectives are not to serve the public interest, but to run a commercially profitable event. Atkinson and Laurier's (1998) analysis of Bristol's Festival of the Sea provides a good example. The event was initiated and organised by private interests and was intended as a profit making festival. According to Atkinson and Laurier (1998: 201), the organisers were 'granted full and exclusive use of Bristol's docklands for the duration of the festival, along with the right to charge an entrance fee to Bristol citizens for access to areas they already supported with their local taxes'. It is easy to see why some Bristolians objected.

The increased use of parks for events is regarded by some as part of the creeping privatisation of these public spaces. In London, Jenkins (2013a) bemoans the way in which 'concert promoters, fair organisers and product salesmen can now purchase the Royal Parks for money and close them to the public'. In some instances privatisation for events is obvious and dramatic. For example, Lowes (2004: 73) describes the use of Albert Park in Melbourne for a Formula 1 Grand Prix as 'a privatisation' in line with other privatisations introduced by the state government in the mid-1990s. This case is discussed further below. Similarly, the projects that have converted Valencia's waterfront areas into major events venues to stage the Formula 1 Grand Prix and America's Cup Yacht Race are regarded by Prytherch and Maiques (2009: 112) as 'experiments with the private development of public lands'. In other instances, event-led privatisation is a much more subtle process. To allow them to stage commercial events, responsibility for managing many public spaces has been transferred to private companies. Users might not even notice but in this way events have helped to alter the way are our public spaces are governed. For neoliberalists, this is a positive trend rather than negative one. Privatisation via events allows a 'cleansing of cityscapes' (Foley et al., 2012: 72) – something which is attractive to city authorities. The individual responsible for the introduction of events in Bryant Park, New York, embraces privatisation as a good thing: 'our belief is that every service provided by the government can be improved upon' (Biederman, cited in Madden, 2010: 200). However, most commentators rightly argue that anything that distances public spaces from democratically elected organisations need to be treated with great suspicion.

A key issue when assessing events as tools of privatisation is whether we should deem major events as public or private functions. If tickets are publically available and if there are wider public benefits, should we see major events as public occasions? The answer to this question is no. For many events there is limited availability of tickets, and even if some tickets are available they are often expensive. A ticketed event contradicts the definition of public space developed in Chapter 2: by definition any form of ticketing restricts accessibility. Even when tickets are free, the very act of issuing tickets limits the accessibility and looseness of a space. Tickets impose conditions of entry, and they mean that users of the space are contractually obliged to behave in a certain way. Many events in New York's Central Park are free and open to the public, but the ticketing is 'heavily monitored' and the Park's management agency 'employ a myriad of rules regarding the distribution of tickets' (Nevarez, 2007: 164). Rules are implemented to restrict the lucrative secondary market for free tickets (Sandel, 2012). Therefore, although the notion of publicness is often used in the discourses used to help justify events, it would be mistaken to see ticketed events as public occasions. These events tend to tighten urban spaces, rather than loosen them. As Foley et al. (2012: 30) argue, major event strategies further emphasise the 'closed city' as the demands of event owners require the exclusion of citizens.

When events are staged there are many parts of the site which are not publically accessible even to ticket holders. This further erodes the ideas that event spaces are public spaces. These privatised spaces include VIP zones and those areas reserved for performers and support staff. During the aptly named 'build up' to the Olympic Games, Jenkins (2012) wrote 'London parks this summer have become industrial estates, crammed with business enclosures, containers, marquees and car parks'. Hagemann's (2010) analysis of the 2008 European Football Championships staged by Austria and Switzerland provides another good example. Hagemann (2010: 732) notes how urban space was 'dissected into more or less exclusive privately organised viewing locations, hospitality areas and VIP lounges with restricted access or paid admission'. This is a temporary iteration of splintered urbanism (Graham and Marvin, 2001).

Using the 'power of video and social media' the University College London project 'Whose Olympics?' documents examples where public open spaces were privatised by the London 2012 Olympic Games (Whose Olympics, 2012). Boykoff and Fussey (2014) also highlight some of the same cases. The Olympic Delivery Authority (ODA) requisitioned a protected green space (Leyton Marsh) to house a temporary basketball training facility. Another valuable green space nearby (Wansted Flats) was used to provide briefing and mustering facilities for

12,000 officers drafted in to police London during the Games. These private uses contravened existing legislation that aimed to protect these spaces, but they were sanctioned because they were part of a public project – the staging of the Olympic Games. During the London Games the reservation of road lanes for officials (the so called Zil lanes) provided another example of the privatisation of public space to facilitate the organisation of an event. There were other examples too. Special laws were implemented (London Olympic and Paralympic Games Act 2006) to protect the commercial interests of sponsors which restricted advertising and commercial activity in the public realm. Jenkins (2012) suggests that the overall effect of these initiatives was to turn London into an 'Orwellian world of . . . private regulators and LOCOG inspectors roaming the streets tearing down political banners and Pepsi ads'.

Privileging corporate sponsors erodes a key justification for staging events in public spaces – the idea that this allows local businesses to benefit more. As Foley et al. (2012) state, local objectives and interests are usually 'sidelined' by sponsor agreements which make it harder for local businesses to benefit. Companies are not allowed to make connections to the event if they are not official sponsors. The rationale for staging events outside traditional arenas often includes the premise that more local businesses get access to event related spending. However, event organisers often make it very difficult for non-official companies to profit from events: something that is achieved through the regulation and organisation of space. Tactics include heavy handed treatment of informal traders in designated areas, corralling people along certain corridors between transport nodes and venues, and restricting what people can take into venues. Because they are unable to benefit from event-related business, and because of the disruptions to normal trade, many city centre businesses suffer negatively from events. Events privatise urban space but they also privatise event benefits.

Despite its deserved reputation for staging free events, New York's Central Park is sometimes used for large private events. These are often justified by the fact that they are 'fund-raisers' either for good causes, or for the Park itself (Nevarez, 2007). Using the same logic, the Central Park Conservancy (the organisation which manages the Park) justifies a small number of private, ticketed events via the notion that they help to fund the numerous free events that are staged in the Park. This policy is linked to the wider argument that citizens can only have good public spaces if citizens are prepared to fund them. In the absence of generous government grants, one of the most viable ways to fund parks is to semi-privatise them by staging lucrative events. Few people would have a problem with occasional private events staged to raise much needed funds. The problem is that ticketed events are now staged so regularly in many parks. For example, the events programme in Bryant Park (New York) means that the space, in the view of one prominent campaigner 'is effectively closed to the public for most of the fall and winter. The park's whole central lawn has been sublet to commercial entities for private events limited to ticket holders' (Kent cited in Madden, 2010: 199). A similar situation exists in many UK parks. Parks have entered into contracts with event promoters to stage series of events over several years, effectively locking out the public for large periods of time. This is a pertinent example of how events privatise public space.

Securitisation

Urban development is driven by economic priorities but elite anxieties and insecurity are also important drivers (Wood and Abe, 2011). The result is the securitisation of cities. Most of the literature on this trend is negative – it assumes that attempts to secure urban spaces have been unnecessarily stringent, driven by paranoia about the perceived dangers of urban spaces: terrorism, violence and public disorder. The previous chapter explained how some events can help places to feel more secure in a positive way, by animating space (at night) and making them more accessible. Events are also associated with securitisation of urban public space, but in a more negative fashion. When major events are staged in public spaces they contribute to the tightening of space. Traditionally, public events were seen as times during which policing and regulations were relaxed – authorities turned a blind eye to behaviours that were not normally tolerated – e.g. drunkenness, gambling and prostitution. However, contemporary events often result in the introduction of tighter controls than would normally be the case. This is caused by fears about terrorism, demonstrations and unrest. The threats posed by terrorism are perceived to be higher during major events. High profile events staged in public spaces are attractive to terrorists for the same reason as they are attractive to urban authorities – their symbolic value. The bombing at the Atlanta Olympic Games (1996) and the recent attacks at the Boston Marathon (2013) provide troubling – although isolated – examples. The place marketing value of events means there is an added incentive for authorities to ensure that demonstrations, disorder or illicit behaviours don't infiltrate media coverage and contaminate the messages they are trying to communicate. The result is higher security and tighter spaces.

During major events, controls and restrictions are often implemented which are beyond the standards of criminal law (Palmer and Whelan, 2007). New constraints are placed on what people can do in public spaces, what can be brought in and what can be consumed. Whilst these tighter restrictions are often justified on safety grounds, they are also designed to protect the commercial interests of sponsors and to increase sales of items within temporary event venues. This is where commercial and security agendas become blurred. During mega-events the greater control exerted over public spaces can extend well beyond the confines of event venues. During London's Olympic Games in 2012, dispersal zones were created across the city where police could exclude anyone deemed to be engaging in anti-social behaviour and disband groups without reasonable levels of suspicion (Boykoff and Fussey, 2014).

Despite the concerns about over-securitisation and the effects this has on public space, there are isolated examples where events seem to have (accidentally) liberated spaces from over-zealous security measures. Prominent public spaces are already heavily controlled even when they are not staging events, so in some instances, events can help to change the dynamics of these spaces. Kennelly and

Watt (2011) describe how a prominent public space in Vancouver was altered by the imposition of a big screens and related festivity during the 2010 Winter Olympic Games. One interviewee described how she had been continually moved on from this location prior to the start of the Olympics. However, once the Games started her experiences changed. Her presence was suddenly tolerated because she was perceived to be watching the Games on the big screen, rather than merely 'loitering'. Kennelly and Watt (2011: 774) conclude that 'the Olympic Games spectacle had transformed this central urban space from a site of intense surveillance and policing into a space of consumption'.

Streets and squares are securitised during events, but so are parks. Security in public parks was traditionally provided by park keepers and other forms of 'secondary social control' (Palmer and Whelan, 2007). The withdrawal of these staff has diminished open space and its use according to Burgess et al. (1988). In recent years there has been a formalisation of control – via the employment of dedicated security personnel. These personnel are even more evident during events. Indeed, whilst some events may be justified as ways to encourage the self-regulation of urban space by introducing more users (see Chapter 4), during major events there are more security personnel than there would be normally be. These include conventional guards and officers, but less conventional security staff too. Roberts (2010) feels that event volunteers are part of a 'secondary police force' used by urban authorities during events to help identify nuisance behaviours. Roberts' (2010) analysis of the securitisation of Durban during the 2010 FIFA World Cup also helps us to understand the motives for security arrangements: here, the obsession with eradicating nuisances was linked to city image considerations. New byelaws were also introduced to regulate public open spaces during the event.

The result of all this extra surveillance is that urban public spaces are more rigidly controlled during events, reducing their permeability or looseness. Tightened security and tightened space are event effects illustrated well by the case of Central Park, New York. This Park stages a series of major events every year including concerts, movie screenings and sport events. One effect of these events is that security is temporarily extended. Nevarez (2007: 165) feels that 'the aesthetics of order is more evident during major events than during more everyday life moments . . . control spreads through the whole park including areas which usually have less surveillance'. As Degen (2003: 870) notes, surveillance can be 'ingrained in the physical environment and in the social relations it facilitates'. Nevarez (2007) identifies that during major events, boundaries in Central Park are more rigidly marked – via fences but also through more subtle mechanisms (e.g. the positioning of rubbish bins) making the space feel less accessible and penetrable. This is a technique perfected by Disney theme parks where objects are used to direct visitors away from or towards certain locations (Degen, 2003). Controls of this kind suggest park space during major events represents the antithesis of loose space. According to Nevarez (2007), the reasoning behind the heightened security is clear, with authorities adopting the same rationale as Durban (Roberts, 2010). During major events Central Park is on display – it becomes a spectacle rather than a 'backyard' for local residents. Therefore, everything is done to control the space, and the image of the space, so that its status is not diminished. Even though major events have traditionally been enjoyed as disruptions to the normal order, in Central Park these events provide an opportunity for the authorities to display a well ordered public space.

Racing in the streets

The processes of commercialisation, privatisation and securitisation discussed above are inherently interlinked. As Klauser (2012) argues, there has been a fusing of commercial and security interests, with both benefiting from splintering urbanism and the tight controls implemented when major events are staged. Privatisation, commercialisation and securitisation are can be furthered simultaneously when certain events are staged in public spaces. The next section focuses on a type of event which seems to contribute to all these processes: street circuit motor racing. Despite attracting a dedicated following, this is an event genre that is particularly hard to justify. Certain authors – particularly Mark Lowes and Paul Tranter – have been instrumental in drawing attention to the problems associated with these events. The issue is not whether motor races should be staged at all, but whether governments should be seen to be sanctioning them by staging them publically in a city's streets.

Tranter and Lowes (2009: 155) suggest that staging motorsports in important public places helps to promote this sport and its commercial interests and 'advances a city culture that favours the consumer over the citizen'. This is true of most major sports events staged in public spaces which tend to be heavily sponsored and commercialised. But motor sport and its sponsors have particularly problematic associations. The 'glorification of the car' is at odds with contemporary public policy and this message is unhelpful with regards to key priorities like road safety (Tranter and Lowes, 2009). A spectacle that glorifies speeding seems hard to justify especially if the sport and its sponsors are being subsidised by public funds. It is even harder to justify if you consider research evidence that suggests that young males who are interested in motor sport are more likely to engage in risky driving behaviours (Tranter and Warn, 2008).

Beyond safety issues, motor races are events associated with negative environmental impacts and they undermine efforts to promote environmentally friendly transport modes. Most cities around the world are trying to reduce levels of air pollution and carbon emissions and staging motor races contradicts such objectives. The motorsports industry has tried to address this problem by launching new races that feature more environmentally friendly vehicles: 2014/5 saw the launch of Formula E – a series for fully electric cars. An edition of this new event was staged in London's Battersea Park in June 2015. But unlike cycling events and running events (which are also staged on city streets), conventional motor races pollute cities. They are the antithesis of sustainability and urban authorities' attempts to encourage responsible behaviours amongst their citizens are undermined by staging motor races in public spaces.

There are various examples of street races that have caused problematic impacts. Residents of Canberra, Australia felt that staging three day V8 races in 2000 and 2001 on the city streets compromised the dignity and meaning of their urban spaces (Tranter and Keefee, 2004). Similarly, residents of Melbourne objected to the use of one of their parks for the Melbourne Grand Prix. Albert Park is an historic urban public space (est. 1876) and one which has traditionally provided a space for relaxation and recreation. According to Lowes (2004: 73) 'having a Grand Prix in Albert Park was counter to the integrity, purpose and core philosophy of this profoundly public space'. Lowes (2004) thinks the staging of the Melbourne Grand Prix in Albert Park represents a privatisation of the space, and given the fact it takes four months to set up and dismantle this annual event, this is more than a temporary privatisation. The event has resulted in permanent structures being installed in the Park (e.g. a two storey pit building), even though there were assurances that race facilities would be temporary (Lowes, 2004: 76). The event caused other negative effects too: including environmental degradation (1,000 trees were removed) and the loss of public amenities (13 sport fields). Attempts to resist the use of the Park as a race track were obstructed by the Australian Grands Prix Act (1994) which gave the state government special powers to hinder protests and demonstrations. Therefore, as well as illustrating the way events can commercialise and privatise a precious public space, the Melbourne Grand Prix also highlights how major events are used to usher in new security regimes. Such regimes erode the notion that public parks are democratic places of protest and resistance and affirm the notion that they are spaces for passive entertainment and consumption.

Events and the physical denigration of space

The discussion above highlights that events can denigrate public space symbolically; and they can also alter the accessibility of space and what people can do in those spaces. Staging events in public spaces can denigrate public spaces in other ways too. Events may inconvenience regular users and they may damage physical environments. These issues are discussed in this next section. All events cause negative environmental and social impacts so the discussion deliberately avoids impacts that are generic to all events. Instead the analysis focuses specifically on issues caused by staging events in public spaces rather than conventional venues. Although many public spaces have been adapted to stage events (see Chapter 4), most are not designed as venues and this means they usually are ill-equipped to deal with the volumes of traffic and different behaviours associated with events. This can exacerbate negative environmental impacts.

Physical damage

When events are staged in parks, there are usually concerns about the environmental impacts caused. As many parks have a conservation mission, authorities are under pressure to ensure that measures are taken to mitigate negative impacts.

One of the main issues is the damage to turf and other vegetation. During periods of wet weather, events turn green space brown. Even if protective surfaces are used, the grass underneath suffers from the compaction and lack of sunlight. Some parks now have to be regularly re-turfed because of the number of events they stage. This is expensive and disrupts park use for long periods after events have finished. There is also damage to flora and fauna. Major events have been used as excuses to remove trees in parks, and the noise they make disrupts wildlife as well as local residents. Flowers and plants are inevitably trampled. The effect of large crowds on carefully planted vegetation was visible in the Olympic Park during the 2012 Games in London. On day one of the Games, everything was pristine and spectacular. A week later, the beds had been decimated.

Damage to parks is not just caused by people, it is caused by the vehicle movements needed to allow events to take place (see Figure 5.4). This is also a problem for events staged in other kinds of public spaces too. Flecha et al. (2010) explain how the vibrations caused by trucks supplying the Ouro Preto Carnival (Minais Gerais, Brazil) are causing fissures in historic houses. The problem is so acute that the Director of National Heritage has advocated the withdrawal of the events from the historic core. Since 2007, organisers have moved part of the festivities from the historic centre – a decentralisation that is designed to prevent physical damage resulting from the 30,000 extra people that are hosted on each day of the carnival (Flecha et al., 2010). This case shows that, although we presume urban

Figure 5.4 A lorry servicing a temporary event venue in Hyde Park, London.

streets and squares are more robust environments than natural ones, but they are still vulnerable to physical damage. Urban spaces may suffer from collateral damage when they are used to stage events but they can also be denigrated by vandalism. Large sport events and cultural festivals often involve hedonistic or extreme behaviours and this can increase the chances that streets and squares are damaged deliberately. After an event it is not unusual to find that shop windows and street furniture have been broken, or that graffiti has been sprayed on signs, walls and monuments. These are relatively minor issues but many squares and streets are important symbols, so even minor damage may be perceived as a major problem.

Noise

When events are staged indoors, or in purpose built stadia, noise is not really a problem. However, when events are staged in public spaces, residents and other users often complain about the noise levels – particularly if performances last until late into the night. Much of the noise is caused by public announcement systems and the use of powerful speakers. Decibel levels at events are usually regulated by public authorities. In the UK, the Noise Council's 'Code of Practice on Environmental Noise at Concerts' is used in licensing procedures. This stipulates that the average music noise levels should not exceed 65 decibels over a 15 minute period for 'other urban and rural venues'. This limit is deliberately set 10 decibels lower than the 75 decibel limit set for 'urban stadia and arenas'. However, many of London's parks and squares use a limit of 75 decibels: in other words they are treated as stadia or arenas rather than urban venues (Vanguardia, 2014). For example, Victoria Park and Trafalgar Square in London are regulated via premises licence conditions that restrict noise levels to 75 decibels. In these sites, sound is recorded 1 metre from the façade of any noise sensitive premises (Vanguardia, 2014). This 10db difference might not sound like much, but it is worth noting that when sounds differ by 10db this means one is twice as loud as the other.

Reducing noise levels does not necessarily result in an optimal outcome as it can reduce people's enjoyment of the event, leaving both spectators and residents dissatisfied. At many music events staged in public spaces the crowd have been frustrated by how quiet performances are. Hyde Park is a good example. As one UK comedian recently put it: 'in recent years huge audiences have come together in Hyde Park to shush each other at some of the quietest rock concerts the world has ever seen' (Williams, 2015). The noisiest events staged in public spaces are motor races. Whilst the citizens of Melbourne, Monaco, Singapore and Valencia might be relieved to note that Formula One cars have been deliberately quietened in recent years, it is interesting to note that this change has attracted complaints from race enthusiasts. This highlights a key issue with events – they are deliberately designed to provide heightened experiences, so any attempts to regulate them so that they fit in with everyday urban life may be counter-productive.

In extreme cases, authorities have switched off speakers to ensure that stipulated noise levels are not contravened. The most famous instance happened in Hyde Park, London, in 2012 when Bruce Springsteen's microphone was turned off during a duet with Paul McCartney. The US artist was delivering an extended encore and had gone over his allotted time. Despite the status of the performers, local Council officials were unwilling to let the show continue. This type of regulation is becoming a major problem for event organisers and may restrict further growth of public spaces as concert venues. John Reid, European President of Live Nation, suggests London's parks are increasingly difficult to use as concert venues because of licensing laws and noise controls. Showing a certain disdain for those who oppose his events, Reid argues that: 'it seems odd that a small number of concerned residents can dictate to loads of people' (cited in Blackhurst, 2015: 44). Controlling unpredictable artists and performances is just one part of the problem. The noise created by large crowds is often underestimated. This is a problem during events when the noise of crowds can't really be regulated. It is also a major problem as crowds leave and make their way home through residential districts. However, as the next section illustrates, for local residents, this may be the least of their worries.

Public urination

One of the more odious impacts of staging events in public spaces is public urination. Many of the complaints about these events by local residents can be dismissed as conservative NIMBYism, but it is hard to argue that someone should have to tolerate strangers urinating in their front garden. This is a particular problem with events staged in public spaces because often these do not have the facilities required to accommodate the thousands of people who need to use toilets and other basic facilities. Music and street festivals feature high levels of drinking – which means that people want to use the toilet even more regularly and for longer than they usually do. Many running events held in public spaces also face this problem. Runners tend to drink lots of water in the build up to the race. They are often held for a time at the start line, so as soon as the race begins participants immediately start to look for somewhere to urinate. Organisers of the London Marathon now put up signs requesting that runners do not urinate in people's gardens.

There is now extensive provision of temporary toilets at most events, including al fresco 'pissoirs' for the men at some, but there is never enough capacity to satisfy large crowds. Some people will always avoid queuing by making their own arrangements. When events are over, a large proportion of people want to use a toilet and the lack of availability means that people urinate wherever they can: in the park, on the street, in doorways or in people's gardens. When Finsbury Park in London staged two controversial Stone Roses concerts in 2013, one of the main issues was public urination. The high number of complaints and negative press coverage about the events prompted the local council to undertake a consultation exercise on staging events in Finsbury Park. During this exercise one local resident complained that 'The Park stank of urine for days after' (Haringey Council, 2013). Another stated that the event meant 'excrement, urine, vomit and rubbish in our front garden' (Haringey Council, 2013).

Littering

The size of an event is often measured by the scale of the items consumed – how many bottles of water sold, how many pints of beer consumed, how many bananas eaten etc. Unfortunately, when these items are consumed in public spaces, those spaces are denigrated by the waste created. It seems as though the only time it is socially acceptable to leave litter in streets, squares and parks is during events. Sports events participants throw water bottles recklessly on to the ground, festival goers leave empty beer glasses in the gutter and concert attendees don't think twice about leaving food wrappers behind. This mess is usually cleared up fairly quickly, but in the meantime urban public spaces look dishevelled and tarnished.

Restricted access

One of the most obvious impacts of staging events in public spaces is that the people who would normally inhabit these spaces are not able to do so. This includes local residents and workers, but also visitors who may want to see a park, street or square in its everyday form. Whilst regular visitors and residents may like to see a space transformed by an event, these transformations are less desirable for irregular users. Tourists visiting a city for a limited time many want to visit a park or square in its usual guise and their experience may be negatively affected by restricted access. An extreme example of this occurred in Trafalgar Square, London in 2011. The Square was used as the venue for the premiere of the final instalment of the Harry Potter film franchise and people travelled from all over the world for the event. Disruption was not just caused on the day of the screening, but for days previously as thousands of fans camped overnight to ensure they were in a good position to see the event. This highlights another practical problem with staging large events in public spaces – it is hard to know how many people will attend. If more people than expected turn up, and because access may be unrestricted, this can cause major disruption and safety issues.

Events displace everyday uses of public spaces (e.g. dog walking, jogging) causing disruption and inconvenience to many people. This disruption is not just limited to the time of the event: most events take some time to set up and dismantle. In these instances people are forced to alter their routines. However, when cities stage events in public spaces there is a more deliberate displacement of people deemed 'undesirable'. Homeless people and informal traders are 'moved on' from city squares, parks and streets. These people rely on public spaces to provide shelter and income, so for them the effects of staging events are more fundamental than mere inconvenience or disruption.

Many street events, but also other events staged in public spaces, result in the closure of local roads. Whilst this is generally a positive thing (see Chapter 4), it obviously inconveniences businesses, residents and employees who would normally use the thoroughfares. For these reasons, and because of the recent growth of street events, officials in London now believe that the city cannot stage any more street events than it currently does. The World Triathlon Finals staged in Hyde Park and the surrounding streets in 2013 (see Figure 5.5) 'caused five days

Figure 5.5 Disruption to road users caused by the 2013 World Triathlon Finals in Hyde Park, London

of congestion and delay across West London, culminating in total chaos as the Royal Parks and Hyde Park Corner were shut over the weekend' (Jenkins, 2013b). Jenkins (2013b) feels that when these projects are conceived, 'no one speaks up for the ordinary commuter or city user'.

Street closures can be annoying and inconvenient if you are not interested in the event, but for some city users they are also damaging financially. The extent of this cost is hard to estimate. A Freedom of Information request sent to Transport for London revealed that the authorities simply did not know how much it costs to close London's roads for major events (Carey, 2013). Sometimes London's roads are closed for a day or, in isolated cases, for a whole weekend. Other cities, for example those that stage motor races in urban streets, suffer the inconvenience of more extensive road closures. To stage the 2008 Grand Prix, many of Singapore's roads were closed for 12 days. Henderson et al.'s (2010) research found that over half their sample of residents (n = 338) felt that their everyday lives had been disrupted by the staging of this event. In some instances, for example the St. Valentines Fair in Leeds (see Chapter 1), this disruption has led to the event being moved to a more peripheral location. This reflects Tallon et al.'s (2006) research which notes that if events are too successful, they 'outgrow' city centres. Therefore, although there has been an urbanisation of events in recent years, and welcome attempts to close city streets to traffic, cities may not be able to sustain this.

Public safety

Staging events in public spaces rather than traditional venues also has other knock on effects. As well as the deficient provision of basic (e.g. transport or toilet) facilities, there are more general concerns about public safety. Parks, streets and squares are designed to accommodate large numbers of people, but not necessarily at very specific points in time. Over-crowding can cause inconvenience but it can also result in more fundamental consequences. There have been multiple instances of death and injuries in traditional venues too, but since the Hillsborough football stadium disaster (1989) better safety measures have been introduced. Similar measures can be applied to events staged in public spaces, but these spaces are harder to regulate.

There have been several high profile instances where events staged in parks, squares and streets have resulted in death and injury to participants. At the 2000 Roskilde Music Festival, an event staged annually in this Danish city's park since 1971, nine spectators were killed. Conditions were slippery and fatal injuries were sustained when the crowd pushed forward during a Pearl Jam set. Love Parade, a techno music festival staged 1989–2007 in Berlin and 2007–2010 in the Ruhr region of Germany, was cancelled permanently in 2010 following the death of 21 people. Attendees were crushed following a stampede in Duisberg. The deaths occurred when festival goers entered tunnel that was too narrow to cope with the crowds. This incident had similarities to the appalling tragedy in 1990 just outside Mecca, Saudi Arabia, where over 1400 pilgrims celebrating Eid al Adha died in a pedestrian tunnel.

Safety issues are not just caused by overcrowding. Most traditional venues now conduct searches and security checks at points where spectators enter the venue, but it is harder to prevent weapons from being taken to events staged in public spaces. In 2012, the organisers of Toronto's Irie Music Festival cancelled all the concerts planned in Yonge-Dundas Square (see Figure 2.2). The city had recently experienced a series of gun crime incidents and organisers could not figure out a way to search the large numbers of people expected to attend.

Temporary or more permanent effects?

This chapter has explored the detrimental effects of events and the ways events can denigrate public spaces. Even if we accept that these negative effects occur, it needs to be acknowledged that in many instances these are temporary effects. Public spaces are restored to their former status once events are over. Any commercialisation, privatisation, securitisation or physical denigration many only last as long as the event in question. However, in many instances these negative effects do persist. As Johansson and Kociatkiewicz (2011) state, practices adopted for events provide 'blueprints' for future spatial practices. Within this is mind, it is important to explain the mechanisms through which eventification can result in more permanent changes.

One issue with many of the events discussed in this chapter is that they represent a re-territorialisation of space, rather than a de-territorialisation. The previous chapter discussed how events can helpfully destabilise and loosen the identity and meanings of spaces. In other words, some events can assist the de-territorialisation of urban space. But when public spaces become regular venues for commercialised, ticketed events they are effectively re-territorialised as venues. These spaces have more in common with tight spaces, rather than the loose spaces advocated by Franck and Stevens (2007). Space identities are changed by these events but not necessarily in a positive way. Whereas some looser events challenge fixed meanings and determined functions, staging major events can re-fix meanings and provide new determined functions. Hence many people now assume parks and squares are obvious spaces to stage events because they have become accustomed to this new meaning/use. For example, many Londoners now accept that Trafalgar Square and Hyde Park are event venues. They have become used to not being able to use these spaces at weekends or in the summer and so their meaning has changed. Alongside other effects, this undermines their significance as political sites – as democratic places and sites of resistance (Jenkins, 2013a).

There are other ways that temporary events cause negative effects that persist long after events have finished. Many large events staged in public spaces are sold to the public as exceptional occasions. They are justified not only by their impermanence but by their irregularity (Smith, 2014). Any controversy associated with staging the event is dampened by rhetoric emphasising that this is a one-off. However, once staged these exceptional events becomes *precedents*: because it has been done before there is a clear justification to do it again. If an event has gone well, or even if it is presented as being successful, then this provides a man date to stage similar events in the future. From one event we get a cycle of events. Adapting Agamben's (2005) ideas, we get a permanent state of exception.

In certain instances urban authorities *want* to commercialise, privatise and securitise public spaces. As previous parts of this book have explained, they many want to realise revenue (see Chapter 3), restrict access for certain groups (see above) or deal with persistent safety issues (see Chapter 4). Knowing that changing spaces in these ways can be controversial, major events are a good way to introduce changes which are then retained post event. In other words events are used as 'Trojan horses' – convenient ways to push through controversial changes. When public spaces are commercialised, privatised and securitised through events, it also helps to *normalise* these processes and their outcomes. People get used to seeing corporate logos in these spaces, they get used to the fact that they can't use them on certain days and they become accustomed to the measures introduced to control behaviour. In others words, what was once regarded as unusual becomes the 'new normal'. As Hagemann (2010) argues, 'temporary reconfigurations' can become 'a new state of normality'.

Summary

This chapter highlights how events can affect public spaces in detrimental ways: by contributing to their commercialisation, privatisation and securitisation. These processes produce a tightening of the spaces used to stage events, a re-territorialisation that typifies eventification. The processes discussed here are interlinked: event organisers and their commercial partners require exclusivity and security. Urban authorities seeking place marketing benefits control the messages disseminated by restricting access and behaviours. Obviously, public spaces are already commercialised, privatised and securitised, so it is important to emphasise that events are not solely responsible for these processes, but the analysis in this chapter shows that events can exacerbate these trends. Mega-events and their associated activations – such as fan zones and sponsor installations – seem particularly culpable. There are also problems with the regularity with which events are staged: this merely introduces a new pre-determined event function for public spaces. Few would object to occasional events in their parks, streets and squares but regular events represent major restrictions on accessibility. Ticketing also undermines the other defining attribute of public space – that it is free to access. Sometimes the negative effects discussed here are incidental and unfortunate by-products of staging events. However, in other cases events are deliberately used as vehicles for commercialisation, privatisation and securitisation – either as high profile precedents to sanction future changes, or more surreptitiously, as an attempt to introduce new arrangements using the 'cover' of an event. The general idea that events are a 'good thing' is undermined by this chapter, but this prevailing view is an important vehicle used to justify controversial practices. Organisers of commercial events use the traditional traits of events (festivity, sociability, escapism) to justify installations and restrictions in public spaces that wouldn't otherwise be tolerated.

6   Using public spaces as events venues

Greenwich Park becomes an Olympic Park

Introduction

Previous chapters of this book discuss events and their effects on public spaces at the general level. One disadvantage of this approach is this that the various cases mentioned are covered relatively briefly. To compensate, it is helpful to examine one case in more detail. This chapter helps to illustrate key issues through an in-depth analysis of the use of Greenwich Park as the venue for the equestrian events during the 2012 Olympic and Paralympic Games. Staging *Olympic* events in a *Royal* Park hardly represents a typical scenario. However, we can learn much from this example which involved intense debates about the merits of using public spaces as event venues. Although Greenwich Park is a Royal Park (owned by the Crown), since the early nineteenth century the public have had the right to use it for recreational purposes and contemporary research shows it is a well-used and highly regarded public space (Burgess et al. 1988). Despite the availability of alternatives, including established venues, organisers of the 2012 Games decided to stage the equestrian events here. The aims of this chapter are: to examine the ways in which this decision was justified and resisted and; to assess the impacts and outcomes of staging the events for the Park. Although the 2012 Games has been the subject of an unprecedented amount of academic research, the Greenwich Park dimension has only received very limited attention. This chapter helps to rectify this.

Methods

A mixture of primary and secondary data is used to explore the Greenwich case study. Observations were undertaken regularly 2010–2014 in the Park, and at several meetings that were held in the run up to the events, including the two most significant meetings: 'Save Greenwich Park from Olympic Events' on 17th January 2010 (the largest of the public forums convened by those opposed to the event); and the 'Meeting of the Greenwich Council Planning Board' on 23rd March 2010 (when the proposals to stage the events in Greenwich were ratified). Observations were also made at the events themselves, within the venue on the 30th July, 31st July, 2nd August, 4th August, 30th August and 1st September, and at other times outside the venue. More formal research was also carried out:

234 surveys were undertaken over two days when Park was used for the equestrian events. This research exercise was conducted jointly with Professor Graham Brown from the University of South Australia. Findings from these surveys are also included in this chapter.

To supplement the primary research, official documents and newspaper coverage produced 2008–2014 were analysed. The official documents reviewed included publications and communications produced by the three main stakeholder groups involved in the controversy:

1   The company who were responsible for organising the event:

   • The London Organising Committee for the Olympic and Paralympic Games (LOCOG).

2   The organisations responsible for the site:

   • The Department for Culture, Media and Sport (DCMS) – the National Government Department with responsibility for managing Royal Parks;
   • The Royal Parks – the agency appointed by DCMS to manage the Parks;
   • Greenwich Council – the Local Planning Authority.

3   The community action group who led the opposition movement:

   • No to Greenwich Olympic Events (NOGOE).

The history of Greenwich Park

The origins of Greenwich Park can be traced back to the early fifteenth century when the Duke of Gloucester obtained a license to enclose 74ha of land on Blackheath in South East London (Bold, 2000). Deer were introduced in 1555 and the site was used as hunting grounds by members of the aristocracy and royal family. Over time, various built structures have been added. During the period 1619–1625 a wall 12 feet high and two miles long was built around the Park that still exists today. From the late seventeenth century, several important buildings were added: including the Queen's House (designed by Inigo Jones) and The Royal Observatory (designed by Christopher Wren). The public were allowed in from 1705: with access limited to holiday periods; including during the infamous Greenwich Fair (1683–1857). This Fair was staged twice a year; for three days in May and three days in October.

The use of Park for the Greenwich Fair during the early nineteenth century provides an interesting precedent to help contextualise contemporary debates. Charles Dickens' (1836) account of the Fair pre-empts the twenty-first century controversy discussed in this chapter: 'if the Parks be the lungs of London we wonder what the Greenwich Fair is'. Greenwich Fair was originally a cattle fair but it evolved into a more raucous event involving amusements such as theatrical and wax work shows, menageries, prize fights, rope tricks, fortune tellers and various stalls. Attractions included looking through telescopes and 'tumbling' – rolling down the hills in the Park. According to Aslet (1999) tumbling and those dubbed the 'tumbling classes' represented the 'organised mayhem' of Greenwich Fair. By the late eighteenth century the crowds were so great they could not easily get through the entrances of the

Park (Aslet, 1999). For affluent locals who lived nearby it was all very unseemly. From 1825 onwards they campaigned to close the Fair down and it was eventually abolished in 1857. This provides a parallel with the twenty-first century controversy: during the build-up to the 2012 equestrian events, a campaign to prevent them from being staged in Greenwich Park was led by affluent residents.

Some authors have written that the use of Greenwich Park for equestrian events was inappropriate because the site lacks established links with equestrian sport (Hayes and Horne, 2011). This argument ignores the fact that one of the original uses of the Park was as an equestrian venue. Webster's (1902: 24) history of Greenwich Park notes that in 1552 'there was a great number of horsemen before King Edward VI in Greenwich Park'. His successor, Henry VIII, also used the Park for equestrian activities and links to horses continued after the Royal Household departed upstream. During the Greenwich Fair, equestrian shows were one of the main attractions and horse riding was a popular leisure activity in the surrounding area well into the twentieth century. Indeed, Rhind (1987) notes that the last riding school on Blackheath closed at the start of World War II. This history doesn't justify using Greenwich Park for Olympic equestrian events, but it does suggest that the proposal wasn't entirely divorced from the established identity of the space or its origins.

Contemporary status of Greenwich Park

Greenwich Park is now managed by The Royal Parks. This agency is funded by an annual government grant and revenues generated by commercial activities. The Royal Parks has two core objectives:

1   Conserve and enhance the natural and built environment, historic landscape and biodiversity of the Parks for the benefit of our diverse audiences and future generations.
2   Strengthen the organisation and its effectiveness by continuing to deliver better value for money and exploring commercial opportunities.

(The Royal Parks, 2013a)

These two objectives are not necessarily compatible. For example, plans to generate more revenue sit awkwardly with the wider mission to conserve the environment of the Park. The current Business Plan (The Royal Parks, 2013b) identifies that: 'tensions remain between those who believe that too much commercialisation threatens the intrinsic qualities of Parks and those who accept that . . . more income must be generated'. As corporate objective 2 (above) highlights, cuts to government funding mean that the Royal Parks are being placed under greater pressure to increase commercial revenues. The Royal Parks now generates over half of its own income and their latest Annual Report 2012/13 suggests that approximately one third of this is derived from events (The Royal Parks, 2013a). This reflects the discussion in Chapter 3 about the financial drivers of event projects. Like other public spaces, Greenwich Park has started to stage more ticketed events over the past few years, including film screenings, music concerts and theatrical performances. The decision to stage the London 2012 equestrian events in Greenwich Park need to be addressed with this context in mind.

As Carmona (2010: 171) notes, Greenwich Park is a public space, but not necessarily an open one: 'although open to the public during daylight hours, restrictions on public rights and access remain'. The Park is completely surrounded by walls and railings with gates only open at stipulated times. The Royal Parks and Other Open Spaces Regulations (1997) provide the statutory instrument that controls access, use and behaviour. Ironically, given the use of the park for equestrian events in 2012, these regulations prevent people riding horses except on the road that connects the two main entrances. The 2012 events were meant to generate spectacular media imagery, so it is also ironic that taking commercial photographs is forbidden. A Parks Operation Command Unit polices the Royal Parks and there is a police station inside Greenwich Park near to Blackheath Gate. Regular police patrols take place and CCTV cameras have recently been installed. Therefore, like many other examples of contemporary public space, Greenwich Park is highly regulated.

Greenwich Park's status as a Royal Park signifies that it belongs to the nation; and its inscription as a World Heritage Site (1997) communicates its status as a global asset. This confuses the answer to a question commonly asked of public space: who is it for? The Park is a major tourist attraction but, like other parks, it remains an important amenity for local use. Burgess et al.'s (1988: 469) extensive research into open spaces within the Borough of Greenwich found that Greenwich Park was regarded as the most important local example by Borough residents because it is well managed and 'offers a mix of environments and attractions'. This is important for the subsequent analysis here; parks are not merely for relaxation and escape but for entertainment and recreation. People in Greenwich use them mainly to get out of the house, as somewhere to take their children, and for exercise (Burgess et al., 1988). Greenwich residents also want 'something unexpected' when engaging with park spaces (Burgess et al., 1988) which suggests that events could help to make Parks more enjoyable.

The choice of Greenwich Park as an Olympic venue

Although London was not awarded the rights to stage the 2012 Games until 2005, provisional planning began several years earlier. A temporary venue in Greenwich Park was earmarked from a very early stage as the venue for the equestrian events. In their 2003 feasibility study, the British Equestrian Federation (BEF) indicated Greenwich as their preferred option; and the venue was a key part of London's bid. In the Candidate File submitted to the International Olympic Committee (IOC) London's bid team wrote: 'we have selected locations that provide excellent facilities and spectacular backdrops: the World Heritage Sites of Greenwich, the Palace of Westminster and the Tower of London' (London 2012, 2004: 10). The opportunity to incorporate Maritime Greenwich (and views of Canary Wharf and the City of London) into the venue was the most compelling reason for staging the events in Greenwich (see Figures 6.1 and 6.2).

The inclusion of Greenwich Park in London's bid for the Olympic Games was something favoured by organisers who knew it would increase their chances of success. Competition to stage the 2012 Games was exceptionally fierce with Paris, Moscow, Madrid and New York also short listed. Using a World Heritage Site as a venue provided a unique selling point and the officials responsible for the Site were keen to remind the Government about this. According to their submission to a Parliamentary Report 'the decision by the IOC to award the 2012 Games to London may well have been assisted by the special qualities of Maritime Greenwich which featured strongly in the submission' (Maritime Greenwich, 2011: section 4.5). The Observer newspaper reported a more blunt interpretation 'London organisers threw in Greenwich when they thought Paris might win' (Moss, 2012a).

Alongside image considerations, the most commonly cited reason for designating Greenwich Park as the equestrian venue was its proximity to Stratford where the main Olympic venues and the Athletes Village were to be located. As McLaren (2012: 132) notes, LOCOG 'wanted to host the events at Greenwich Park because it would ensure it was close to the majority of the other London Olympic sites'. This was important for practical and symbolic reasons. Greenwich Park is only 4.5km from Stratford and this proximity also aided the logistics of staging the modern Pentathlon; an event that required participants to use the Aquatics Centre at the Olympic Park and the equestrian facilities on the same day. Because they are the only disciplines involving animals, the equestrian events are widely regarded as presenting highly complex logistical challenges for Olympic host cities. In 1956 Olympic equestrian events were staged separately (in Stockholm) because quarantine rules prevented them taking place in the main host city (Melbourne). In 2008 Olympic equestrian events were staged in Hong Kong – 1000 miles from the host city, Beijing. This geographical separation had a detrimental effect on the athletes' experience: riders didn't feel part of their national teams, they weren't able to attend the opening ceremony and they didn't stay in the Olympic Village with other athletes (Dashper, 2012). The IOC is an organisation that takes athletes needs very seriously; so to please the athletes and the IOC, London wanted to stage equestrian events that felt part of the wider Games (Dashper, 2012). This mission also contributed to the decision to use Greenwich Park as the venue. A subsidiary aim of staging the equestrian events in Greenwich was to take the sport outside its normal (rural) setting to attract a new, younger, more urban audience. This was in keeping with the motto of the 2012 Games; 'Inspire a Generation'.

Staging the equestrian events required a large stadium for the dressage and show jumping events plus space for a cross country course. Initially, the plan was to build the main stadium in the grounds of the National Maritime Museum, but this was changed and the arena was built on an adjacent site within Greenwich Park (see Figures 6.1 and 6.2). Extensive support infrastructure for competitors, spectators and workers was also required – including stables for hundreds of horses. Organisations responsible for the proposed site – The Royal Parks and the National Maritime Museum – supported the use of the Park as an Olympic venue. This was to be expected as both are governed by the national government department responsible for organising the 2012 Games (DCMS). Greenwich was a Host Borough and was hosting other events in the North Greenwich Arena and at Woolwich (see Chapter 7). And during the build up to the Games, Greenwich was seeking to acquire the status of a Royal Borough, a title that was awarded in

2012. So, unsurprisingly, the local authority also backed the use of Greenwich Park as an Olympic venue.

Objections and opposition

Once the Olympic Games were awarded to London in 2005, and it became clear that the newly formed Organising Committee (LOCOG) intended to stage the equestrian events in Greenwich, an opposition movement emerged. No to Greenwich Olympic Events (NOGOE) was formed in 2007 as a 'community action group'. NOGOE benefited from the professional skills (legal, IT, communications) of

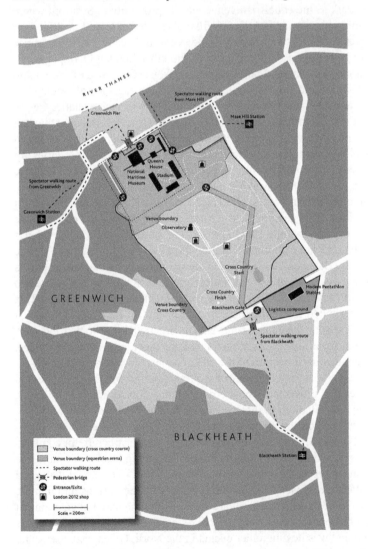

Figure 6.1 A map of Greenwich illustrating the configuration of the area during the London 2012 Olympic and Paralympic Games.

Source: Mason Edwards

many of its supporters and it also received publicity and support from well-known writers, such as David Starkey (a royal historian) and Andrew Gilligan (a prominent journalist). The group were not opposed to the Olympics per se, they were opposed to staging events in Greenwich Park. However, NOGOE received support from other groups and networks formed to resist the 2012 Games: including Games Monitor, 'a network of people raising awareness about issues within the London Olympic development processes' (Games Monitor, 2015). NOGOE adopted the generic slogan 'Save Greenwich Park' which highlighted the rather hyperbolic tone of much of their work; a trait dismissed by their opponents as 'scaremongering'. Olympic boosters are often accused of hype (Waitt, 2008), but this community action group used similar tactics to get their views heard.

Although NOGOE expressed multiple concerns about LOCOG's plans for Greenwich Park, their campaigning was dominated by two main issues: the environmental impact of the events and the way they restricted park access. Environmental problems were framed by the idea that the event presented an 'unnecessary risk' to important natural environments but also to archaeological heritage. NOGOE consistently advocated Windsor Park – an established equestrian venue – as a less risky alternative. There were understandable worries about constructing a 23,000 seat arena in historic parklands (see Figure 6.2) and campaigners were concerned that the cross country course would damage valuable grasslands and ancient trees.

Figure 6.2 The construction, use, dismantling and after effects of the arena used to stage the equestrian events. These pictures were taken in May 2012 (top left), July 2012 (top right), November 2012 (bottom left) and January 2013 (bottom right).

NOGOE's campaigning often highlighted temporal contrasts between the historic Park and the temporary event; and the 'lunacy' of risking permanent damage from an event that was only scheduled for a few days. They felt there was an inherent contradiction in the rationale of the organisers who wanted to make Greenwich Park better known by desecrating it. One contributor to the public meeting felt this was equivalent to gaining celebrity by beating yourself up.

The principle of park access was also prominent within NOGOE's campaigning. This issue wasn't just raised on behalf of the privileged residents who live next to the Park. Burgess et al.'s (1988) detailed research found that, unlike other local sites, Greenwich Park is used by residents across the Borough, which is one that is relatively deprived compared to other London and English territories (see Chapter 7). NOGOE emphasised that the Park is used extensively by Greenwich's disadvantaged residents, many of whom do not have gardens. This argument is supported by contemporary data. Figures from the 2011 Census suggest that access to gardens is relatively restricted in the Royal Borough of Greenwich: 46.4 per cent of the population live in flats, maisonettes or apartments (London Borough of Greenwich, 2011). The envisaged closures/part-closures to stage the equestrian events were scheduled over the summer months; prompting local opponents to ask where their children were supposed to play during this time (public meeting, 2010). NOGOE also claimed that the Park was too small to host the event; as there was insufficient space to route a full length cross country course. These practical arguments were supported by some within the UK's equestrian community. Subsidiary arguments highlighted by NOGOE included the potential for threats to public safety, transport congestion and disruption to local businesses.

LOCOG's response

LOCOG and affiliated stakeholders responded to NOGOE's opposition by promising that Greenwich Park would be returned to the public in pristine condition. They also tried to emphasise the positive impacts that would supposedly accrue. LOCOG stated the events would 'increase the global profile of the Borough'; '[provide] inspiration for its residents'; and 'bring sport to a new audience' (Smith, 2014). More substantial justifications for staging the events in Greenwich were needed because estimates of the cost had been severely underestimated. A figure of £6 million was quoted in the initial documentation, but the final costs of the temporary venue were estimated to be £60–120 million. The BEF had hoped that using a temporary venue would help to convince the IOC that equestrian sport was an affordable and manageable part of the Games. However, the costs and controversies associated with the 2012 Games undermined this mission.

Emotive rhetoric was used to justify staging the equestrian events in Greenwich. One narrative that reappeared during public meetings was the notion that using the Park was 'in the national interest'. Advocates were heard saying 'we have all got to do our bit for Britain'; with restricted access to Greenwich Park justified as a sacrifice worth making. The notions of 'borrowing' and 'sharing' were also apparent within the discourses used by those keen to see Greenwich Park become an Olympic venue (Smith, 2014). Supporters claimed they wished merely to 'borrow' the Park for a good cause and urged Greenwich residents to show 'generosity of spirit' to 'share the Park with the world'. Therefore, rather than trying to appeal to the self-interest of residents by offering positive impacts, the rhetoric of Olympic boosters implored local people to offer something to the event. This fitted with the spirit of volunteering – dubbed Games Making – that infused London's staging of the 2012 Games.

The planning process

The controversy regarding Greenwich Park's designation as an Olympic venue reached a critical point in late 2009/early 2010. On the 30th November 2009, LOCOG submitted planning applications to stage equestrian events in Greenwich Park. The documentation submitted by the organisers was voluminous: if you asked for it in a local library you were presented with several large boxes filled with reports. At the public meeting staged to discuss the proposal one contributor noted 'I specialise in responding to planning applications and I have never seen a planning application so large'. Initially, responses were required within 28 days. This appeared to be a tactical ploy to limit objections, particularly as the deadline coincided with the Christmas holidays. However, the window for consultation period was eventually extended to 27th January 2010.

During the consultation period NOGOE campaigned intensively to garner local support and the public meeting mentioned above was staged during this period (January 2010). This meeting began with an opening address and a melodramatic film that implied there was a real danger that Greenwich Park would be closed indefinitely. At the end of the meeting NOGOE representatives distributed templates of letters which their supporters could send to Greenwich Council's planning officers.

The letter stated:

> I wish to object to the above planning applications relating to the use of Greenwich Park for the 2012 Equestrian Olympics, and I wish these objections to be taken into account; the principal objections which I have are the likely damage to Greenwich Park, the lengthy periods when the park will be closed or partly closed, the traffic congestion, the disruption to the lives of local residents and the lack of any significant legacy.

Council records indicate that 2,099 responses to the planning application were received; 236 in favour and 2,063 against. 51 per cent of the submissions used the standard template disseminated by NOGOE. A petition with over 13,000 signatories was also presented to the Council. However, of the 2022 responses to a council letter sent in October 2009, 58 per cent supported staging the 2012 Games at Greenwich Park. LOCOG also completed their own survey that suggested 85 per cent of local people were in favour of staging the events. All this evidence was taken into consideration by Greenwich Council's Planning Board along with submissions from a range of third parties including local amenity groups, and national sport, heritage and environmental organisations. After considering the applications, planning officers recommended that permission be granted albeit with

38 conditions imposed (see Box 6.1). This unusually large number of conditions can be interpreted as both a reflection of the level of concern about the original proposals and as a productive outcome of the objections raised by civil society groups during the planning process.

Box 6.1   The conditions attached by Greenwich Council's Planning Board to the planning permission to stage Olympic and Paralympic equestrian events in Greenwich Park.

1   The site has to be restored
2   The hours of the event should not extend beyond 09:00–18:30 hours
3   Organisers must stick to submitted plan
4   Organisers must submit drawings for the Test event structures
5   Plans for spectator/vehicle/waste management must be prepared
6   Work in sensitive areas cannot commence until approved by Local Planning Authority
7   A site specific environmental management plan must be produced
8   Heritage management plan must be produced
9   Community mitigation plan must be produced
10   There can be no excavation without written permission
11   An archaeological plan must be produced
12   Approval must be given for archaeological plan
13   Ground protection measures must be introduced
14   Fencing must be approved
15   Back of house facilities must be approved
16   Archaeological remains must be preserved
17–19 Various archaeological stipulations
20–23 Archaeological conditions regarding field of play
24–27 Archaeology and other installations
28   Safety conditions with respect to movement of vehicles during construction
29   Transport movements only during 08:00–18:00 weekdays and 09:00–17:00 (Saturday)
30   Unloading/loading restrictions
31   Ensure field is restored and equestrian equipment has a legacy use
32   By December 2012 all structures removed and all given legacy role
33   Alternative provision made for cricket and tennis
34   Flood risk assessment
35   Work to be suspended if contamination found
36   Traffic management plan/transport plan required
37   Local labour scheme must be used
38   Proposal should not commence until Local Planning Authority is satisfied.

To provide democratic accountability the decision needed to be agreed by Greenwich Council's Planning Board (comprising elected councillors). A meeting of the Board was convened to discuss the application on 23rd March 2010. This meeting lasted for almost five hours and was attended by a large number of people including NOGOE campaigners and representatives from LOCOG – including its chair, Lord Coe. In their statement NOGOE reaffirmed their concerns about environmental and social impacts, but afterwards they were also subjected to their own criticism. Some present complained about NOGOE's NIMBYism and scare-mongering with one contributor stating: 'thank god NOGOE weren't around to prevent Inigo Jones from making physical changes to the Park'. This argument highlights Greenwich Park's evolution and the justification of the Olympic eques-trian events as something that could add a new dimension to the Park's identity. NOGOE was dismissed as a 'vocal and well-resourced minority' by one contribu-tor, and as unrepresentative of local people by another. This reflected previous comments at a public meeting where supporters of the Olympic project had dis-missed NOGOE's campaigning as 'anti-youth conservatism'.

The significance of the application, its timing (it was too late to nominate an alternative venue) and the role of Greenwich Council as a key supporter of the Olympic Games always made it unlikely that the Board would reject LOCOG's proposals: they voted (by 10 votes to 2) to approve the application. Each member justified their vote and several cited the Olympic Games in general – rather than the suitability of the proposal under consideration – when explaining their deci-sion. One councillor stated that he was 'looking forward to watching the greatest show on earth' as a reason to vote for the application, whilst another cited the importance of having Olympic events in the Borough of Greenwich to justify his support. These justifications were inappropriate reasons to support a plan-ning application, but were entirely predictable. A year previously, a planning expert had predicted that 'anything involving the Olympics tends to seduce oth-erwise sensible people . . . and the Council might think that the kudos of having an Olympic venue would be worth overriding policy' (cited in Cuckson, 2009). The justifications given by the dissenting councillors are worth considering fur-ther. One felt the proposed closures were too long. The other suggested media/ global considerations cited by advocates were not appropriate reasons to support a planning application. One dissenting councillor also implied that his colleagues were a little starstruck by Lord Coe's interventions and stated he was a 'lot less starry-eyed than other members of the committee'. These comments reinforce the problems with giving individual planning applications appropriate consideration when they are part of wider, high profile projects.

NOGOE must have anticipated that they would lose the vote at the Planning Board meeting as they gave out flyers on the way out that stated: 'do not lose heart as we will continue to fight through legal channels'. The environmental objec-tions for the event had been neutralised by LOCOG's voluminous documenta-tion, so NOGOE's focus switched to the legality of closing and enclosing public space. There were precedents for enclosing space in Greenwich Park and other Royal Parks. However, LOCOG's need for extra space provided an opportunity for a legal challenge. In their planning application, organisers had expressed their wish to use Circus Field on Blackheath as an access and holding area (see Figure 6.3). This site was outside the Park walls and objectors claimed that enclosure of this land was illegal under the 1871 Blackheath Supplement to the Metropolitan Commons Act (1866). Olympic organisers sidestepped objections by buying a lease for the land using the London Olympic and Paralympic Games Act (2006). This allowed the London Development Agency to use common land to stage the Games – a rather underhand way of circumventing a law which existed to protect access to public open space. Despite protests by NOGOE, permission was granted to use Circus Field by Greenwich's Planning Board in January 2012.

The evidence outlined above demonstrates some of the issues associated with regulating mega-events. These events are best understood as complex networks of individual events and projects underpinned by a powerful brand/ideology. In such circumstances it is difficult to separate the parts from the whole – meaning processes to sanction individual elements are confused with the rationale for the wider event. Conversely, legislation designed for the whole can be used erroneously to sanction specific proposals for which they were not intended. The enclosure of Circus Field under the auspices of The London Olympic and Paralympic Act 2006 provides an illustrative example. A further example of the selective

Figure 6.3 Circus Field on Blackheath during the London 2012 Olympic and Paralympic Games.

use of the parts and the whole was the justification of the equestrian events using wider London 2012 rhetoric about assisting young, disadvantaged Londoners. As the subsequent analysis suggests, this ignored the inconvenient truth that this specific event was unlikely to be consumed by underprivileged audiences.

The events

The events – staged between 28th July and 9th September 2012 – were lauded by the media and equestrian enthusiasts as a great success. The spectators surveyed certainly seemed to enjoy them: 92 per cent were satisfied with their experience, with 65 per cent exhibiting very high satisfaction levels. Overall, 80 per cent felt that the event could not have been held at a better venue. Although this seems like a positive outcome, about 10 per cent thought the event could have been held at a better venue, with a further 10 per cent exhibiting a neutral stance. This meant Greenwich Park was rated below other high profile London 2012 venues in terms of its perceived suitability (Brown and Smith, 2012). Knowledgeable spectators knew that there were suitable alternatives and deemed the Park too small for a cross country event. The course was seen as slippery and overly 'tight and twisty' by the riders (see Figure 6.4), several horses lost shoes and 15 of 74 starters failed to make it round.

Figure 6.4 A competitor tackles the 'tight and twisty' cross-country course installed in Greenwich Park for the London 2012 Olympic and Paralympic Games.

The transport chaos, safety problems and other disastrous scenarios predicted by NOGOE failed to materialise during the events. Organisers had limited the number of spectators to 50,000 – fewer than the 75,000 that had been envisaged in the planning stages and this contributed to the relative ease with which spectators moved to, from and within the venue. This, and other amendments made by organisers, can be traced back to concerns expressed by local amenity groups (The Blackheath Society and the Westcombe Society) during the formal planning process. Inspections of Greenwich Park after the cross country event had been completed revealed only superficial damage had been caused by the horses and spectators.

Previous chapters of this book emphasise that events can represent innovative uses for parks, but they can also encourage new users. With this in mind, it is interesting to see whether the equestrian events in Greenwich Park brought different people into the space who wouldn't normally engage with it. Despite the pre-event rhetoric about assisting young, disadvantaged Londoners, audiences for the equestrian events were predictably dominated by middle class enthusiasts from different parts of Britain. The profiles of the people surveyed in the Park (n = 234) suggested that, compared to other Olympic events, the equestrian spectators were slightly older with a high proportion of females and a greater representation of UK residents from outside London. Only 1 per cent of the sample was unemployed, which does not represent the economic composition of the Borough of Greenwich's population, 6 per cent of whom are unemployed. This rather privileged profile of spectators is corroborated by data collected by the organisers via an email survey of ticket holders. This data also suggests there was a disproportionately high number of females at the events and a high average age. More worryingly, and despite London's diversity, black and minority ethnic spectators were very poorly represented. Although the Royal Borough of Greenwich has a large proportion of black, minority and ethnic citizens (47.7 per cent of the Borough's population at the last census), only 4 per cent of spectators were from these groups.

So, despite the pre-event rhetoric, young and disadvantaged Londoners were poorly represented in the audience for the events in Greenwich. The events didn't change the socio-economic profile of park users, although it did extend the geographical reach of the Park to people who live outside London. The idea that staging the events in Greenwich would bring equestrian sport to a different audience was also undermined by the data collected: almost half of the people surveyed were already regular participants. More positively, there were some indications that experiencing the event would inspire more people to take up riding. Whilst 49 per cent of the spectators surveyed were already riding regularly, 57 per cent said that they would ride regularly over the next 12 months.

The data cited above are further corroborated by media reports regarding the composition of the Greenwich crowd. The Guardian reported that 'the crowd at Greenwich is a mix of equestrian aficionados and people who had really been hoping to be at the gymnastics down the road' (Moss, 2012b). A day later the same paper reported 'Greenwich feels like a more than usually expert crowd' (Hyde, 2012). Moss (2012c) tried to sum up the atmosphere; 'think Ryder Cup and add the high pitched screams of 10,000 horse mad teenage girls and you get some idea'. The conspicuous presence of 'aficionados' somewhat undermined the LOCOG and BEF mission to introduce equestrianism to a new (more urban) audience. Media obsession with members of the British royal family who were conspicuously competing and spectating at the events exacerbated this problem. Regal connections assisted Greenwich's re-imaging as a Royal Borough, but did little to erode equestrian sport's reputation as a pastime for the privileged. More could have been done to allow more local and less privileged people to access Olympic events. However, during the Paralympic Games younger and more diverse audiences were able to access the venue.

Greenwich Park is now an Olympic Park as well as a Royal one. In the weeks and months following the events, many visitors could be seen trying to work out where the events had taken place. So staging Olympic events has added a rich layer of meaning to the Park. However, the 2012 Games did not destabilise its established identity or de-territorialise it in the manner suggested in Chapter 4. The events did not make space here more inclusive either; they temporarily privatised the space and they excluded regular users who were unable to get tickets. Ultimately, Greenwich Park's established identity as a spectacular, highly controlled and regal space was reinforced rather than reconfigured by the events.

Impacts

Two years have passed since the London 2012 equestrian events were staged and it is now possible to reflect on their enduring impacts. The events haven't resulted in the kinds of permanent environmental damage to Greenwich Park feared by NOGOE, although tree branches were removed and the grass resurfacing will have had some impact on the Park's ecological stability. The most visible damage was done to the turf, with some sections of grass taking a long time to regrow. This was not helped by the weather: the timing of the event, combined with unusually large amounts of rainfall meant it was Spring 2013 before the main sections of turf were restored (see Figure 6.2). It was not only the grass under the arena that was damaged. Because eventing requires soft turf, grass on the cross country course had to be re-laid. This highlights that, although very little damage was caused by the horses, there were long term environmental effects of preparing a course that met Olympic specifications.

Apart from environmental issues, the other key concern of NOGOE was the impact of the events on the accessibility of Greenwich Park. The cross country competition meant minor restrictions over several years as organisers needed to prepare the course from 2010. The need to construct a large arena (see Figure 6.5) meant disruptions lasting approximately two years: from Spring 2011 (when preparations for the test event began) to Spring 2013 when returfing was completed. LOCOG were quick to restore access to parts of the Park once the events had finished and they just about kept their promise to remove installations by the end of November 2012. Some re-opening dates were put back, but generally disruption was minimised. Severe restrictions were confined to a three month period in

Figure 6.5 One of the enormous temporary stands erected in Greenwich Park for the London 2012 Olympic and Paralympic Games.

2012 (July–September), although there were partial closures during several other months. Somewhat ironically given the mission to use the 2012 Games to increase sports participation, the stakeholders who were most affected were those who play sports regularly: the cricket pitch and tennis courts were unavailable for an entire season.

Symbolic effects were central to the rationale for staging the events in Greenwich and these seem to have been realised, particularly amongst those who attended in person. Of the spectators surveyed, 69 per cent agreed (including 24 per cent who strongly agreed) that Greenwich Park would be a symbol of the 2012 Games and 80 per cent (including 38 per cent who strongly agreed) felt that staging the equestrian events in this particular venue made the experience more memorable. The media coverage generated was both extensive and positive, suggesting effects will extend well beyond the limited number of people who attended in person. Before the events the Maritime Greenwich World Heritage Site predicted; 'there is no doubt that the outstanding setting provided by the Old Royal Naval College and the Royal Park will feature very prominently in the world wide coverage of the Games' (Maritime Greenwich, 2011) and this proved to be accurate. The cross country course was designed to frame the view across London, and many of the photographs of the event used the image of riders jumping with Canary Wharf in the background. Other media coverage tended to feature views of the arena set in the context of the World Heritage Site, although critical pieces emphasised that configuring this eventscape had come at considerable cost: 'Greenwich is a £60 million picture postcard' (Moss, 2012a). Extra efforts were made to maximise the visual impact for those watching on television: a tower was constructed to support an overhead camera. The outcome was a type of 'mediascape'; an intensive and strategic mediation of a landscape that was already established as 'iconic' (Kolamo and Vuolteenaho, 2013).

To placate local opposition to staging the Olympic and Paralympic equestrian events in Greenwich, organisers had promised that local businesses would benefit. This is a common way that staging events in public spaces, rather than peripheral venues, is often justified (see Chapter 3). However, economic benefits failed to materialise with businesses complaining that takings were lower than they would normally expect. This is a noted problem with major events: they often disrupt regular business and their short term economic effects can be negative unless spectators use local traders. Local businesses were particularly aggrieved because many felt they had suffered unfairly from the way ticket holders were corralled from train stations to the venue. In seeking to manage the expected transport problems, LOCOG inadvertently made it harder for local businesses to benefit. On the busiest days the nearest stations were closed because of fears of over-crowding, so spectators were asked to travel to either Blackheath station or Greenwich station (see Figure 6.1). People were then kept to specified routes. In Blackheath spectators were deliberately routed from the station round the back of Blackheath Village to the venue, meaning local shops were bypassed. In Greenwich this channelling was achieved using physical barriers (see Figure 6.6). This tactic was designed as a safety measure but it discouraged people from using local shops and services. People went straight into the venue and, on leaving, went straight back to the station. The result was that Greenwich and Blackheath were unusually quiet during the equestrian events with local trade down as a result. This shows how difficult it is for event organisers to fulfil multiple promises: in seeking to manage the negative impacts of overcrowding, they restricted the potential for economic impacts.

As airport-style security measures were adopted at the two main entrances to Greenwich Park during the events, people were unable to take liquids inside. This was another reason why spectators did not purchase items in local town centres. Although ticket holders were given plenty of warning about this, there were complaints because of the deficient provision of free water inside the Park. People were told they could fill up empty water bottles, but difficulties finding the taps, and the long queues, meant most people were forced to buy water from the concession stands. This reflects general concerns about the way security measures are often conveniently aligned with commercial agendas when events are staged in public spaces (see Chapter 5). Other modes of commercialisation noted in Chapter 5 were less apparent. Aside from the visible presence of merchandise stalls, concession stands and the London 2012 logo there was little evidence that the Park was demeaned by its role as an Olympic venue. The IOC deliberately restricts the visibility of sponsor logos inside venues. This is a stipulation which protects the

Figure 6.6 Route march. Spectators walking along one of the designated routes constructed
to take them from Greenwich station to the equestrian venue in Greenwich Park.

Games from over-commercialisation, but a knock on effect is that it encourages
sponsors to display their logos in the host city more generally (see Chapters 5
and 7).

Implications

The Olympic and Paralympic events in Greenwich Park were spectacular. They
were staged in a beautiful location not normally used as a horse riding venue. The
temporary transformation of the Park allowed those already familiar with it to see
it in a new way and others to see it for the first time. Greenwich's World Heritage
Site was showcased to the world and there may now be extra interest in visiting
the Park and the surrounding area. In surveys undertaken during the event, 40
per cent of spectators indicated they would return to the Park during the next 12
months. However, the controversial decision to make Greenwich Park an Olympic Park illustrates some important issues. Amongst the hyperbole and melodrama
that characterised some of the objections were some extremely important arguments about the appropriate use of public spaces.

In Chapter 2 of this book public spaces are defined as those which are available
to any citizen without charge. Opponents of the equestrian events in Greenwich

Park felt that it was inappropriate to restrict access to a public park to stage an exclusive event. If we follow this interpretation, Greenwich Park was turned into a semi-public (Conway, 1991) or pseudo-public space (Banerjee, 2001) for several months during 2012. However, rhetoric from advocates of the events highlights a very different interpretation of the public space implications. Supporters felt that staging Olympic events was in the national interest and, rather than restricting access, the events allowed the Park to be 'shared' with the world. The interpretation is further justified if the Royal (i.e. national) and World Heritage Site (international) status of the Park is acknowledged. Negativity was countered with the notion that public space was merely being 'borrowed' by public agencies for a good cause (Smith, 2014).

In the absence of objections from established stakeholders, a community action group (NOGOE) was one of the few organisations that challenged proposals in the public sphere. This group was highly organised and well resourced, allowing them to gain the visibility and credibility normally denied to single interest groups. NOGOE's work meant that proposals to stage events in Greenwich Park were debated more extensively than in other examples where public spaces were used to host the 2012 Games (see Chapter 7). The post-event reaction of NOGOE (2012) to the events was that:

> The peace of the Park has been disrupted and the public have been excluded from it; a great deal of damage has been, and will be, done to it; and a dangerous precedent has been set for future commercial exploitation of it.

The public were excluded, and the equestrian events did diminish the public realm in this part of London. Rather than reducing the total amount of public space available, the events shortened the amount of time people have had to enjoy that space. As NOGOE's concern about a 'dangerous precedent' highlights, there is also a risk that staging the equestrian events (and their perceived success) provides the justification for further incursions into the spatial and temporal availability of public space. These incursions are discussed further in Chapter 7. As funding for Royal Parks in London is set to be reduced it is likely that Greenwich Park will stage more events in the future. During preparations for the Games, one of the Park's main gateways was removed, cleaned and replaced with a wider opening. According to Rhind and Marshall (2013) Blackheath Gate (see Figure 6.1) was widened to allow large vehicles to turn in to Greenwich Park – which suggests authorities are expecting to stage major events in the future. Greenwich Park's Manager has reassured local people that the environmental integrity of the Park will be protected. However, the way the Olympic events were staged in Greenwich Park contradicted The Royal Parks policy to offer affordable public access to events. Even Greenwich residents who could afford to attend were excluded by the limited number of tickets and large portions of space within the Park were reserved for corporate guests. These characteristics suggest that the equestrian events were ultimately an exclusive event (see Chapter 5), something that contradicts The Royal Parks policy that they do not 'normally consider private events of any kind'.

The analysis here has also highlighted wider issues associated with staging events. Many of these relate to the difficulties using established planning procedures to regulate proposals that are part of wider 'mega-events'. In the Greenwich Park case gaining approval to stage the events was straightforward – because all the main stakeholders were governed by one government department. The local planning board was the only obstacle between event organisers and securing their preferred location. Democratic planning procedures were followed but it was somewhat inevitable that permission would be granted: Greenwich Council was a key stakeholder in the London 2012 project, and if Councillors had rejected the proposal there would have been insufficient time to find a replacement venue. The amount of resources LOCOG had at their disposal to prepare their case also contributed to the outcome of the planning decision. LOCOG boasted powerful figures and a large budget which it used to disarm opposition.

The status of the Greenwich events as Olympic events caused other complications. Councillors on the Board appeared to conflate the application for the installations in Greenwich Park with the 2012 Games project in general. This reaffirms existing evidence suggesting that it is difficult to conduct objective impact assessments within the emotive context of staging a mega-event (McManus, 2004). In this case, planning assessments were also complicated by the ultimate design rationale for the proposal under consideration – to produce spectacular media images. Councillors in Greenwich seemed unclear whether or not this was a legitimate reason to justify a planning application. Once in motion, the Olympic 'machine' driven by relentless delivery/management agencies was hard to counter. However, it would be a mistake to think that the efforts of opponents were inconsequential. NOGOE's persistent campaigning held LOCOG to account in the public sphere, forced them to improve their plans and provided a forum for concerns to be expressed. The group generated social capital by bringing local people together to discuss proposals and, by encouraging a debate about what Greenwich Park was for, NOGOE highlighted the important role it plays in many people's lives.

Summary

The case study presented in this chapter suggests that when events are staged in prominent public spaces this benefits the event, more than the spaces used. Staging these types of events causes a series of intended and unintended consequences for public space availability. When events are ticketed, and where they require large installations, they exclude people symbolically and physically. Some legitimate arguments are used to justify event projects, but these are no consolation to those who feel their everyday spaces have been appropriated. However, to critically judge overall outcomes for the provision of public space requires us to establish who and what we think public spaces are for: existing or potential users, established or possible uses. Major events can promote a form of inclusivity and accessibility through the associated mediation of public spaces and by encouraging future visitation. They engage different audiences than would normally use these spaces and 'borrowing' them for events can add new dimensions to public spaces with established identities. As Taylor (1995: 220) argues, new layers of meaning for park spaces are created over time: 'historic public parks should not be recovered and pickled in aspic'. In other words, we shouldn't restrict park activity to traditional uses and users. If Franck and Stevens (2007) are right to advocate non-fixed meanings then events can be interpreted as ways of adapting the identities of public spaces, opening them up to different groups, uses and interests. However, it seems inappropriate to consider the sort of events analysed in this chapter in this manner. Tightly programmed, heavily controlled events aimed at privileged audiences do not loosen space, they restrict it.

A core theme emanating from this chapter is the long term significance of short term events. We live in an era where the permanent is increasingly being rendered temporary (as in pop-up installations), but temporary phenomena can become permanent. Events justified by temporally constrained discourses ('borrowing', 'one-off', 'once in a lifetime') have the potential for long term changes. By allowing temporary infrastructures and restrictions, precedents are set. Cities are urgently seeking ways to generate revenue from public resources, and staging events provides opportunities to do so. Events generate revenue, they promote future visitation, and successful events provide the mandate, knowledge and reputation required to stage more events in the future. Events cause other long term changes too. They may be used as 'Trojan horses' to usher in other forms of commercialisation: sponsorship and retail provision (see Chapter 5). Parks are particularly vulnerable, something highlighted by Zukin's (1995: 261) question, 'does anyone know, in these days of entertainment, security and retail shopping what a park is?'

Borrowing parks for individual events seems acceptable, but using them to host recurring seasons of commercial events (as now happens in Hyde Park, London) is not. This commercialises and urbanises parks, and undermines any notion that events loosen public space by challenging conventional interpretations of them. Just as Agamben (2005) thinks the 'state of exception' has evolved into a permanent phenomenon, there is a danger that staging exceptional events becomes the norm for public parks. This is when revenue-driven eventisation does impinge upon public space provision. The key issue is whether 'borrowing' public spaces for events lays foundations for appropriation.

The case analysed here also provides useful material to evaluate the procedures used to protect public space. Despite concerns raised about the way event projects override established practices, the evidence presented in this paper suggests that a regulatory 'state of exception' is not inevitable. There are some awkward aspects of assessing event projects within conventional planning systems, but no fundamental reasons why event projects shouldn't be subjected to the same rigorous planning procedures as other proposals (see Chapter 8). The Greenwich Park case demonstrates both the possibility and the value of civil society input in these processes. Within the growing body of critical literature on international events, the role of local planning procedures is often neglected. Unaccountable event agencies and rights holders are often blamed for malign and inappropriate actions, but if host cities/nations have sufficiently developed regulatory frameworks, and if they can resist the temptation to make events exceptional cases, then public interests can be protected. However, even when the integrity of regulatory processes is maintained, exceptionality is still an important factor within event projects. The exceptionality of events creates a culture and set of discourses – and a coalition of interests – that can push inappropriate projects through the planning process. Indeed, the evidence presented in this chapter supports McManus's (2004: 164) conclusion that 'the control of space is built on the ability to control the discursive terrain'. Event discourses and their implications for public space are explored further in the next chapter.

7 Enclosing open space

Event legacies in the Royal Borough of Greenwich

> Right at the heart of capitalist modernity . . . has been a process of endless enclosure.
>
> (Retort Collective, 2005: 193)

Introduction

The Greenwich Park case needs to be considered alongside other controversies that unfolded in the Royal Borough of Greenwich during the period 2007–2014. Many of these were linked directly and indirectly to the Greenwich's status as an Olympic Host Borough. This chapter explores a series of events and event legacies in this part of South East London. The discussion provides a spatial extension of the Greenwich case introduced previously, but it also helps to illustrate many of the wider issues discussed in this book. Between 2007 and 2014 a wide range of events (music festivals, opera screenings, sports events) affected a wide range of public spaces (parks, streets and squares) in the Borough of Greenwich. This provides a fascinating context in which to study the relationship between events and public spaces.

The chapter begins with an analysis of how the legacy discourses noted in the previous chapter were materialised and how this affected the provision of open spaces in other localities. A series of other projects that collectively comprise the public space legacies of Greenwich's status as an Olympic Borough are then discussed. These include alterations made to Charlton Park, the reconfiguration of a public square in Woolwich, and events staged on the Borough's streets (see Figure 7.1). The Chapter finishes with a detailed discussion of a new event and a new events policy for Blackheath – an open space which is partly in the Borough of Greenwich, but which mostly lies in neighbouring Lewisham. The general aim is to provide detailed and up to date illustrations of the issues discussed in previous chapters. More specifically this chapter aims to highlight the complex, subtle and controversial legacies of events staged in public spaces.

The Royal Borough of Greenwich

Before the different cases and spaces are discussed, it is important to provide a brief introduction to the territory that provides the geographical focus for the

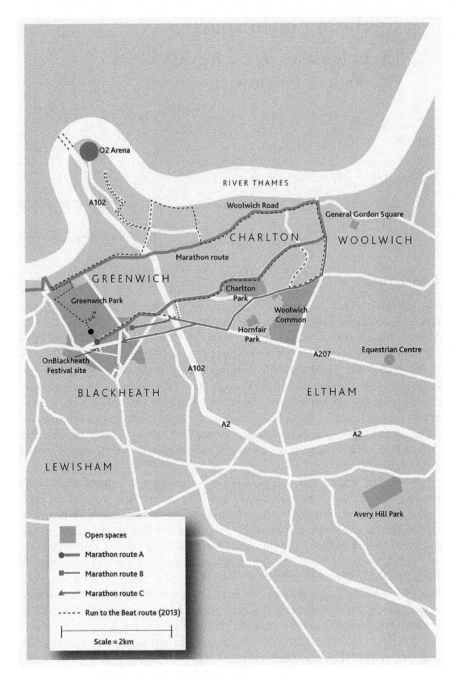

Figure 7.1 A map of South East London illustrating the locations of temporary event sites in the Royal Borough of Greenwich.

Source: Mason Edwards

chapter. The Royal Borough of Greenwich is a very diverse and highly polarised socio-economic urban area. This administrative territory was created by amalgamating the Metropolitan Boroughs of Greenwich and Woolwich in 1965 and it was made a Royal Borough in 2012 to mark the Queen's Diamond Jubilee. Areas of great affluence and famous tourist sites (mainly in the West of the Borough) are located close to areas of poverty and deprivation (mainly in the East). This social polarisation is a common feature of world cities. In 2010 the Borough of Greenwich ranked as the 28th most deprived out of 326 local authorities in England. This shows how disadvantaged some parts of the area are. Over a quarter of a million people (254, 557) live in the Borough, making this part of London equivalent in size to a small city. Apart from its prestigious royal, military and scientific history, one of the characteristics that differentiates Greenwich from other London Boroughs is the availability of open space. There are over 50 parks, several large sections of common land, and a long stretch (13km) of riverside space. Much of the public space in Greenwich is open space and, following the trend introduced in Chapter 3, these sites are increasingly used as venues for events.

Materialising legacies: implications for open space

Legacy is a key theme in much of the event policy work and academic research published in recent years. In one sense, event legacy is a relatively straightforward notion that refers to the residual (i.e. long term) effects of a staging a transient event. However, the term has been appropriated and used by different interests, and it is now a highly contested and ambiguous concept. Event legacy is now best understood as a discursive device that is used to justify event projects. In the Greenwich Park case analysed in the previous chapter, one of the most significant factors was the legacy discourse that pervaded the 2012 Olympic Games. This was employed by Olympic advocates, but it was also adopted by opponents who saw an opportunity to undermine the rationale for staging the events in Greenwich Park. The use of legacy discourse is analysed further below, to help understand the subtle effects of the temporary venue used to stage the London 2012 equestrian events.

In seeking to justify their use of Greenwich Park, LOCOG and their supporters initially emphasised that the legacy of the equestrian events would be nonphysical: they aimed to leave no trace to protect the environmental integrity of this World Heritage Site. Instead, they emphasised the soft legacies of inspiration and imagery – they said the events would inspire residents to take up sport and would showcase the Royal Borough of Greenwich to the world. These intangible legacies were also emphasised in media accounts:

> the legacy will be amazing photographs that encapsulate both Britain's glorious past – represented by the Queen's House next to the arena and what we hope will be a vibrant commercial future, embodied by the glassy heart of the City across the river.

> (Moss, 2012a: 16)

This imagery fitted well with destination marketing at the time that aimed to position London as a historic city that was forward looking (London Development Agency, 2009). However, the lack of any physical legacy was capitalised on by opponents of staging the equestrian events in Greenwich Park. NOGOE argued that staging the events in temporary facilities restricted opportunities to provide positive legacies; and argued it would be better to build permanent facilities in a more suitable location (Smith, 2014). Media critics also emphasised the futility of a disposable venue that 'would leave nothing at all in its wake except a churned up park' (Heathcote, 2012). This argument was also made by several high profile people within equestrian sport. For example, Nick Skelton, one of Great Britain's Gold medal winners at the 2012 Games stated: 'I had always thought the equestrian events should have gone to an equestrian venue, such as Hickstead, so as to ensure some kind of legacy' (Sport, 2012: 46).

In response to these criticisms about the lack of positive physical legacies, LOCOG began to emphasise that the Park would not only be restored, but improved, after staging the Games. This stance was maintained into the post-event era. In 2013 the Manager of Greenwich Park claimed the Park's pathways and roads had been improved 'beyond their pre-Games condition' (Dear, 2013). LOCOG – with support from the London Marathon Trust – upgraded the children's playground with new timber play equipment, better seating, planting and pathways. They even installed one of the equestrian jumps as a feature. LOCOG also organised and part-funded the return of a Henry Moore statue that had been removed from the Park. These tangible effects were not necessarily sufficient to placate opponents. Local stakeholders were hoping for further physical improvements as compensation for the inconvenience they experienced. For example, Rhind and Marshall (2013) suggest that Olympic organisers should have provided funding to solve problems with coach parking near Blackheath Gate in return for using Circus Field as a logistical compound, 'but this legacy did not materialise'. There are surprisingly few visible remnants of the 2012 Games in Greenwich Park. The scaled down model of Nelson's Column that featured in the show jumping arena is now an exhibit in the National Maritime Museum next door, but otherwise there is little evidence the event ever took place.

Like LOCOG, the local authority was also keen to counter accusations that the equestrian events would leave no tangible legacies for sport, so in the build up to the Olympic and Paralympic events, Greenwich Council responded by introducing some new projects. Complaints that the equestrian legacy was non-existent were countered with a project to establish an Equestrian Skills Centre nearby at Shooters Hill. This new facility opened in 2013 and features a horse therapy centre, an equine swimming pool, stabling for 20 horses, an all-weather arena, and an indoor arena. It was funded by Greenwich Borough, Sport England and the BEF and it is run in partnership with a local college.

The Equestrian Skills Centre was a controversial project in itself, mainly because it was constructed on Metropolitan Open Land – this is undeveloped, but not necessarily publically accessible land. Metropolitan Open Land is defined in the London's overarching spatial plan as:

Land which has more than Borough significance, generally because of its size and catchment area. MOL provides breaks in the built up area, provides open air facilities and contains features . . . which benefit the people of part or all of London.

(Greenwich Council, 2006: 74)

There were already some buildings on the site, but the plans for the Equestrian Centre involved extending the footprint of existing development. The loss of Metropolitan Open Land meant there were multiple objections to the proposal, including opposition from a community farm situated next door: 'we don't understand why the Council are so adamant to use this protected site' (Gray cited in Massey, 2011). The Council consulted 199 local residents and, of the 32 that responded, 30 were against the proposals (Massey, 2011). Despite these objections, and although the proposal contravened official planning policy which recommends a 'presumption against inappropriate development' on Metropolitan Open Land (Greenwich Council, 2006: 74), the political imperative to deliver a legacy from the equestrian events in Greenwich Park helped to push the Equestrian Skills Centre through the planning system. There is plenty of evidence to help justify this claim. For example, in the planning application for the Centre, the developers included the statement:

Due to the historic and environmentally important nature of Greenwich Park, its equestrian events facilities will be removed after the event. The potential to create an accessible Equestrian Centre which could provide both a physical sporting and educational legacy from the 2012 Games has therefore been identified.

(Campbell Reith, 2011)

When planning permission for the Centre was approved in November 2011, Greenwich Council (2011) stated that 'the proposed development is only considered acceptable due to the special circumstance associated with the proposed use'. The designation of Greenwich Park as an Olympic equestrian venue seems to have been regarded as this special circumstance. Thus, the perceived need to create a permanent legacy from a temporary venue in one part of the Borough resulted in the loss of open space in another.

In balancing this assessment, it should be noted that various conditions were attached to the planning approval of the Equestrian Centre that (if enforced) should ensure some public benefits: for example, the College is required to provide 82 hours of community access each week (Condition #3, Greenwich Council, 2011). In one sense, what was previously an inaccessible space is now accessible by a larger number of people. There are other benefits of having an Equestrian Centre in Greenwich, particularly for the British Army who have horses stabled nearby at Woolwich barracks. The Equestrian Centre employs several people and educates many more, which are also positive contributions.

The supposed benefits of the new Centre haven't placated Greenwich residents worried about the incursions into their public and open spaces. The temporary loss of public space in Greenwich Park led to the permanent loss of Metropolitan Open Land nearby. In this regard, the Equestrian Skills Centre provides a fascinating example of the enduring outcomes of transient events, and highlights how legacy discourses have real effects on places. The case also reflects the way the discourse of event legacy is inherently oriented towards material outcomes. The 2012 Games was infused with rhetoric about physical legacies: for example, the promise to 'transform East London' (Marrero-Guillermon, 2012). So, even though Greenwich Park was always envisaged as a temporary venue, there was a perceived need to deliver long term physical effects (i.e. a legacy) from the events staged there. This agenda was driven by media narratives as well as pressure from NOGOE. Major events are often associated with wasteful expenditure and this is deemed even more problematic when facilities are removed post-event. In the case of Greenwich Park, journalists criticised 'Spending £60 million on facilities that will be dismantled' (Moss, 2012a). This pressure led to the Equestrian Skills Centre, and therefore to the development of open space. It also led to other changes to open spaces in the Royal Borough of Greenwich which are reviewed below.

Park programmes: improvements or incursions?

Greenwich Council's mission to provide material legacies associated with the 2012 Games also resulted in some new sports facilities and improvements to several parks. The 'Playground to Podium' programme involved £4.8 million worth of investment from the Council and their partners in outdoor gyms, cricket and tennis facilities, plus 23 refurbished playgrounds. This programme also involved committing resources (£850,000) to ensure that 12 local parks met the standards required for Green Flag status – a national accreditation scheme for open spaces. Unsurprisingly, the Council have been quick to publicise these relatively modest levels of investment. Large signs proclaiming these sites to be 'Our 2012 Legacy' have been installed in the improved public spaces.

Hornfair Park in Charlton is the site that has received most investment. The Park is named after a local event which was suppressed in 1874 because of over-excess. In the build-up to the 2012 Games, £4 million was spent improving the facilities here; including £3 million on reviving an outdoor swimming pool. Money has also been spent installing new changing rooms and a BMX track. The changes made are justified by the claim that the Park was previously under-used. Greenwich Council suggests that Hornfair Park has been 'transformed' by Olympic-related investment with physical changes linked to social benefits. According to the Council, anti-social behaviour has been reduced and 'many new users' attracted (Royal Borough of Greenwich, 2012).

The improvements outlined above seem very positive. However, a deeper analysis reveals more complex and controversial changes. The new outdoor gyms cited above provide a good example. These include an AdiZone – installations that were developed as a community-level legacy of the 2012 Games. AdiZones are outdoor gyms and sports facilities that are branded with the logos of the

London 2012 Games and their sponsors. Reflecting the prominence and influence of legacy discourses outlined above, the justification for the facilities was to ensure that the 2012 Games left a legacy of increased sports participation in the Host Boroughs. The main justification for staging the 2012 Olympics in London was to encourage young people to take up sport, something emphasised by the London 2012 slogan: 'inspire a generation'. To help achieve this objective, fifty AdiZones, each costing £150,000 have been built in the UK since 2008 (Weber-Newth, 2014). These provide publically accessible recreational facilities, but they also represent three dimensional (i.e. experiential) advertisements for Adidas – one of the Tier 1 sponsors of the 2012 Games. Accordingly, AdiZones have been criticised by several academics such as Duman (2012) and Weber-Newth (2014) on the basis that they represent a 'corporatisation' of urban space. As Duman (2012: 60) notes, for Adidas they offer 'unique penetration in otherwise brand free public spaces'. They also involve the development of green/open space: AdiZones are 25 x 25 metres installations featuring brightly coloured gym equipment, a climbing wall, and concrete flooring.

One prominent AdiZone was constructed in Charlton Park, an important public space in the Borough of Greenwich. This site has been a public park since Greenwich Council acquired 43 acres of land from a family estate in 1925. The facility includes a wall featuring Adidas-sponsored athletes and artists, a small basketball/ football court and an outdoor gym. The floorspace of the site is dominated by a very large 2012 logo (see Figure 7.2).

AdiZones are not events, but they are event legacies and they help to illustrate many of the issues discussed in previous chapters of this book. Like many forms of privatisation/commercialisation, these facilities are justified on the basis that they provide resources that local councils can longer afford to provide. In reality, these facilities are 100 per cent state funded: local authorities contributed 50 per cent of the development costs, with national government making up the other 50 per cent (Weber-Newth, 2014). Local authorities are also required to pay 50 per cent of the maintenance costs (£5,000 a year) so, effectively, local authorities are paying to host glorified corporate advertisements. Local users don't seem to have a problem with this – indeed Adidas connections make them seem 'cool' (Duman, 2012) and the facility in Charlton is popular and well used. As Weber-Newth (2014) notes, the Charlton Park AdiZone has become a new social space, as well as a sports facility, so in some ways the space has become more public because of the new installation. Despite this, the overriding effect is one of creeping commercialisation. The main beneficiaries are not the residents of Charlton, but Adidas and LOCOG. The zones helped to activate Adidas's status as an Olympic sponsor and allowed the firm to circumvent strict IOC rules on venue sponsorship (Duman, 2012). Allowing firms to sponsor public space in this way legitimises the companies involved (see Chapter 5). It is valuable for Adidas to be associated with the provision of accessible community facilities and it is beneficial for the company to be physically embedded within urban communities. Taking all this into account, the £5000 a year the company pays to maintain this site seems to represent very good value for money.

Figure 7.2 A literal form of place 'branding' in Charlton Park and Greenwich Park.
     Whilst the London 2012 logo in Greenwich Park (below) was temporary, the
     one in Charlton Park (top) is now a permanent fixture.

Whilst the 2012 Games made a very visible, but temporary, imprint on Greenwich Park, the imprint on Charlton Park is more permanent because of the installation of the AdiZone (see Figure 7.2). For Weber-Newth (2013: 234) the facility
represents 'a symbolic extension of the Olympic Park'. This is an understatement:
the Charlton Park AdiZone represents both a spatial and temporal extension of
the 2012 Games. It extended the reach of the Games further into London and it
now provides a (semi) permanent monument to Greenwich's status as an Olympic
Host Borough – the facility can only be removed with the permission of Adidas
and has a life span of 20 years (Duman, 2012). AdiZones represent significant
event legacies. These installations create a long term relationship between events

sponsors and event hosts, and provide another vehicle through which events have long term effects on public spaces.

The common and the square: Olympic Woolwich

Greenwich Park was not the only open space in the Royal Borough of Greenwich used to stage Olympic events. Woolwich Common was also a key venue, although the events here received far less publicity. Several shooting ranges were constructed on Woolwich Common and the road that runs along the north side of the common was closed for the duration of the events (see Figure 7.3). This temporary use of the site seems fitting: the site was used to test ordinance during the 1720s and Woolwich has a long history as a military town. Army barracks were constructed at the north end of Woolwich Common between 1776 and 1802 and for a long time land here has been owned and controlled by the Ministry of Defence. Anyone visiting the site would assume that this is a typical piece of common land, but the public have no official access rights. As Jefferson (1970: 213) notes, 'it is generally conceded that Woolwichers have no rights at all as commoners'. This makes Woolwich Common a very interesting example of government owned 'public space'.

The military history of the site may have resulted in the lack of public resistance to using Woolwich Common for the 2012 Games. It is also significant

Figure 7.3 The 10/50m Shooting Range installed on Woolwich Common during the London 2012 Olympic and Paralympic Games

that Woolwich is a much less affluent area than Greenwich. Greenwich Park is surrounded by expensive houses worth over £1 million, whereas Woolwich Common is surrounded by military barracks, a hospital and a social housing estate (see Figure 7.4). The lack of debate about the use of Woolwich Common for the 2012 Games fits Boyle's (1997) contention that less educated and less affluent groups are less likely to get their views heard during debates around event projects, and thus are more likely to suffer negative outcomes. There are various examples that illustrate this, including some involving disputes about the development of public spaces. Drawing upon Owen's (2002) work, Waitt (2008) uses the opposition to the temporary beach volleyball arena on Bondi Beach in Sydney to illustrate the greater influence of middle class opposition movements. At Bondi, as in Greenwich Park, a well-loved and much used public space was used to stage Olympic events. The outcome was similar too – the event went ahead, but vocal middle class opposition meant original plans were modified (Waitt, 2008). Local benefits were secured for residents in Bondi, but for less affluent areas of Sydney (e.g. Auburn), outcomes were negative (Owen, 2002; McManus, 2004; Waitt, 2008). These examples from Sydney and the Greenwich Park case suggest local campaign groups may help to protect public spaces. However, spaces that serve less organised / affluent populations like those in Woolwich are more vulnerable.

Figure 7.4 Inspired or ignored? A view towards the Woolwich Common Estate during the London 2012 Olympic and Paralympic Games.

The lack of resistance to staging Olympic and Paralympic events on Woolwich Common meant that – compared to the Greenwich Park project – events were staged without the same level of scrutiny and protection. Although Greenwich Park has a more prestigious history and landscape, Woolwich Common is also a large open space comprised partly of acid grasslands. There was pressure to conserve these in Greenwich Park, but no one seemed too bothered about the acid grasslands further east. The lack of concern in the public sphere meant that the restoration of the space to its former condition was very slow. Indeed, one by-product of the sluggish efforts to restore Woolwich Common was that the army troop stationed in Woolwich was required to exercise their horses in Charlton Park, providing another unexpected open space legacy of staging the 2012 Games in the Borough of Greenwich. And unlike Greenwich Park, Woolwich Common was not fully restored to its former condition after the Olympic events – a new all-weather horse ring has been constructed at the north end of the site.

General Gordon Square

Other legacies of staging the 2012 Games for Woolwich include the changes made to General Gordon Square, the town's main plaza (see Figure 7.1). Major events are often associated with improvements to the public realm. For example, public plazas were one of the positive outcomes associated with the improvements made to Barcelona in advance of the 1992 Olympic Games (Smith, 2012). However, the Woolwich project was a particularly interesting example of an event-driven public space project. In 2009, a collaborative venture between Greenwich Council, the BBC and LOCOG installed a 25 m² screen in General Gordon Square (see Figure 7.5). Subsequently, £3 million was spent improving the Square as part of the town's preparations for the 2012 Games. These improvements included the construction of granite/grass terraces facing the new screen which created a shallow amphitheatre (see Figure 7.5). The aim was to provide 'a vibrant animated square filled with music, dance and games' during the Olympics (Greenwich Council, 2012). According to Greenwich Council (2012), 2,000 people attended the screening of the Opening Ceremony and 12,000 people visited General Gordon Square on some days during the 2012 Games. Reflecting the concerns raised in Chapter 5, Cadburys – one of LOCOGs main sponsors – featured prominently.

What makes this case particularly interesting is that the screen is permanent (see Figure 7.5). A permanent fan zone has been created here which now stages screenings of sports events and cultural events. These events are advertised as 'accessible to all', but 'in the interests of public safety' several conditions often apply (Royal Opera House, 2015). For example, during the 2015 opera screenings in General Gordon Square (sponsored by BP), event stewards were 'entitled to search persons on entry to the Square', and more controversially the organisers reserved the 'right to refuse admission to the event enclosure for whatever reason' (Royal Opera House, 2015). Such stipulations mean that, although these screenings are meant to animate and enliven the Square, they can also be used as a mechanism to exclude people from a space they are normally allowed to enter.

Figure 7.5 General Gordon Square, Woolwich, just before the start of a screening of La Bohème.

The screen also shows regular BBC output, reflecting the way the Corporation has supplemented its public service broadcasting remit with a public space broadcasting one (Mcquire, 2010). The everyday use of the screen suggests that Greenwich Council is trying to recreate the feel and function of a communal living room in Woolwich town centre. This is a noted tactic in cities seeking to create a sense of shared identity and sociability in an era when people have withdrawn to their own private spaces. For example, Thörn (2011) notes how authorities in Gothenburg presented the city and its public spaces as 'a common living room'. In several newspaper advertisements the city centre was depicted in this way; something that was designed to make people feel that the city centre was a public home. In this context, installing a large screen like the one in Woolwich makes perfect sense: after all, every modern living room features a screen.

Thörn's (2011) work has wider implications too – her research notes how ambience is used as a form of control in contemporary public spaces. Drawing upon Degen's (2003) ideas of sense scapes, she argues that the design and management of public spaces produce environments which are 'seductively inclusive' for some, but which make others feel uncomfortable. This fits well with the ideas discussed in Chapter 5: events animate places, but they always include some people and exclude others. Opera screenings are designed to provide a sense scape which is more attractive to middle class users and less attractive to 'undesirable' people who have traditionally inhabited the Square. Indeed, given the reputation of Woolwich as a hotspot of crime and delinquency, the installation of a permanent fan zone and the staging of regular events needs to be viewed as a typical attempt to 'civilise' the space. Events staged in General Gordon Square are used to create a more sociable space and to increase the number of people using the Square – particularly at night. Hence there are clear parallels with the discussion in Chapter 4 about the security rationale for staging events in public spaces.

Fun running and big running

The discussion thus far has mainly focused on parks and squares. However, events have also affected the *streets* of the Borough of Greenwich. The most significant event that takes place every year on these streets is the London Marathon: Greenwich Park has been used as the starting point for this event since the inaugural edition in 1981. The London Marathon is broadcast live on the BBC, providing an annual vehicle with which to showcase Greenwich. Over a quarter of the route (approximately the first seven miles) is within the Borough boundaries (see Figure 7.1) and runners circumventing the Cutty Sark ship in Greenwich has become one of the defining images of the race. This eventscape is also a valuable promotional tool for Greenwich in general and the Maritime Greenwich World Heritage Site in particular. The Marathon is not just staged in Greenwich town centre but also through the streets of Charlton, Woolwich and other less familiar parts of the Borough (see Figure 7.1). Local traders complain that the event isn't good for business, but generally the London Marathon is seen as a positive event by the people of Greenwich. Runners raise millions of pounds for charity and some of the funds generated by event organisers have been used to provide playing fields and other recreational facilities in the Borough.

The London Marathon attracts people from all over the world to participate in the race. People who are 'running away from home' (Shipway and Jones, 2007) get to experience urban space in a different way than conventional tourists who visit Greenwich. Running tourists get to look at different places and get to look at places differently. This fits with recent trends in tourism. Tourists are becoming less passive and desire activities and places to 'stimulate the senses to a pitch beyond everyday experience' (Bell and Lyall, 2002: 27). Running is an activity that can accelerate and heighten tourism experiences, something that can be understood via the idea of the accelerated sublime. Because of the crowds and due to the presence of fellow competitors, a running event is an even more heightened experience. Even when runners go quite slowly, this provides a different experience because of the extended time they spend in unfamiliar urban environments. Sugden provides a useful example in his ethnographic research on the Marabana-Havana Marathon in Cuba:

> The full 42 km Marabana requires two laps of the city. It will take me more than four and a half hours to complete, giving me plenty of time to study and reflect further upon the city and its people.
>
> (Sugden, 2007: 243)

Like many other street events, the London Marathon attracts more spectators than participants. The people who line the roads are an essential component of the event: they create the festive atmosphere and runners appreciate the support. The combination of spectators, elite runners and amateur runners (many of whom wear fancy dress) transforms the urban public realm into a spectacle. As Wilson (1995: 175) notes, events like the London Marathon 'transform urban space into cultural places in which theatrical forms can be offered for the gaze of spectators'. The roads are closed to traffic, parties are staged at different points along the route and the large numbers of people running plus the diverse range of athletic abilities on display mean that the spectacle lasts for several hours.

There are also some problems with the London Marathon too, many of which reaffirm the issues highlighted at the end of Chapter 5. Greenwich residents are inconvenienced by the extensive road closures, and there are some issues with public urination, litter and noise (from helicopters, motorbikes and amplified sounds that accompany the race). Parts of Blackheath and Greenwich Park, which are used as the assembly points at the race start, are inaccessible to the public for short periods and they are strewn with litter and clothing discarded by the runners. But generally the people of Greenwich are happy and proud to host the London Marathon every year. The event encourages sociability: people congregate out-side their homes, chat to their neighbours and for a short time before the race starts they are able to walk or cycle along streets emptied of motorised traffic. In line with the discussion in Chapter 4, the event *produces* public space.

Whilst they are happy to host an annual marathon, Greenwich residents have been much less impressed with other events that have begun to appear in the Borough's streets. As one contributor to a local online forum, put it: 'I am getting a bit fed up with the assumption of all and sundry that because we host the start of the London Marathon, we must also be happy to host every other sporting event that needs roads closed' (Greenwich Forum, 2013). This is not a necessarily a representative view. On the same forum another resident had posted: 'I think the hosting ethos we embraced during London 2012 should continue with these smaller events' (Greenwich Forum, 2013). There is clearly a difference of opinion here, but both comments indicate the way existing events are used as a mandate to expand the provision of events in Greenwich's public spaces. The main legacy of events seems to be more events. This is a recurring theme in this chapter and one neglected in other analyses.

In the run up to the 2012 Games, more street based sports events started to appear in the streets of Greenwich. These new events reflected the rise of public events generally during this period (see Chapter 3), a trend that was particularly noticeable in London (see Chapter 1). However, other local factors were significant too. Greenwich was an Olympic Host Borough and organisers were keen that events were staged in the period between winning the rights to stage the Games (2005) and the Olympic events (2012). These events helped to build momentum, but they also served as test events. For example, in 2007 when the first part of the world's most famous cycle race – Le Tour de France – came to London, Greenwich was used as the starting point for Stage One (see Figure 7.6). The roads were

Figure 7.6 The streets of Greenwich during Stage One of the 2007 Tour de France.

closed and the route that was chosen was almost identical to the one used for the London Marathon – albeit in reverse (Smith, 2008).

Run to the Beat

From 2008–2013 the Royal Borough of Greenwich also staged an annual half marathon every September. This race was particularly controversial. 'Run to the Beat' was organised by IMG – a global sport, fashion and media company which operates in 25 countries around the world. IMG officials responsible for mass participation events had spotted a gap in the market: the company was already organising a duathlon (run/bike) event in Richmond Park (also a Royal Park) but at that time there was no half marathon in London (Karageorghis, 2014). Given its experience of staging road races, and its iconic public realm, Greenwich was seen as an ideal location for this new venture. The race was distinctive because it featured live musical accompaniment along the entire route – hence the name. This wasn't an entirely original idea: many existing road races featured some live bands – e.g. the Philadelphia Marathon and the Great North Run (Karageorghis, 2014). The London Marathon has always featured music and sound along the route – albeit organised in an informal and ad hoc manner. This entertainment is often used to direct members of the public away from pinch points, and so this is an event management strategy as much as event experience one. Despite these precedents, Run to the Beat's dedicated focus on music was original. IMG worked with a UK based academic who had been researching the benefits of music on athletic performance to add academic credibility to the musical theme.

The idea of a musical running event fits into the wider trend of de-differentiation in the events and leisure sectors. Many sport events are now infused with content and rituals normally associated with cultural events and vice versa. Run to the Beat worked with an organisation that aimed to help unsigned artists (Karageorghis, 2014), so the link between art and sport was more than a superficial marketing stunt. The strategic use of music was a nice idea but it didn't really work – even the runners weren't impressed. The academic who helped conceive the idea admitted many participants thought the musical accompaniment provided on the day was 'rubbish' (Karageorghis, 2014). Predictably, the inclusion of amplified music also increased the potential for complaints from local people. The route included Greenwich Park which, in light of the discussion in Chapter 6, was a particularly sensitive context in which to operate events at this time. One account posted to an online forum highlights this well:

> I came across Run to the Beat for the first time last year when on the first occasion I was able to visit the Park after it had been closed for the Olympics I found it had been occupied by an intrusive and dreadful noise, I don't want to see it in the Park again.
>
> (Greenwich Forum, 2013)

Another resident highlighted the problem with staging noisy events in public spaces rather than traditional venues: 'could they perhaps hire The Valley or The Den [local football stadiums] for the day and run round that with their music blaring' (Greenwich Forum, 2013). Combining a road race and a music festival seemed like a good idea, but it ultimately created an event that caused complaints about road closures *and* excessive noise. Noise was an issue for residents but it wasn't the main reasons residents objected to the race. Most opponents were concerned about the way the race 'trapped' them in their homes. The design of the route (see Figure 7.1) meant that if you lived within the circumference of closed roads you were unable to use your car for that day. Using the same streets as the London Marathon (see Figure 7.1) contradicted UK Government regulations designed to prevent the closure of the same roads more than once per year. Residents complained about the lack of information and consultation about road closures, particularly as the route changed slightly from year to year.

In considering the complaints above, it should also be noted that many residents liked Run to the Beat. Some people could see beyond their own inconvenience and think about the wider benefits. One resident highlighted the charitable beneficiaries, and felt that 'we should welcome events that encourage people to take up running' (Greenwich Forum, 2013). However, this dimension of the event also needs to be scrutinised carefully. Although fun runs are generally very positive events for participants and hosts, some commentators highlight that they are ultimately commercial events that involve commercial exploitation. Wilson (1995: 184) describes the fun run as 'a spectacular manifestation of the commercial restructuring of leisure and sport'. These types of events are criticised by authors who feel they are too far removed from the essence of running. For example, Featherstone (1991: 185) suggests 'the notion of running for running's sake . . . a sensuous experience in harmony with embodied and physical nature is completely submerged amid the welter of benefits called up by the market and health experts'.

The commodification of running is a key theme in a recent book 'Running Free' in which the author outlines and bemoans the rise of 'big running' – the advent of running as a commercial business (Askwith, 2014). Askwith notes how running has become monetised: and the author asks an important question: 'running hasn't become more expensive so why are people paying more to do it?' (cited in Love, 2014). This can be linked directly to running events staged in the public realm: people now pay a lot of money to complete a route that they could run for nothing whenever they wanted. Fun run organisers hire public space and add value by offering road closures, and the promise of fellow participants and spectators. In other words, the streets are commodified as a venue and the

Figure 7.7 The streets of Greenwich during the 2013 edition of Run to the Beat.

involvement of sponsors means they are also commercialised. As the analysis of Run to the Beat below highlights, 'big running' does not merely encourage the commercialisation of leisure, it results in the commercialisation of public space.

The involvement of IMG and its corporate sponsors highlights that 'Run to the Beat' was ultimately a commercial venture. The 2013 edition of the race provided a good example. The event was 'powered by' – i.e. sponsored by – Nike and the race fee (£30) included a Nike running shirt which the 19,000 participants were required to wear. This meant that when the runners hit the streets of Greenwich, a dramatic live advert for Nike was created in the public realm (see Figure 7.7). Whether they wanted to be or not, runners were participants in an embodied form of experiential marketing, creating a 'brandscape' (Osborn and Smith, 2015). Because this event took place in the public realm the event sponsors became associated with urban space in general (the street), as well as Greenwich in particular. This reinforces the arguments made in Chapter 5 about the motives and issues associated with event sponsorship. The event also included some more traditional forms of advertising and marketing By sponsoring the race Nike were able to plaster their logo all over Greenwich Park – which for the 2013 race served as the start and finish point and as the site for a 'festival village'. Perhaps the most extreme example of this was a three dimensional manifestation of their slogan (Just Do It) that was placed prominently in the park (see Figure 7.8). The deep sponsorship of other companies was also criticised by participants. The event was sponsored by

Figure 7.8 Greenwich Park during the 2013 edition of Run to the Beat.

a company who sell coconut water – and runners complained that this was inappropriately offered to them at some points during the race.

The 2013 race was the last time 'Run to the Beat' was staged in Greenwich. Greenwich Council was unprepared to sign a new five-year contract to host the race and IMG moved the event to Wembley. However, there remain issues with 'big running' in Greenwich. Chapter 6 highlighted that one potential outcome of the Olympic equestrian events was that more events might be staged in Greenwich Park. It seems that after its use as a sports venue during the 2012 Games, the Park has become a regular venue for other events, particularly 5km and 10km 'fun runs' (see Figure 7.9). As Figure 7.9 illustrates, these are organised by a range of commercial enterprises, and these companies pay a fee of £2.75 for every race entrant plus a 'disruption' charge of between £1000–£4000 (The Royal Parks, 2015). Therefore, staging a race involving over 500 runners generates thousands of pounds in revenue for The Royal Parks.

As the very notion of a 'disruption charge' highlights, these events also result in various negative effects. Although they are relatively confined in time (weekend mornings) and space (roads and pathways); they are responsible for noise, disruption, littering and the installation of temporary structures in the Park. Although signs are placed warning about potential disruption, runners navigate Greenwich Park when it is fully open to others. This creates potential user conflicts and there are regular altercations between runners and regular park users. Running races and exercising dogs seem to be particularly incompatible uses of park space. These might be deemed minor irritations, rather than major issues, but there is the potential for more serious incidents. In March 2015 there was a major accident when a runner participating in a Greenwich Park fun run collided with a cyclist. Although the runner was unhurt, the cyclist sustained critical head injuries and was airlifted to hospital. This might have been just a freak accident, but it highlights that sport events are not necessarily compatible with everyday use.

Figure 7.9 Notices fixed to the gates of Greenwich Park forewarning users of forthcoming running events.

Parkrun

One event organised in another park within the Royal Borough of Greenwich provides useful antidote to the issues associated with 'big running' in public spaces. Like 318 other parks around the UK, Avery Hill Park (see Figure 7.1) hosts a weekly timed 5km run which is free to enter. The Greenwich Parkrun staged here attracts over a hundred participants every week. The event is part of the Parkrun series: a network of events that are established and organised by local volunteers. The events work for both participants and the spaces because they are not too big, because they free to enter and because sponsorship is not visible within the spaces. Parkruns are very inclusive – not just because they are free, but because the emphasis is on participating, rather than competing. There are still issues with accommodating some of these events within public parks. The Greenwich Parkrun reinforces the message: 'Please remember that the Parkrun uses shared paths. For the continued success of the event, please give way to other park users' (Parkrun Greenwich, 2015). The events are valued by those involved, but some parks are reluctant to host them because they don't generate any revenue. More commercially-oriented park authorities are more interested in staging 5km and 10km races where commercial race organisers pay to stage events. For example, a London resident recently complained that 'my attempts to launch free community Parkruns in Battersea Park have been blocked by Wandsworth Borough Council which only sees this park as a cash-cow and wants payment – even for free runs' (Cook, 2015). This highlights that seemingly innocuous running events are part of the broader agenda to generate revenue from open spaces – an agenda that inevitably leads to commodification and commercialisation.

Blackheath events: a tragedy for the commons?

One of the most important arguments made in earlier sections of this book was the idea that events can be part of the de- and re-politicisation of public spaces. As Jenkins (2013a) argues, the traditional role of public spaces as sites of protest has been usurped by staging planned, official events. Evidence of this can also be found in the Royal Borough of Greenwich during the period 2009–2014. The local public space which is most associated with political activism is Blackheath (or the Heath as it is known locally). In 1381, Watt Tyler and Jack Straw assembled 100,000 men here during the Peasants Revolt – a rebellion provoked by the imposition of a Poll Tax. There were also other famous instances of political resistance on Blackheath. In 1450, just after the Duke of Gloucester has enclosed 74ha of the Heath to create Greenwich Park, Jack Cade camped on Blackheath with 40,000 followers and prepared the Blackheath Petition. From the late seventeenth century Blackheath had its own Fair, occasions which were feared by authorities because of their riotous and counter-cultural elements (see Chapter 1).

Blackheath's political tradition was temporarily revived in 2009 when climate protestors organised a three day occupation – the so-called Climate Camp. This demonstration against climate change was deliberately staged on Blackheath because of its history as a site of political protest. A spokesperson for the group who organised Climate Camp explained the decision to use Blackheath: 'It is really exciting to be able to look back through history and see this as the site of the uprising of thousands of people' (The Daily Telegraph, 2009). The organisers also chose Blackheath because it boasts views over Canary Wharf – the eventscape was deliberately designed to incorporate this symbol of corporate power. Climate Camp was peaceful and celebratory. Most events staged in public spaces attract hundreds of complaints, but interestingly there were only three complaints made about this 'event' (JWP annual public meeting, 2010). Rhind and Marshall (2013: 77) provide a succinct appraisal of the Climate Camp: 'no mess and no fuss'.

Governance and policy

Blackheath is officially 'manorial waste' that has been controlled by local government bodies for almost 150 years. In 1871 London County Council assumed responsibility and an 1871 Supplement to the Metropolitan Commons Act (1866) was passed to regulate its use. Since the dissolution of a London-wide council in 1986 the open space on Blackheath has been governed by the two local authorities: Lewisham and Greenwich which is seperated by the A2 – a major road which dissects the Heath (see Figure 7.1). This busy artery causes various complications when staging events on Blackheath as authorities are very reluctant to close it – even for large one-off events.

In 1986 a Joint Working Party (JWP) involving the two Boroughs was established to provide co-ordinated management of Blackheath: an arrangement which was needed 'for the co-ordination of any events'. Events had caused considerable damage to the surface of the Heath in the 1970s and 1980s and fewer funfairs are now staged. The largest and most important public events staged on the Heath are the Fireworks display held in November (c. 50,000 people) and the London Marathon (c. 35,000 runners) staged in April. These events are free for spectators, involve few access restrictions and attract a wide variety of people from the different neighbourhoods that border the Heath. There are also various charity runs staged every year, and these attract few complaints apart from some concerns about the noise created by 'over-enthusiastic rabble rousing' (JWP public meeting, 2010). From 2008–2010 a Kite and Bike Festival was organised on the Heath by Lewisham Council. This free festival attracted 25,000 people in 2010 but was discontinued thereafter because of local authority budget cuts. This highlights that the decision to invite private companies to stage events on the Heath (see below) is linked to the reduced capacity of the public sector to fund their own festivals and events (see Chapter 3). As London's most famous open spaces are now being used as venues for commercial events it was perhaps inevitable that there would be pressure to use Blackheath for such events too.

The use of the Greenwich Park for the 2012 Games had major implications for Blackheath. The section of the Heath controlled by Greenwich Council (Circus Field) was used as a logistical compound (see Chapter 6). On the other side of Blackheath, Lewisham Council erected a fan zone, albeit a smaller and less commercialised version than those installed in other parts of the capital (see Chapter 5). New Olympic connections supplement a prestigious sporting history (Inglis, 2014). Rhind and Marshall (2013: 4) suggest that Blackheath has been 'one of the most popular places of recreation and sporting activity in the capital' since the thirteenth century. The Heath was the site of England's first golf course and the first Rugby Club and, although these have both been relocated, Blackheath still hosts formal and informal sports every weekend.

In 2011 Lewisham Council granted an events company a license to stage a music festival on Blackheath. This decision was challenged by the local amenity group – The Blackheath Society – and a lengthy and expensive legal dispute followed. The Council's decision was eventually upheld, but this legal challenge, the Climate Camp, local authority budget cuts and the growing number of requests to stage events on the Heath encouraged the JWP to prepare an 'Events Policy 2011–2016' for Blackheath. This Policy was published in late 2011 (and amended in 2015). One of the main objectives was to direct decisions on applications made to stage major events on Blackheath. The Blackheath JWP reported that they were receiving 'weekly' applications for music festivals and for large events involving screenings (Blackheath JWP annual meeting, 2010). This is in line with the trend noted in Chapter 3. Staging the Olympic Games in Greenwich Park provided a key precedent; and if a Royal Park could be used for major events, key stakeholders saw no reason why Blackheath shouldn't be utilised in this way too. Lewisham Council had already outsourced responsibility for managing their section of Blackheath to a private company (Glendale) and this provided a governance model that was conducive to staging events. Therefore, it was perhaps inevitable that one of the main elements of the Events Policy 2011–2016 was to sanction major events for the first time. This limits the provision of these major events to 2 x 2 day festivals per year which are to be staged on the Lewisham side of the Heath. The Events Policy stipulates that a 'Large Music Festival' is an 'enclosed event, free or ticketed', held over one or two consecutive days which involves more than 10,000 people (Lewisham Council, 2015: 1). The first of these events was staged in 2014 – the ONBlackheath music festival.

ONBlackheath

Lewisham Council gave organisers the go-ahead to stage ONBlackheath in 2011 but the new festival experienced a few false starts. The first edition was originally scheduled for 2011, but the legal challenge by the Blackheath Society against the decision to award the organisers a license prevented it from being staged that year. The Olympic and Paralympic Games meant that plans to stage this festival in the summer of 2012 had to be postponed too. In February 2012 organisers announced that:

> After careful consideration, and taking into account the additional usage of Blackheath in this Olympic year, the directors of ONBlackheath have taken the decision to postpone their inaugural two day music event until September 2013. We have looked long and hard at the challenges that this unique year presents and believe that Blackheath and its residents will be best served by moving the event back to 2013.

The 2013 event was also postponed, leading to the event being dubbed 'Off Blackheath'. However, the inaugural edition of ONBlackheath finally took place on 13th and 14th September 2014. The event was staged on a large fenced off section on Dartmouth Field (see Figure 7.1) which was licensed to accommodate up to 25,000 people. The event was sponsored by a major retailer – John Lewis – and featured a food related theme which differentiated it from other London music festivals. The organisers were targeting middle class audience as highlighted by the choice of headline sponsor. This marketing strategy was confirmed by the prices of the tickets: a two day weekend pass was priced at £99.00 plus booking fee, with under 16s charged £60 plus booking fee. Following the trend for rural events to be relocated to urban locations (see Chapter 3), the organisers stated 'the event looks to bring a sense and space of the countryside to this urban village location' (ONBlackheath, 2014a: 3). The organisers also claimed that the event would involve 'capturing the locality of Blackheath and Greenwich – its artists, its traders, its people' (ONBlackheath, 2014a: 3). Other attempts were made to placate the local community, including funding an urban beach during the summer of 2014.

Despite these attempts to garner local support, many local residents opposed the staging of the event for many of the same reasons they opposed the equestrian events in Greenwich Park. People were worried about the noise, the disruption to local transport and the potential damage to the Heath (once again, an environment mainly comprising acid grasslands). At a broader level, residents worried whether ONBlackheath was an appropriate use of common land. The Heath has traditionally been used for fairs and demonstrations, so a free music festival or other open access event would have been relatively uncontroversial. But many felt that enclosing Metropolitan Commons for a commercial event was illegal and contravened the terms of the 1871 Supplement to the Metropolitan Commons Act. Lewisham Council's legal justification for the event was provided in Point 6.6 of their Event Policy:

> The Council has powers to . . . provide amusement fairs and entertainments including bands of music, concerts, dramatic performances, cinematograph exhibitions and pageants; provide meals and refreshments of all kinds to sell to the public; and set apart or enclose in connection with any of the matters referred to in this article any part of the open space and preclude any person from entering that part so set apart or enclosed other than a person to whom access is permitted by the local authority. The part of any open space set apart or enclosed for the use of persons listening to or viewing an entertainment (including a band concert, dramatic performance, cinematograph exhibition or pageant) is not to exceed in any open space one acre or one-tenth of the open space, whichever is greater.

The space 'set apart or enclosed' for ONBlackheath was very large. But the Heath is enormous (112 hectares) so the festival site did not take up more than 10 per cent of the open space. The Council have taken this legal justification from the Greater

London Parks and Open Spaces Act 1967. However, some argue Blackheath is entitled to special protection from enclosure because it is not merely a park or open space but Metropolitan Commons. The Metropolitan Commons Act (1866: s5) states that 'after the passing of this Act the Commissioners shall not entertain an application for the inclosure of a Metropolitan Common, or any part thereof'. To stage ONBlackheath, Metropolitan Commons was enclosed (albeit temporarily) – between Sunday 8th September 2014 (when production staff began preparing the site) and Thursday 18th September 2014 (when the site was handed back).

Fencing off a site and charging high ticket prices made the space inaccessible and these arrangements sit uncomfortably with the idea of events as phenomena that can loosen or animate public space. ONBlackheath seemed to be a private event staged for the benefit of organisers and attendees. Those unwilling or unable to pay the high ticket prices were automatically excluded – not just from the event, but from common land. There was also evidence of symbolic exclusion. As Thörn (2011) suggests, people can also feel excluded by the ambience and positioning of a space. Staging a very middle class music festival had this effect on many people who live in the Boroughs of Lewisham and Greenwich. Staging an elitist festival was inappropriate at a time when local people were suffering from cuts to welfare budgets. With this in mind, some juxtaposed ONBlackheath's food theme with the recent rise in demand for food banks cited to emphasise how inappropriate they thought the festival was. One local blogger and anarchist described the event as:

> A fenced-off foodie fest on what's supposed to be 'common land' in ever such close proximity to communities in Deptford, Peckham and the like, that are getting screwed over by ongoing austerity – well if that's not a provocation, I don't know what the f*** is!
>
> (Bone, 2014)

The event was justified through the Council's remit to provide 'amusement and entertainment' for local people, but ultimately this was an initiative driven by financial motives. Lewisham Council is heavily indebted and staging a commercial music festival every year is expected to bring much needed funds. Organisers paid £30,000 for the hire of the Heath in 2014: with half of this money dedicated to a fund used to maintain the space.

Local assessments of the event

The inaugural edition of ONBlackheath attracted 25,000 people and the event was regarded as a success by the organisers; a verdict underlined by the fact it will be staged again in 2015. A post-event survey (n = 641) of residents carried out by a local amenity group highlights how the event was regarded by local residents (Blackheath Society, 2014). Around a third of respondents (189) had attended the event, suggesting that ONBlackheath was not staged entirely for the benefit of external interests. Even though many of these respondents lived very close to the Heath, their responses regarding the impacts of the event were surprisingly positive. Respondents were asked about their attitude towards the festival when it was announced and after it had finished. A large number indicated they were more positive post-event, suggesting many of their concerns has been allayed. Responses to the survey indicated that festival goers were very well behaved, with 54 per cent of those responding giving the maximum positive rating for crowd behaviour (Blackheath Society, 2014).

The most significant negative impacts were deemed to be the associated road closures and noise. Around two thirds (65 per cent) of local people indicated they were inconvenienced by the road closures, with one fifth (19 per cent) feeling they had been 'very inconvenienced' by the event. Nearly two thirds (63 per cent) of local people were aware of the noise created by the event and a third (34 per cent) found the noise to be 'intrusive' (Blackheath Society, 2014). The survey also addressed the impacts of ONBlackheath on local businesses. Despite the large number of people attending, the event did not have much effect on local trade. 59 local businesses who did not participate directly in the event responded to the survey. When asked whether they benefited or not, 45 stated that the financial impact of the event was 'neither good nor bad'. Of the other 14, seven said they had benefited, with an equivalent number (seven) indicating that the impact on their business had been negative (Blackheath Society, 2014). When considered together these responses suggest a neutral impact overall. This underwhelming outcome undermines the notion that staging events in public spaces is good for local businesses, something that reinforces preceding analysis (see Chapters 5 and 6).

Alongside questions about ONBlackheath in particular, the survey also asked local residents about events and events policy more generally. These responses are particularly significant given the focus of this chapter. Again, responses were more positive than expected. Almost half (49 per cent) felt that *more* events should be staged on the Heath, with only a third (32 per cent) wanting *fewer* events (Blackheath Society, 2014). Unsurprisingly, support for events was weaker amongst people who live closest to the Heath. When they were asked about the types of events they want to see, very few local people opposed the use of the Heath for non-commercial events, but many objected to commercial ones. The Blackheath Society (2014: 3) concluded 'it seems it is the commercialisation of the Heath which raises most strong feelings'. These concerns about commercial events and the commercialisation of public space reinforce ideas discussed previously in this book.

ONBlackheath: conclusions

The 2014 edition of ONBlackheath can be read at a number of different levels. At one level, it represented a successful inaugural event for this precious open space and one that didn't cause as many problems for local people as feared. The apparent 'success' of the event now provides a precedent for staging similar events in the future. This sounds like a problematic outcome but local people want the space to be used for more events. Although negative impacts were relatively minor, the positive effects for those not attending the event seemed to be somewhat insignificant too. Indeed, it is hard to see what the positive outcomes for the citizens of South East London were, other than the modest payment made by organisers to the local authority for the hire of the site. The main beneficiaries were the event organisers who were able to trade on Blackheath's image and environment; something that was obvious from their promotion of the event: 'a unique celebration of good food and fantastic music, set on stunning Blackheath, one of the capital's most beautiful open spaces' (ONBlackheath, 2014b).

ONBlackheath can be read at a deeper, more critical level too. Music festivals are associated with alternative cultures, but this festival almost represented the antithesis of this tradition. Indeed, the event helped to reaffirm Blackheath as a place for the privileged. A free music festival with less restricted entry may have helped to make Blackheath feel like a more inclusive space. This type of event might have invited different users. But an expensive, fenced event helped to reaffirm Blackheath's reputation as an island of affluence separated from the disadvantaged citizens that live nearby. Even though thousands of disadvantaged people live within walking distance of Blackheath they don't tend to use it because of its exclusive feel. ONBlackheath reinforced this exclusive ambience.

ONBlackheath was a highly commercialised and exclusive festival that was aimed squarely at the privileged classes. By staging an exclusive music and food event the space was effectively appropriated as a one for commercial uses and privileged users, rather than one which provides a platform for alternative cultures and inclusivity. This is in line with Madden's (2010) idea that many urban public spaces have been 're-politicised' as 'the home of a public of consumers'. Rather than being loosened or de-territorialised by the event, Blackheath has been re-territorialised as a space for the few, rather than for the many, and as one for formal rather than informal uses. Using the space for official events erodes its traditional identity as a site for unofficial events. Just as the authorities have 'seized' London's other traditional sites of protest (Hyde Park and Trafalgar Square) by turning them into events venues (Jenkins, 2013a), ONBlackheath represents a seizure of Blackheath.

Summary

Despite the focus on a relatively confined urban area during a relatively confined period of time, this chapter has covered a wider range of relevant cases, controversies and issues. At a basic level the volume of cases discussed emphasises how events have become an increasingly common function of our public spaces. More specifically, the discussion highlights the effects of Greenwich's Olympic events on the Borough's public spaces. The perceived need to materialise the legacy of events staged in a temporary venue resulted in the controversial development of open space. This is merely one example of how events and their legacies have enclosed Greenwich's open spaces. As Stevens (2007) notes, we can think of open spaces as spaces without buildings, but also as those which are loosely configured and accessible. The examples noted in this chapter highlight how events can erode both these aspects of open-ness. Events have resulted in temporary and semi-permanent installations and they have restricted the (physical and symbolic) accessibility of public spaces.

Through the analysis of specific examples in this chapter, several of the key issues addressed in this book are explored further. The introduction of an AdiZone in Charlton Park and the way Run to the Beat created a Nike brandscape high-lights the way events can commercialise public spaces. The chapter also provides good examples of how events commodify public space. Blackheath, Greenwich Park and the streets of the Borough are now offered for hire to commercial event organisers to raise money for authorities struggling to cope with budget cuts. Open spaces which were presumed to be protected from enclosure such as Black-heath have been privatised – albeit temporarily. This case and the relative neglect of Woolwich Common are good examples of the way that more affluent areas/ groups tend to be privileged in events planning and policy making. This reminds us of the importance of undertaking political analyses of the way public spaces are being used as events venues. Indeed, the case of ONBlackheath provides an illustration of the way events re-semanticise spaces for passive consumption, rather than political activism. Although discussed less extensively, there was also evidence of the securitisation rationale for staging events in public spaces. The changes made to Woolwich's main square were motivated by the need to provide an environment that feels safer.

8 Regulation and resistance

Introduction

The previous three chapters emphasise some of the problematic aspects of staging events in public spaces. These include reduced access (privatisation), inappropriate sponsorship (commercialisation) and the imposition of excessive controls (securitisation). This chapter explores if anything can be done to address these problems. One obvious solution would be to fund public spaces more generously. This would help to counter commercial pressures and associated privatisation/securitisation, but it doesn't seem likely in the prevailing political and economic conditions. In this context, there seem to be two mechanisms that have the potential to 'protect' public spaces from excessive eventification: robust regulation and resourceful resistance. Most developed cities have expansive regulatory systems that could be used to ensure that poorly conceived events do not go ahead, or to ensure that events that do happen are organised in a more appropriate way. These systems usually involve event licensing procedures, but also more general development control systems. Inappropriate events can be prevented or reconfigured by less formal means too. Civil society organisations, social movements and other campaign groups can exert pressure which can stop some events from happening. At an even more informal level, when events are staged people can appropriate them and the spaces they occupy. Event-goers can negotiate and resist dominant meanings and practices so that they work in ways not envisaged by event organisers.

Two examples of where regulation and resistance have prevented inappropriate events from being staged in public parks are discussed in detail in this chapter. These cases have been selected because of their comparability with the extended case explored in Chapter 6: the use of Greenwich Park for Olympic equestrian events. It is worth emphasising that regulations and resistance do not represent ideal solutions to many of the dilemmas noted in this book. Hence, the analysis of each of these mechanisms is accompanied by a discussion of their inherent limitations.

Regulation

To stage events in public spaces, organisers usually require a license and this procedure provides an obvious opportunity to regulate events. Licensing arrangements vary according to an event's size, duration, location and content. They also vary according to the stated purpose. In the UK under the Licensing Act (2003), small events (fewer than 500 people) require a Temporary Event Notice whereas larger events require a Premises Licence, which involves providing an assessment of anticipated impacts. These permits are awarded by the relevant local authority. When public spaces are used regularly for events they often have a pre-existing Premises Licence attached: this illustrates both the extent to which public spaces are now envisaged as venues, and the inherent limitations of licensing procedures. When events are staged, organisers usually require various other licenses too, for road closures, for temporary structures and for permission to sell or distribute various items. Most cities also have controls on outdoor advertising and these can also be used to regulate the commercial dimension of events. For example, the City of Westminster in London restricts sponsor logos on banners to 10 per cent of their area (for large media screens, this 10 per cent rule still applies; advertising is restricted to 6 mins per hour). In the UK, city councils permit temporary signs to advertise charitable events 'which may be religious, educational, cultural, political, social or recreational, but not commercial events' (DCLG, 2007). Therefore, anyone wanting to put up large advertisements in association with a commercial event needs to apply for 'advertising consent'. These types of measures, if properly enforced, can be used to address concerns regarding over-commercialisation. However, as previous chapters have shown, the distinction between commercial events and other events is often unclear or even deliberately conflated to help justify events installations. This limits the effectiveness of this type of regulation.

The discussion above highlights the complex 'red tape' that exists to protect public spaces form over-commercialisation. In many cities the issue is not the lack of suitable regulation, but the failure to apply and enforce it properly. Toronto's 'Illegal Signs' group works hard to hold advertisers to account by checking whether their installations have full planning approval (Iveson, 2012). Enforcement is not the only issue. The effectiveness of advertising control mechanisms is also undermined by the way 'outdoor advertisers and urban authorities have become partners in regulating and restricting the use of urban public space' (Iveson, 2012: 162). Cities are very reliant on the income from outdoor advertising, so a lot of their enforcement resources are used to protect their official advertisers from others who try to advertise in public space (e.g. flyposters). Clamping down on informal advertisers allows city authorities to monetise their own space by reducing the amount of free sites available to others (Iveson, 2012). This reflects a wider concern whereby the regulation of the city is often configured in a way that protects event interests, rather than public spaces (see Chapter 5). In the contemporary era, these commercial interests include local authorities who generate large amounts of financial and symbolic capital from commercial events staged in public spaces (see Chapter 3). This perhaps undermines the capacity for local authorities to be impartial regulators.

Legal measures should protect public spaces from inappropriate incursions: constitutional laws (to protect a citizen's rights) and municipal laws (those designed to govern a particular location) can serve this purpose. However in many instances, legal systems have been reconfigured and manipulated to make it easier for cities to stage events in public spaces. As governments are key stake-holders they often introduce legislation that usurps any controls that might have prevented or restricted incursions by commercial events. The New South Wales Major Events Act 2009 is a good example. Here, legislation has been introduced to attract and facilitate major events in New South Wales. One of the objectives of this Act is to prevent commercial exploitation, but it is not designed to prevent urban spaces from being inappropriately exploited; instead, it mainly serves to protect event sponsors from ambush marketing. Other Australian legislation has also facilitated the appropriation of public space for events: the Melbourne Grand Prix in Albert Park (see Chapter 5) was sanctioned by the Australian Grands Prix Act1994. This legislation exempted the event (and the works required to stage it) from environmental impact studies and pollution / planning controls. It effectively gave the government a license to do anything they wanted at Albert Park (Lowes, 2004).

When large events are staged in public spaces they may require planning per-mission. This is often the case if events require complex structures, if they cover a large amount of space, or if they last for an extended period. In the UK, for cases where event structures are in situ for more than 28 days, event organisers need to apply for planning consent in the same way as they would if they were proposing a permanent structure. This effectively defines a temporary structure as one that exists for no longer than four weeks. This sounds like a long time, but it takes several weeks to build and dismantle a large temporary arena. Hence, planning permission – and the conditions imposed by planning authorities – can be effec-tive tools with which to regulate major events. The conditions imposed on event organisers in the Greenwich Park case outlined in Chapter 6 illustrate this to some extent. However, there have been instances where planning permission for events in urban public spaces has been refused. An insightful case where this occurred is analysed below.

The Global Champions Tour in Kensington Gardens

Kensington Gardens is a Royal Park located next to Hyde Park in central London. The public space here (242 acres) is adjacent to Kensington Palace, a residence cur-rently occupied by the Duke of Cambridge and other members of the Royal family. The site is within the territorial boundaries of the Royal Borough of Kensington and Chelsea local authority (hereafter RBKC). In 2013 a fascinating controversy unfolded here when SEL UK Ltd applied to host a major equestrian event in part of Kensington Gardens. The event was envisaged as a London leg of the Global Champions Tour – a show jumping competition that involves the world's best rid-ers competing for lucrative prize money. This event is particularly relevant to this book given the rights holder's vision 'to bring show jumping to as many people as possible, and that means being in the centre of the great cities of the world' (Global Champions Tour, 2014). The Global Champions Tour has been staged in various city centres across Europe (e.g. in Hamburg, Cannes, Lausanne, Vienna, Valencia) and further afield (e.g. Doha). According to the British Equestrian Federation, the organisers of the event 'have demonstrated time and again that they can stage competitions in the very heart of iconic cities' (BEF, 2013).

The controversial construction of an equestrian arena in a public space for an elite event means this example has obvious parallels with the Greenwich Park case analysed in Chapter 6. Indeed, there were direct connections between the events: campaigners who opposed the Kensington Gardens event sought advice from NOGOE and their campaign materials were remarkably similar. The case is interesting for other reasons too. It is a good example of the potential for existing regulatory systems to address the problems noted in this book. The competition was only due to last for four days, but the structures required to stage it (including grandstands, stables and a retail village) were scheduled to be built and dismantled over a period of more than 28 days. Hence the organisers needed to apply for planning permission. Refusing consent seemed unlikely given the formidable status of the applicants and their supporters. The application was made by SEL UK Ltd, whose managing director is Peter Phillips (the Queen's grandson), and the event was supported by both the Royal Household and the Royal Parks. These organisations own and control the space on which the event was due to be staged: The Dials and Broad Walk which are parts of the Royal Park (see Figure 8.1), plus Perks Field to the north of Kensington Gardens owned by The Royal Household. It is hard to imagine a more imposing planning application: the Queen's grandson was applying to the local authority to stage an event in a Royal Park and on a site

Figure 8.1 The part of Kensington Gardens earmarked for the Global Champions Tour event.

that was partly owned by the Royal Household. The brave decision by the planning authority to turn down the application, plus some of the interesting ways the event was justified by the organisers, means the case deserves further analysis.

Legacy discourses

Following a trend noted in the previous two chapters, the organisers tried to use 'Olympic legacy' as a justification for staging the event in Kensington Gardens. The Global Champions Tour is a relatively small-scale event dominated by corporate hospitality, but that did not stop the organisers trying to claim the London edition was a natural successor to the 2012 Games. Indeed, SEL UK Ltd positioned their project as 'a later phase of the Olympic and Paralympic Games' (BPTW, 2013: 1.12) and the 2012 Games was a recurring theme in the Planning Statement submitted to RBKC (BTPW, 2013). The Games were used in various ways to help justify this controversial project. Firstly, the organisers cited them as a precedent that sanctioned further exploitation of public space: 'major sites within London have demonstrated their credentials in hosting high quality events and in providing a suitable environment for exhibiting sporting excellence' (BPTW, 2013: 1.8). There were also obvious instances where legacy discourse was employed more explicitly. The organisers felt their event was one that would result in the 'fulfilment of an integral part of the Olympic/Paralympic Games legacy' (BTPW, 2013: 1.12). According to organisers, the event would 'provide a strategic platform to enhance interest and activity in all sports'. More specifically, the event would provide a 'durable legacy for equestrian sport', and build 'on legacy of the Games' by 'developing the public's enthusiasm' for equestrian sport (BTPW, 2013: 2).

Where the event was to be staged was deemed to be integral to achieving these Olympic legacy ambitions. According to advocates of the Global Champions Tour, delivering an accessible equestrian legacy could only be achieved by staging the event in a city centre location. One of the letters of support that accompanied the application was provided by a Team GB gold medallist who wrote that 'to provide an enduring legacy from London 2012 these events are best held in the centre of cities' (Skelton, 2013). Placing the event here would 'make the sport more accessible to the public', opening it up to an 'audience that would not normally consider equestrian sport as a recreation option' (Skelton, 2013). The empirical evidence provided in Chapter 6 suggests this is a spurious argument. In any case, although it is an urban park, Kensington Gardens hardly represents a space that is far removed from the privileged surrounds in which equestrian sport normally takes place. Indeed, the accompanying media narrative was that the event would take place in the Duke of Cambridge's 'front garden' (Lydell, 2013).

Grounds for refusal

The decision by RBKC's planning department to refuse permission for the Global Champions Tour event was accompanied by a report which seemed to explode many of the dubious justifications used by event organisers seeking to exploit public space (RBKC, 2013). Perhaps unsurprisingly, alongside legacy considerations, economic and promotional justifications featured prominently in the event organiser's planning application (BTPW, 2013). Previous sections of this book emphasise how image enhancement and local business benefits are commonly cited as reasons for bringing events out of traditional venues into public spaces (see Chapter 3). According to organisers, this 'world class event' was 'a unique opportunity to showcase Kensington Gardens and the Royal Borough' (BTPW, 2013: 8.23). The planning authority dismissed this idea: 'Kensington Palace and Kensington Gardens are already popular tourist attractions and leisure destinations in their own right. As such the need for showcasing is not agreed' (RBKC, 2013: 4.54). In a similarly refreshing way RBKC planning officials felt that economic justifications for staging the event were overstated: they felt the event would discourage general use of Kensington Gardens, offsetting any positive impacts. Planners felt that the organisers had not taken into account 'losses from people discouraged from visiting by the proposed events' (RBKC, 2013: 4.55). The failure to acknowledge this 'crowding out' effect is a noted weakness of ex-ante event impact analyses (Smith and Stevenson, 2009).

The decision by RBKC to turn down the Global Champions Tour application was ultimately one directed by concerns about the temporary loss of public space. In their 'reasons for refusal', the most prominent reason cited was that the events would 'result in inappropriate and protracted loss of scarce and high quality Metropolitan Open Land that makes an important contribution to the health and well-being of the community' (RBKC, 2013: 2). Planners were concerned not only about the presence of intrusive installations in the Park, but also the amount of time it would take to restore the site. Their concern was influenced by previous experiences where reinstatement works had taken longer than intended. On this basis RBKC planners estimated that the four day equestrian event would result in 74 days of disruption to public space provision (RBKC, 2013: 4.7). Because the proposed events were scheduled for the period June 6–9th, closures would take place at the times when the Gardens were heavily used. Concern about the loss of this public space was also influenced by the relative lack of alternatives for RBKC residents to use: 'there is a comparatively small amount of publically accessible parks, gardens and open space' (RBKC, 2013: 4.7). RBKC (2013: 4.7) also recognised that events such as the one proposed were beginning to affect the provision of public space:

> ... some of these spaces have come under increasing pressure from temporary uses for special events, often in large structures to accommodate commercial activities. The form of these means that some open spaces are not accessible to the public for large parts of the year ...

This comment reaffirms concerns noted throughout this book.

Successful precedent or failed trial?

Previous Chapters have noted how 'one-off' events staged in public spaces can be used as a justification for staging future events. The issue of precedent was also a key consideration in this planning dispute: organisers used other events staged in

Kensington Gardens to help justify their event. During the previous year (2012) parts of the site had been used to house a temporary theatre (May–September) and Russian officials had been given permission to install an exhibition and hospitality facility during the Olympic and Paralympic Games (July–August). Rather than considering these events as precedents, RBKC (2013, 4.52) asserted they were 'trial runs' as they were the 'first temporary events that the Council has permitted on those sites'. And RBKC felt that these experiments demonstrated that the loss of access to public space was more protracted than had been anticipated. Hence, these previous events were used as reasons to turn down the application, not reasons to sanction it. RBKC felt the Global Champions Tour event would *become* the precedent if planning consent were given: making it difficult for the Council to refuse future events applications. According to the Council, granting permission 'would establish the principle that The Dials can be used for largely private purposes rather than as an area of public open space' (RBKC, 2013: 4.14). In effect, RBKC were using existing planning regulations to protect the public space from creeping privatisation.

RBKC felt that the previous events staged in 2012 needed to be regarded as 'special circumstances' because the Olympic Games were staged in London that year. The applicants tried to deal with this by arguing that their event represented 'very special circumstances' because it sought to capitalise on the legacy of the Olympic and Paralympic Games. SEL UK Ltd argued that the 'strategic importance of fulfilling legacy is no less fundamental' than staging the Olympic Games (BTPW, 2013: 1.12). This was a fascinating – if rather fanciful – position to take. Organisers were attempting to extend the exceptionality of staging the Olympic Games beyond the life of that event to help justify other smaller events. Letters of support that accompanied the application to stage the event also emphasised this was a 'unique' opportunity, providing the justification to stage this event in a particular place at a specific time. Letters of support for the event were outnumbered by the 300 objections sent to RBKC, and by the 390 people who signed an online petition (Change.org, 2013). These contributions also influenced the outcome.

Outcomes and implications

Ultimately, the controversy cited here is interesting because the planning authority refused permission for the event and organisers were forced to find a more suitable venue. The RBKC decision was announced in March 2013, less than three months before the event was due to be staged. This suggests the decision was also brave because, unlike in other event projects (Smith, 2012), time pressures weren't used as an excuse to override proper scrutiny of the proposal. The inaugural London edition of the Global Champions Tour was eventually staged on the fringes of the Olympic Park, something which rather undermined the organiser's original claim that Kensington Park was the only suitable site available (BTPW, 2013). Intriguingly, the Head of Events and Filming at the Royal Parks who had supported the use of Kensington Gardens for the event left his position soon after the controversy to set up an events company. This company (Major Live Events) is now reportedly helping SEL Ltd to find a venue for the Global Championships Tour in London from 2015 onwards (Edwards, 2014).

Despite the rhetoric about Olympic legacies and local benefits, and despite the involvement of powerful people and influential organisations, RBKC officials refused permission for the event. Sceptics might say this was because the local authority had no financial stake in the decision: any revenues earned from the hire of the space would go to the Royal Household and The Royal Parks. The absence of a vested interest perhaps made it easier for the local authority to refuse permission. However, this would be an unfair assessment of a courageous and enlightened decision. In this case, what is sometimes dismissed as bureaucratic 'red tape' helped to ensure that public space remained accessible.

The RBKC decision may represent a watershed. Local authorities have come to realise that opposition to commercial events staged in public spaces is not merely conservative NIMBYism, but genuine concern about the way some events restrict access to and enjoyment of public spaces. The case has a wider significance too. It emphasises the growing significance of legacy discourse in event projects and demonstrates the way the term has been appropriated as a vehicle for event justification (see Chapter 7). The case also highlights how one event (in this case The Olympic Games) can be used as a justification for staging other events (The Global Champions Tour). This reaffirms the idea discussed in Chapter 7 that one outcome of staging major events in public spaces is more events in the future.

The limitations of planning controls

The Kensington Gardens case analysed above shows that planning controls can be used to regulate event projects. However, it is perhaps unwise to rely too heavily on the planning system. In the UK, planning consent is only required for structures that will be in situ for more than 28 days, hence development control mechanisms only apply to certain types of events – those that last for a long time and those that involve complicated or extensive builds. There are other reasons to be sceptical about statutory regulation of event projects, particularly as there is also noted tendency for event projects to be exempted from normal planning procedures (Smith, 2012). For example, in the V8 motor races staged in Canberra's streets (see Chapter 5), 'there was a complete absence of due process and reckless regard for the ordinary conventions of good government' (Reese cited in Tranter and Keefee, 2004: 184). Deficient implementation seems particularly common when projects are accompanied by the powerful discourses that surround the Olympic Games or other events labelled as 'world class'. Sánchez and Broudehoux (2013: 136) argue that 'the hosting of world class events legitimises the adoption of an exceptional politico-institutional framework that authorises the relaxation of certain rules and obligations'; including the 'reformulation of planning regulations'.

McManus (2004) provides a good example in his analysis of a temporary facility constructed in Rozelle Bay, Sydney for the 2000 Olympic Games. Previous proposals for a marina development had been opposed and defeated, but the Games provided the justification for a new super-yacht marina here. McManus

(2004) feels that the discourses surrounding the Olympic Games allowed developers to gain support for a project that in other circumstances would have been considered unnecessary or politically sensitive. The failure to complete an Environmental Impact Assessment and the approval of the project were linked to the powerful Olympic rhetoric that pervaded Sydney at this time. Staging the Olympic Games provided a justification for the project, but also a convenient smokescreen which limited opposition (McManus, 2004).

The exceptionality associated with major events is justified by temporal rhetoric claiming events to be unique, one-offs or once in a lifetime occasions that require special consideration (Smith, 2014). These qualities allow them to be judged as 'special circumstances' which exempt them from planning policy. Such exemptions were evident in the discussion in Chapter 7 which examined the justifications cited for the new Equestrian Centre in the Royal Borough of Greenwich. They were also evident in the City of Westminster's justification for granting planning permission for the extended use of Hyde Park for 'live music performances', 'live broadcasting of the Olympic Games' and 'interactive sports zones' during the summer of 2012 (City of Westminster, 2012). The report prepared for the Planning Committee acknowledged that 'temporary structures and fencing will encroach onto the open parkland character of Hyde Park which will significantly alter its character and appearance' (City of Westminster, 2012: 14). The installations required a large part of Hyde Park to be closed for a long period – for 63 days including assembly and disassembly. Despite these worrying impacts, the City of Westminster (2012: 16) decided that:

> the exceptional circumstances of the London 2012 Games outweighs any harm caused by the proposal, particularly given that any harm caused would be temporary and short term in nature and entirely linked to a single event of global significance.

This fascinating explanation for the planning decision explicitly confirms that exceptions are made for event projects, and that this is justified by their global and time limited status. The quote also highlights another worrying aspect of planning decisions regarding event projects. Inherent within this justification is the idea that because an event is a temporary phenomenon environmental damage will be temporary too. This is a commonly cited assertion in event related planning applications/decisions. However, this is not necessarily the case. Long term damage can be caused by short term events.

There are also more practical temporal factors that influence the way events are regulated. Event projects often have limited time frames; they need to be delivered at specific points in time, and this means that established (time-consuming) planning procedures are sometimes compromised. In most developed countries planning decisions are made by independent planning officials to avoid potential conflicts of interest. However, there is still a tendency for local authorities or national governments to sanction projects that fit with their own objectives – even if they contravene established policies and laws. To assist the staging of the 2012 Olympic Games a 133 year old law protecting Wanstead Flats was changed using parliamentary legislation (Boykoff and Fussey, 2013: 13). The same Act allowed Circus Field on Blackheath to be used as a logistics compound to service the Olympic Games (see Chapter 6 of this book). As previous chapters of this book highlight, urban authorities are not only stakeholders but potential beneficiaries from staging events in public spaces. Therefore, exceptional arrangements are often made to ensure these benefits accrue.

Resistance

If regulatory systems are inadequate, unenforced or abused then public space might be better protected from the pernicious effects of events by more direct means – via 'resistance'. If capitalist modernity inevitably involves processes of securitisation, commercialisation and privatisation, it inevitably generates resistance against those processes. Polanyi (1946) famously identified modernity's 'double movement' whereby processes of enclosure automatically produce forms of resistance. Recently, urban resistance has crystallised around key ideas such as 'the right to the city', with prominent public spaces both the subject of, and platform for, protests (see Figure 8.2).

In the subsequent sections of this book, two different types of resistance are explored: (1) resistance by organised groups prior to events; and (2) more informal resistance by individuals during events. Although neither offers a panacea, these

Figure 8.2 Occupy Vancouver's 'Tent City' outside the Vancouver Art Gallery in 2011.

represent: ways that people can reclaim public space from inappropriate events; and opportunities to restrain the eventification processes that accompany them.

Organised resistance

The analysis of regulatory systems above is organised around an example where statutory regulation was used to protect public space from an inappropriate event project. Following a similar approach, this section of the book identifies an instance where organised opposition to an event project stopped it happening. In 1997 community groups in Vancouver successfully prevented Hastings Park from being used for a series of Indy Car motor races. This case is analysed in detail by Mark Lowes in his book *Indy Dreams and Urban Nightmares* (2002). Cases where opposition movements succeed are not that easy to find, something that illustrates the difficulties faced by groups attempting to block events projects. There is also a 'dearth of detailed analysis of successful opposition to . . . such spectacles' (Lowes, 2002: 11), which makes Lowes's own account particularly valuable. The other reason this example has been subjected to detailed consideration here is because of the clear parallels with the Greenwich Park case discussed in Chapter 6. These similarities provide an opportunity to undertake insightful comparative analysis.

The Battle for Hastings

Hastings Park is a 160 acre site located in the North East of Vancouver. The Park was established by the Municipal Act (1889) which 'set apart and reserved' the land 'for the recreation and enjoyment of the public'. Over time Hastings Park has become more commercialised, with attractions and entertainment facilities added. Many of these are linked to the Pacific National Exhibition; a 17 day agricultural fair which has been staged annually in the Park since 1910. The Park has other event links too: a stadium was built on the site to stage the 1954 Commonwealth Games and this arena subsequently hosted the city's sports team, the BC Lions and the Vancouver Whitecaps. The Park also hosts a major horse racing facility which dominates the north end of the site. All these incursions mean that access to large parts of the park is restricted spatially (by fences and admission fees), as well as temporally (they are only open at certain times).

In the mid-1990s an ambitious plan to 'green' the Park was conceived; this was produced in conjunction with community groups who participated in the Hastings Park Working Committee (Lowes, 2002). This process was interrupted in January 1997 when organisers of the Molson Indy Vancouver motor race announced that they wanted to move their event to a new venue – Hastings Park. Between 1990 and 1997 the race had been staged in the False Creek area of Vancouver (see Figure 8.3), but development in this regeneration zone had intensified and the circuit here was no longer viable. City interests, including the Mayor, were desperate to keep the Indy Car event in Vancouver and so they supported the request to move the event to Hastings Park. This relocation would have given the race organisers 'exclusive control of that site for several weeks each year to prepare and stage the event' (Lowes, 2002: 97).

Figure 8.3 False Creek, Vancouver. This was the venue for the Molson Indy Vancouver
1990–1997. After the proposed relocation to Hastings Park was rejected, the
event returned and was staged here until 2004.

When the plans to relocate the event were made public, they were met with vehement opposition by local community groups. Residents expressed obvious concerns
about the event, especially the noise, crowds and inconvenience that it would generate. Community groups were also aghast that their efforts to secure a commitment to
rehabilitate Hastings Park as a green space were so blatantly undermined by the proposal (Lowes, 2002). Some of their objections resonated with one of the key themes
in this book: the importance of accessible, inclusive and permeable space that the
people can flow through. The plan to have a motor racing track in the Park was
seen as exacerbating the physical restrictions and 'privatisation' that were already
present, and which local people were seeking to remove.

In seeking to get the relocation they wanted, organisers and advocates emphasised the benefits of the race. They used rhetoric in promotional campaigns which
emphasised the symbolic significance of this 'world class event' for Vancouver
and the economic benefits it would bring to the city. Indeed, a recurring theme
was that local residents would be doing their civic duty by allowing their park
to become the venue – thus helping the city keep the race and retain the supposed economic stimulus that came with it. Some residents interviewed by Lowes
(2002: 102) seemed to accept this dubious reasoning: one was quoted as saying
'all communities have to realise that they have to do their full share by hosting
these big sport events and festivals'. However, most local people were offended

by this idea and instead asserted that their civic duty was to defend their recreational space from privatisation (Lowes, 2002).

As discussed in Chapter 7, the socio-economic composition of a community can influence the likely success of resistance movements. In this case, the local community was made up of people who had lived in the area for a long time, but also a younger, middle class and family oriented section who had moved to the area more recently. Lowes (2002) views this group as pivotal to the movement that helped to see off the threat posed by the Indy Car race. The influential involvement of middle class residents links back to previous arguments made about the contexts in which opposing voices tend to be heard (see Chapter 7). The controversy had a galvanising effect on the community, but Lowes (2002) notes that local people already had a track record of activism, and their prior involvement in planning for Hasting Park meant the community were already engaged and organised. Opposition to the event was led by the Hastings Community Association. Fittingly, given their mission to protect the park and rehabilitate its green space, this was very much a 'grass roots' movement led by volunteers. In late January 1997 a public meeting was organised to discuss the Indy Car proposals, and this was the pivotal moment in the opposition campaign. Approximately 700 people attended and the vast majority were opposed to the event (Lowes, 2002). Event officials were surprised by the strength of feeling. The demonstration of local opposition meant the proposal was deemed unviable and a week later the plan to use Hastings Park for motor racing was abandoned.

In his explanation for the success of the organised opposition, Lowes (2002) points to the significance of discourses. This reaffirms analysis in the previous two chapters where the importance of discourses in contested event projects was also emphasised. For Lowes (2002) the Hastings Park controversy ultimately amounted to a discursive struggle between event officials and local community groups. Opponents countered the rhetoric of the entrepreneurial city by deploying 'competing discourses', something that Lowes (2002) feels helped the community groups to succeed. For example, local people responded to the notion that hosting events was a civic duty, by communicating their own interpretation of civic duty. Lowes (2002) suggests that success was also achieved because the community were able to establish and 'frame' a coherent vision of space. This reinforces the findings of wider research that suggests framing processes are key to understanding the role and influence of social movements (Benford and Snow, 2000). Partly because of the pre-existing plans for the future of Hastings Park, residents were able to communicate what the Park was and who it was for. They used powerful discourses within this vision – of family, democracy, nature and inclusivity – which 'struck a deep chord' with other members of the community (Lowes, 2002). Ultimately this vision made more sense to people than the one promoted by event promoters.

Comparative study

To provide an added layer to the Hastings Park case study, it is perhaps useful to compare it directly with the Greenwich Park case analysed previously.

Comparative analyses are helpful as they ensure that case studies go beyond merely description, instead allowing for genuine explanation. This explanatory power is assisted by selecting cases that are similar in many respects, but which differ in terms of certain outcomes. In their attempt to develop a methodology for 'comparative urban political research' Denters and Mossberger (2006: 553) outline the logic of a comparative approach: 'by comparing units that are most similar in some aspects, the researcher is able to control for the variables that are similar and isolate other variables as potential causes of observed differences'. We can apply the same logic to help explain why in two broadly similar cases (major events proposed for Hastings Park and Greenwich Park) the outcome was different: opposition groups were able to successfully block the event in Vancouver, but not in Greenwich.

Similarities Alongside the obvious parallels (both involved using urban parks as the venue for major events), there are many other similarities between the Greenwich Park and Hastings Park controversies. These help to reaffirm the validity of the comparison and, following the logic explained above, they make it easier to identify factors that might provide explanations for the different outcome. In both instances, advocates of the event had a large amount of resources at their disposal to make their case and to counter opposition as it emerged. In each example the rhetoric and discourses employed by the event organisers were replete with references to the supposed image benefits and economic impacts of staging 'world class' events. More subtly, in both cases organisers implied that residents should do their duty by supporting the events: in Greenwich Park, residents were asked to forego their personal enjoyment of the Park to serve 'the national interest' (see Chapter 6); whereas in Vancouver, sacrifices were required for the metropolitan cause.

There were similarities too between the opposition movements that resisted the events. In both cases middle class residents led volunteer movements that boasted meagre resources compared to their opponents. And these groups adopted similar arguments. They opposed the events because of: the disruption they would cause; the restrictions they would impose; their environmental impacts; and the way they contradicted ideas about what urban parks are for. They also used similar tactics: both groups reinforced their case by trying to appropriate the discourses used by boosters. NOGOE appropriated the language of legacy (see Chapter 7) and the Hastings Community Association reconfigured the discourse of civic duty.

Differences So why did the opposition movement in Vancouver succeed? What were the key differences between the cases that contributed decisively to this different outcome? The obvious difference was the contrasting event projects at the centre of the controversies. Motor races seem far more invasive and far less suited to park settings than equestrian events (see Chapter 5), prompting more vehement opposition. There were other pivotal differences too. In Greenwich a community group (NOGOE) was trying to counter a proposal to hold a one-off Olympic event. This was a far more daunting task than opposing a less significant event (Indy Car racing) that was due to be staged every year. To provide a home for a relatively specialised motorsports event, the residents of Hastings were facing the threat of a semi-permanent development that undermined their vision for the

Park. This created a unified and sizeable opposition movement. In Greenwich, a smaller proportion of residents were committed to resisting the proposals. Equestrian events didn't seem as inappropriate and claims that events would deliver symbolic and economic benefits seemed more credible when aligned to staging the Olympic Games. This made boosterist discourse harder to counter.

Another key difference between the cases was the range of interests faced by the opposition movements. In Vancouver, although the Mayor supported the plans of the event organisers, other key officials did not (Lowes, 2002). This contrasts with the Greenwich Park case: NOGOE battled against an impenetrable coalition of interests that included park authorities, local, city and national governments, as well as the event organisers. The organisation of the opposition also differed in the two cases. Communities who lived near to Hastings Park had a long track record of activism and they had been engaged by the ongoing planning process for the Park. This meant they were ideally positioned to deal with the threat posed by the Indy Car race proposals. In his analysis of the case, Lowes (2002) implies that had this controversy not occurred when it did, in this particular community, the outcome would have been different. In Greenwich, although the controversy did galvanise local people, the community was not as unified – nor as engaged – prior to the proposal to use Greenwich Park as an equestrian venue. There was no established community group to lead an opposition movement, and NOGOE – the organisation created to take on this role – was not seen as representative of the community or their views (se Chapter 6). NOGOE was a single issue pressure group rather than a fully-fledged community association. Given the complex identity of Greenwich Park – as a national and international park, as well as a local amenity (see Chapter 6) – it was also harder for NOGOE to frame a coherent vision of what this Park was and who it was for.

Conclusions

The discussion above suggests that organised opposition to events is most likely to succeed when organisations and events take certain forms. If community groups exist prior to events proposals, and if those groups can communicate an argument and a vision that mobilises a large section of local residents then success is more likely. The extent of the opposition faced is also a factor: opposition movements will struggle to defeat proposals that are supported by both event interests (organisers and sponsors) and relevant authorities (amenity managers and governments). Success also depends on the significance of the event and the regularity with which it will be staged. One-off events with universal appeal are more difficult to resist because their supporters can use the exceptionality of the events to justify staging them. Plans for more specialised, regular events are more likely to be considered as akin to conventional development proposals; and are thus more likely to instigate credible opposition.

The Hastings Park case illustrates that organised resistance can defeat plans to use public spaces as event venues. Lowes (2002: 120) suggests optimistically that the case demonstrates that urban development forces 'do not always win' and that 'citizens can take back control over the urban landscape and implement their own local visions of their community's future'. However, the success of the community groups representing Hastings Park does not mean the spaces here are protected indefinitely; or that the long term vision to green the space will be achieved. In 2010 the City Council approved a new master plan for Hastings Park which, according to the President of the Hastings Community Association represents a 'triumph of commercialisation' (CBC, 2010). 'Highlights' of the master plan include the relocation and extension of fairgrounds and new 'celebratory spaces' (City of Vancouver, 2013). This emphasises that, even if isolated proposals are defeated, the threat of incursions from event projects is ongoing.

Problems faced by events resistance movements

Social movements always face tough challenges in seeking to influence political systems and official decisions. Campaigners opposing event projects may face additional challenges. Although there are isolated examples of success, groups that oppose event projects are hindered by various structural disadvantages. These include the coalition of interests that seek to use public spaces as event venues and wider trends that support these interests. Lehtovuori (2010) cites the need for revenue, the touristification of cities and the new reverence for temporary structures as examples of these structural forces. Events have become such an important part of public policy that municipal governments are less likely to bow to resistance. Misener and Mason (2009: 778) quote one official in Edmonton (Canada) as saying: 'opposition never stops an event – they're just too important'.

Event proposals are also harder to contest because of the connotations that accompany them. These are deployed in the discourses used to support events. For example, events are associated with festivity and fun. These connotations and their inclusion in event discourses mean that opponents of event projects are not merely accused of being selfish NIMBYs, they are dismissed as party poopers, spoilsports or killjoys. As Jenkins (2013a) writes, if you try to defend London's Royal Parks from event incursions 'you will be called a killjoy, a fogey and the enemy of growth and jobs'. Because event projects are often used as important vehicles for place marketing at the national level opponents are sometimes labelled unpatriotic. Even when place marketing ambitions are more localised, opponents of event projects can be accused of failing to fulfil their duties as citizens. Temporary event projects are sometimes thought of as ephemeral and insubstantial. However, the analysis above reminds us that they can be difficult projects to contest – because of the mismatch between the coalitions that support them and the movements that resist them, but also because of the discourses involved and the way in which these can be manipulated to support events and dismiss their opponents.

Informal resistance

Public spaces have long been understood as landscapes of power and using them as event venues further embeds power relations. However, power is exercised – not possessed – so it can be subverted (Law, 2002). Landscapes of power are always subjected to resistance. This isn't confined to resistance via organised opposition who seek to influence the political system; there are also informal types of resistance that help to subvert events as they happen. If public space is produced as it is used, or practised (see Chapter 2), then people can create it in their own ways during events, rather than in the ways envisaged by event organisers or city governments. In the analysis below, the supposedly problematic effects of staging events in public spaces – commercialisation, privatisation, securitisation – are addressed in turn with dedicated discussion for each on ways they can be resisted.

Where heavily sponsored events are staged in public spaces, they *commercialise* those spaces. However, spaces are only over-commercialised if they are perceived to be so. People consuming events may not be affected by a sponsor's banners or installations in the ways we might imagine. Iveson (2012) suggests that the hyperpresence of advertising in the contemporary public realm means we increasingly take no notice of it – and what advertisers fear most is being ignored. Research at events has suggested that young people don't see corporate branding as a problem, and those that are aware of it see it as a necessary vehicle to keep events running and ticket prices down (Tickle, 2011). We shouldn't overestimate the extent to which commercial interests can dictate how we think and feel. Efforts to turn events into brandscapes don't necessarily work because they have to compete with other attempts to construct space and because it is impossible to control and territorialise emotions in this way (Wood and Ball, 2013).

Event related commercialisation can be ignored, but it can also be resisted by action. In some instances citizens appropriate commercial advertising in an imaginative way and this helps to reclaim the spaces in which it appears (Iveson, 2012). Anti-advertising has been advocated by groups such as Brandalism – who co-ordinate takeovers of advertising space as part of their mission to end 'corporate control of the visual realm' (Brandalism, 2015). In the same way, people can subvert the dominant meanings of events or the messages of their sponsors. Reconfiguring the dominant meaning of commercial events can also be achieved more subtly. Commercial event spaces are examples of themed spaces and many accounts naively suggest that users are unable to resist the ideological signs designed into them. This is countered by research that emphasises that people negotiate and contest the authorised meanings of the city (Edensor and Kothari, 2004). As Stevens (2007: 206) suggests 'the many playful public performances which occur in urban space highlight that people constantly create new meanings for themselves and others around them, contest meanings or ignore meanings'. Even during very commercial events designed as brand experiences, people can turn them into something that means something to them. Public spaces can still be created within highly commercialised events because it is the informal actions of attendees that produce public space during events, not the event organisers (Stevens and Shin, 2014).

The ways in which events *privatise* public space by restricting access to ticket holders or the 'right sort' of people is perhaps harder to resist. But we should remember that 'there are negotiations and reactions and resistance to every attempt to sanitise, gentrify and privatise urban leisure spaces' (Spracklen et al., 2013: 168). One way that people have resisted private events is by staging a more public version. This 'cultural resistance' is becoming quite common. In many FIFA World Cup host cities, peoples' World Cups have been staged to provide an alternative event accessible to those excluded from the official version. This strategy is employed in smaller events too. During the controversial Festival of the Sea in Bristol (see Chapter 5), an Anti-Festival of the Sea was staged by local multi-cultural arts groups (Atkinson and Laurier, 1998). These events help to create alternative public space, something that compensates for the temporary loss of official public space.

In Copenhagen the Openhagen movement stages their own events to highlight the increasing privatisation of space: and in doing so they create public space. The 'Pirate Parties' they organise 'transform chosen space into a temporary public open space as a protest against the fact that more and more urban spaces have been monofunctional and locked off' (Pløger, 2010: 857). Between 1999 and 2014, Space Hijackers – a group dedicated to 'battling the constant oppressive encroachment onto public spaces of institutions, corporations and urban planners' – performed a similar role in London (Space Hijackers, 2014).

Previous chapters also highlighted the way that events *securitise* public spaces; by introducing behavioural controls which tighten them. These processes can also be resisted. The work of Frew and McGillivray (2008; 2014) helps us to understand how the structures and meanings imposed on events space can be reconstituted by the actions of event attendees. Their work focuses on fan zones – events that are closely associated with security as controlling people was one of the main justifications for creating them in the first place (see Chapters 3 and 5). Using Deleuze and Guatarri's (1987) terminology, Frew and McGillvray (2014) identify 'lines of flight' in these spaces – where people create alternative spaces through creative and/or subversive actions. For example, during the Munich FIFA Fan Fest in 2006, fans ignored barriers, played and paddled in the lake, climbed trees and 'performed' in various ways that contravened the behavioural controls imposed (Frew and McGillvray, 2008). Surveillance deployed via cameras and large screens was playfully countered by fans using their own devices to record what was happening: fans used their phones to distribute unofficial images of themselves doing unofficial things. In doing so they were 'able to subvert (albeit, temporarily) the imposed disciplines and intended narratives associated with the Fan Park space' (Frew and McGillvray, 2008: 194). The 'sophisticated orchestration' and 'governing gaze' of the event was thus resisted (Frew and McGillvray, 2008: 195). This research and the work of others highlights that major events are more complex than they might seem. Indeed, they might be said to exhibit contradictory roles: large events are both spectacles and moments of grassroots appropriation of space (Lehtovuori, 2010).

Summary

This chapter highlights that there are ways to prevent or reconfigure events that are staged in public spaces. The potential exists for regulation and resistance to address, or at least soften, the problematic effects of some events. There are established regulations and regulatory systems which are designed to protect public spaces and public interests, but these are sometimes ignored or usurped for major event projects. Indeed, the discussion here highlights a variety of problems and issues with the ways regulations are conceived and used. However, the Kensington Gardens example shows that planning authorities can use existing systems and planning policy to block inappropriate events. Resistance movements can also prevent event projects from happening – either in conjunction with official procedures or independently. The Vancouver Indy Car case provides a refreshing example of an event project that was successfully resisted through the effective use and appropriation of discourses by community action groups. However, this chapter also highlights the challenges faced by movements seeking to oppose event projects: these include the way event opponents are dismissed as 'kill joys' or 'party poopers'. The final part of the Chapter emphasises that opportunities to resist events exist during events as well as in the pre-event period. There is emerging recognition of the way events and event spaces can be (re)appropriated by people via the subversion of restrictions, by staging alternative events and through negotiation of official meanings.

9 Conclusions

Introduction

Our urban public spaces are increasingly used, conceived and imagined as venues for organised events. Various examples of this trend are cited in this book including many sport events – a genre that is neglected in the emerging literature on events cities. More events are being staged in central public spaces to generate revenue and imagery for host cities, but also because it provides organisers and their sponsors with opportunities to create spectator and brand experiences. Acknowledging this 'urbanisation' of events is important. It helps us to understand wider trends affecting contemporary cities and the events sector and there are specific implications for the availability of public space.

Analysing the spatial effects of the trends noted here is complicated by the multifaceted ways that public space is produced. Formal public space in cities is produced at one level by planners and managers who conceive and maintain parks, streets and squares. But public spaces are also produced by users. Contrived spaces don't always exhibit public qualities in their lived form and some spaces not normally considered as public spaces do exhibit these qualities. Events play a role in both these contexts: they can be used to animate and loosen contrived public spaces such as parks and squares. They can also provide a framework for the production of public space in sites that aren't normally considered to be public spaces. Indeed, events can help to create public places where public-ness has been eroded – for example in busy roads and commercial high streets.

This all sounds very positive. However, the book also notes more problematic effects. Events can socialise commercial spaces, but they also commercialise public ones. Hence, events can erode public spaces as well as produce them. Formal events can undermine the defining characteristic of public space – its accessibility. By introducing ticketing, physical barriers and other restrictions, events exclude people; effectively privatising the spaces they occupy. Even when event spaces are more accessible physically and financially they can introduce symbolic associations and visual cues that indicate only certain people are welcome. These conclusions echo the sentiments of other writers who feel that events are aimed at middle class consumers and so 'marginalise significant sections of society that are not interested in the events, or lack the financial means to experience them' (Tranter and Keefee, 2004: 182).

Time

Events are, by definition, temporary uses of urban public space. So one key issue that needs to be addressed in this conclusion is whether the effects noted above are temporary too – or whether events have more enduring effects on the availability of urban public space. This book highlights that events can leave a lasting impression on the spaces that host them and there are a number of mechanisms that seem to facilitate these effects. Events can change the meanings attached to urban public spaces. The powerful symbolism associated with events means they can de-stabilise existing meanings. In other words, they can help to de-territorialise fixed spaces and loosen tight ones. Where events involve unusual or unexpected transformations, they highlight the possibilities and potentialities of public spaces, something that may invite new uses and users. However, as Tonkiss (2013) notes, it is a fine line between a 'pioneer use' and an 'urban land grab' and this book highlights how events enclose public spaces and the way they are used as precedents or justifications for further incursions. Where events are regularly hosted in certain public spaces they may become a determined use and a fixed meaning and, in these instances, spaces are re-territorialised rather than de-territorialised. Embedding events as an established function of public space thus restricts transformative effects. The visual imagery attached to events is also an important vehicle for lasting effects. Images of event spaces are recirculated via the media, including social media, allowing their transient role as events venues to become enduring ways that certain spaces are represented and imagined.

This book challenges the view that events staged in temporary venues are time limited phenomena with time limited effects. Some events last for a long time, and/or are repeated regularly and this extends their temporal reach. Staging large events in public spaces means building large structures and restoring sites to their original condition. These tasks mean that events exert a material influence over the spaces they occupy for lengthy periods. Some of the cases analysed here resulted in the closure or part-closure of parks for several months or the closure of streets for multiple days. Notable examples include Grands Prix staged in Singapore and Melbourne, and various sports events staged in London's Royal Parks. These events severely reduce the availability of important public spaces. This book highlights other temporal issues too. The temporary nature of events is often emphasised by those seeking to stage them. Chapter 8 notes how negative effects are often justified because they only involve 'temporary harm' – but large projects can cause long term environmental effects on the spaces they occupy. Various social, symbolic and regulatory effects can also persist over long periods of time.

Different events and different effects

In trying to unravel the way events both animate and denigrate urban public spaces it is important to recognise that most events will involve dual effects. Events which require elusive and expensive tickets still produce or 'eventalise' public space to some extent because of the conviviality engendered and the interactions between attendees. And events that are much more accessible and inclusive will still 'eventify' space – they will inevitably involve some commercialisation, privatisation and securitisation. So the processes of eventalisation and eventification outlined in Chapters 4 and 5 are not separate processes associated with different kinds of events. Instead they are related processes that occur simultaneously. This is reinforced by the fact that the same examples are cited in both chapters – the events staged in Trafalgar Square, London and Central Park, New York for example. That said, this book indicates that certain types of events seem to represent more positive interventions for the spaces that host them. In some instances, the balance between eventalisation and eventification is tipped heavily towards the latter. This conclusion is explored further below.

The urban street festival is an event genre where positive effects seem to accrue, with commercialisation, securitisation and privatisation relatively limited. These festivals help spaces to be more sociable, they encourage interaction, they change the rhythm of the street and they encourage different types of flows. They can also encourage different types of people to use certain public spaces. More research is needed to establish whether these people are more likely to return to those spaces as a result of attending a festival, as that would reinforce their long term value. Street festivals allow people to imagine urban space differently: thus, they encourage potentiality, openness and creativity (Pløger, 2010). It is important to explore why. The accessibility and inclusivity of these events are obviously influential, but two other key characteristics seem to be important too: participation and permeability. By participating in the event and by being able to move around the event; festival goers experience the space differently than they normally would. Events with restricted permeability and participation – e.g. cycle races – will have fewer transformative effects on the spaces they occupy. Although these events are often free to access and are relatively inclusive, spectators are usually restricted in various ways. These events don't allow attendees to flow freely within public space and attendees normally adopt a passive role as the audience for spectacle they are witnessing. However, there are some promising examples of cycling events which have tried to break down the barriers between participants and audiences. Events such as RideLondon have emerged in recent years (Chapter 4), which give people the chance to cycle on closed roads and to participate in the event, as well as to watch elite athletes. This makes the events more fluid and participatory and means they don't merely occupy urban public space; they help to produce it.

At the other end of the spectrum are events which seem to represent detrimental interventions for the spaces that host them. Motor races staged on street circuits and mega-events are obvious examples. Designating these events as problematic shouldn't be interpreted as a criticism of these events per se, more a criticism of how and where these events tend to be staged in the contemporary era. The organisers of mega-events are increasingly utilising urban public spaces – for the events themselves, but also for various augmentations and additional elements that surround them including test events, hospitality areas, training venues and logistical compounds. Many large events staged in public spaces are inherently exclusive, so other events have to be organised alongside them to provide a more public version (e.g. fan zones). These activations are staged in public spaces too. Mega-events are also used as justification to stage more events in the future. The overall result is a domino effect where one event leads to others that are staged in parallel and in series – extending the spatial and temporal reach of events.

Mega-events are increasingly influenced by sponsor and media interests and the deep involvement of these stakeholders can lead to the commercialisation of the spaces occupied. Securitisation, privatisation and commodification effects also accrue from the motives of urban authorities and other place based interests who use these events as place marketing tools and who therefore feel they need to control key messages and orchestrate the eventscape. These problematic effects are inherently linked. To commodify something you first have to secure it – this is something that Giulianotti's (2011) work on English Premier League football illustrates. Even in the context of festivals, commercial success relies on providing security and exclusivity (Waitt, 2008). This control results in a type of brand-scape, where space is regulated to maximise economic returns.

Mega-events denigrate urban public spaces temporarily, but effects can persist beyond the scheduled duration of an event. There are various examples where exceptional arrangements introduced have not been removed once an event has ended. FIFA World Cups 2002–2010 are insightful cases: CCTV cameras introduced in Japan (Wood and Abe, 2011) and Germany (Eick, 2010), and new bylaws to regulate public spaces in South Africa (Roberts, 2010) were retained post-event. These provide examples of the pernicious or insidious effects of events staged in public spaces. The detrimental effects of events contribute to existing processes of commercialisation, privatisation and securitisation that are already affecting the availability of public space in our cities. Therefore, we shouldn't exaggerate the negative effects of events or blame them for introducing these changes. However, some host cities use events deliberately to accelerate these processes or to introduce controversial new arrangements which might otherwise be resisted. This reminds us that commercialisation, privatisation and securitisation aren't imposed on urban governments: the regimes that govern cities are often key agents and advocates of these processes.

Staging the city

Chapter 1 introduced the notion that cities are not merely stages but *staged* and this interpretation has been reaffirmed by the discussion in this book. As Merx (2011: 137) states 'when we conceive of public space as nothing more than a stage . . . we tend to overlook the fact that what is at stake in all these performances is the actual and continuous formation of urban public space itself'. In line with this view, the events outlined in this book have not merely been staged in public spaces; they have helped to (re)produce and (re)configure these spaces. In a less abstract sense, this book also demonstrates that the city is not merely the stage, context, or backdrop for events. The role of the city and city space is more fundamental than that. For event organisers, using urban public space not only

Figure 9.1 Staging the city. Glasgow's George Square.

adds value, it is often fundamental to the viability of their events. In many of the cases cited here, it was the opportunity to experience an event staged in the city that was the core attraction; whether it be a film screening in a park, a rock concert in a square or a sport event staged on the street. Following the argument discussed at the beginning of this book, the city is not merely the context for consumption, it is the entity consumed. Event organisers and their sponsors are keen to capitalise on the physical sites and visual imagery that centrally located public spaces offer. They also covet the connotations that are attached to some urban spaces. Ultimately sponsors and event organisers are attracted by the authenticity offered by placing events in city centre sites: this givens them credibility and an official status they would otherwise struggle to command.

In an era of public sector budget cuts (i.e. austerity), urban authorities are particularly keen to hire their spaces as event venues. Some people view this as representing an inappropriate commodification of these spaces or a strategy that is deliberately pursued to deter alternative uses – particularly where sites are renowned for political activism. However, others like the introduction of new uses for spaces which might otherwise remain austere and/or moribund. The final few chapters of this book are quite negative, but staging events in public spaces isn't inherently a bad thing. Indeed, there is evidence in this book and in other texts (e.g. Tallon et al., 2006) that citizens want more events to be staged. Events initiatives will always divide opinion, but if we accept that public spaces will be increasingly hired out as event venues, one practical concern is whether public authorities are undervaluing their assets. Public spaces are hired by private event organisers but the fees charged do not necessarily represent the negative externalities incurred. Rather than staging an extensive programme of commercial events it might be better for cities to stage fewer of these occasions but charge higher prices. This balances accessibility and the requirements for revenue. It seems unreasonable to stage regular succession of commercial events in public spaces, especially if commercial operators are underpaying for the use of these sites. Ultimately, many issues would be resolved if public spaces were funded properly using public finance. This would ease the threat of commercialisation; and would allow events to be used more discerningly - as ways to achieve greater public-ness rather than as revenue generators.

Revenue is just one of several key drivers of the trend to use public spaces as event venues. Staging the city for international audiences is another explanation and one that is often at the root of many of the controversies noted into this book. It is notoriously difficult to reconcile local uses with more expansive (global) objectives. Van Deusen (2002) highlights this, in making the argument that public space design increasingly serves wider interests, rather than the local user. In pursuit of city marketing and tourism objectives, spaces are reoriented to global audiences, something that can conflict with their symbolic and physical accessibility as local amenities. This tension is discussed by Inroy (2000) in his exploration of a new urban park created in Glasgow to mark the city's status as European City of Culture in 1990. The local community wanted a functional space, but the park authorities wanted one which would achieve more ambitious objectives. Inroy (2000: 32) notes that the Park was ultimately designed 'as a vehicle for the promotion of city wide activities and for international and non-local entertainment'. This reflects the prevailing outcome, where external priorities and exchange value usurp local interests and use value.

Potential conflicts between local use/local identities and external objectives/ global imagery can partly be understood by acknowledging the differences between spaces and scapes. Space is produced by designers, but also by users. This contrasts with 'scapes'; these are orchestrated and unified scenes; produced culturally, rather than socially. Space is (partly) produced incidentally via social relations that happen at a particular point in time, whereas scapes are consciously manufactured. The city panorama is the archetypal cityscape: an image of the city set up within the city itself (Boyer, 1992). In this book, various 'scapes' have been mentioned: cityscapes, landscapes, cultural scapes, streetscapes, mediascapes, sense scapes, brandscapes, experiencescapes and, perhaps most significantly, 'eventscapes'. In the context of events staged in public spaces, eventscapes represent instances where events are used to construct, capture and circulate a specific urban imaginary; a staged and enlivened cityscape that simultaneously provokes memorable experiences and spectacular media images.

The Greenwich Park case provides a very good example of an eventscape, but other examples are examined in this book too – in Berlin, New York, Canberra, Singapore and Belfast. Such 'eventscaping' is not merely driven by city interests, but also by corporate ones; private companies benefit from their association with enlivened cityscapes and they are partly responsible for the production and circulation of related imagery. Regardless of the fascinating representations that are produced, the most important consideration is the effects that these eventscapes have. Cities feel that they can encourage tourism and other forms of inward investment to the spaces represented, but also to the city more generally. However, the production of eventscapes has implications for the availability of public space as it can interfere with the experience and meaning of urban space for local users. Producing these eventscapes excludes and constrains local users physically and symbolically, and these effects can persist beyond the duration of the event. Efforts to configure eventscapes sit awkwardly with the normal functions of urban public spaces as places to meet, linger, play or protest. Indeed, these uses are deliberately displaced by event interests who worry that they interfere with the images they want to portray. In staging the city, the public city is sacrificed for the sake of publicity.

Event discourses

A key theme that pervades the latter sections of this book is the significance of certain event discourses. Recurring rhetoric and narratives are used to justify the appropriation of public spaces as event venues. The same discourses are appropriated to resist this trend and to counter any resistance. Certain discourses feature prominently the cases discussed in this book; most notably legacy. Events in public spaces are staged in temporary venues, but more permanent installations have materialised because of pressure to deliver physical legacies. The discourse of legacy is linked to temporal language: rhetoric emphasising an event's irregularity or temporary status is common. This language is deployed by advocates of staging events in public spaces but it is also used by those opposing this practice. For example, within the contemporary 'legacy' discourse building temporary venues which are dismantled after an event is often criticised as wasteful (see Chapters 6 and 7, plus Reid, 2007). Accessibility is also a key discourse that is used to justify staging events in central, public spaces. Organisers claim that placing events in city centres allows the events (and the activities they represent) to reach a wider audience. A discourse of accessibility in this context is also adopted by opponents who highlight the way these events reduce the accessibility of the spaces they occupy. Framing is also an important mechanism through which event projects are pursued. Event advocates frame events as 'festive', 'joyous' occasions, providing a very positive message around which stakeholders can coalesce. This frame also means critics can be dismissed as party poopers or killjoys.

Event discourses are often deployed strategically to divert attention away from some of the detrimental aspects of staging events in public spaces. One of the most recurring discourses revolves around the distinction of events and cities as 'world class'. A wide range of events are justified by the fact that they are 'world class', and in a global economy, cities feel the need to prove that they too are 'world class'. This phraseology and the ideology it promotes help us to understand how cities justify event projects generally, but it seems specifically relevant to event projects programmed in public spaces. This was emphasised by a recent letter published in London's Evening Standard newspaper which supported the increased use of the city's parks, streets and squares for major events despite the disruption this is known to cause. The letter put it simply: 'world class events need world class stages' (Parr, 2013).

Events and the production of loose, open spaces

Franck and Stevens' (2007) notion of loose space is used in this book to help understand what 'good' public spaces might be and how events might help or hinder efforts to produce such spaces. Therefore it is worth reflecting on the validity and implications of this application. The very idea of loose space as that which does not have a prescribed use (or user) contradicts some established ideas about public spaces and the reasons for their supposed decline. For example, some commentators note how many public spaces have been under- or mis- used because there was too little regard for what space was for (Cowan, 2005). The approach adopted in this book inherently rejects this explanation. Public spaces often lack public-ness because their functions are overly determined, rather than because they are too vaguely defined.

When inclusive events are staged irregularly and creatively, they can help to produce loose space. This type of strategy promotes unpredictability and heterogeneity - key characteristics of loose space (Franck and Stevens, 2007). However, when events become embedded and expected features, they lose their capacity to loosen public space. Accessible (i.e. non-ticketed) events which are staged in spaces not normally used for events can help to loosen those spaces. These events provide a framework in which people behave differently and this is important because 'people create looseness' (Franck and Stevens, 2007: 15). The book demonstrates that events can facilitate new uses and users for contrived places which have overly determined uses and prescribed users (e.g. formal parks). Although spaces are loosened via heterogeneous use, social relations and human practices, the managerial and material dimensions of space are important too. For many street based events, closing roads to traffic provides a foundation for the production of public space. The case of the Champs-Elysées discussed at length in Chapter 4 provides a good example (Deroy and Clegg, 2012). Koch and Latham's (2011) research about a more mundane street space in London showed that material improvements to the space were required to allow these events to be staged. Both these examples demonstrate that permeable, participatory events can create looser spaces, but ticketed, commercial events can have the opposite effect. According to Franck and Stevens (2007), tight space is 'aesthetically and behaviourally controlled' and defined by its 'certainty, homogeneity and order'. These qualities characterise the spaces created by ticketed events and the production of commercial eventscapes in general. However, we should remember that people resist and negotiate the aesthetic, commercial and behavioural controls imposed by events. We should also remember that, despite their exclusivity, these events provide enormous fun for the people who are able to access them.

Alongside loose space, the idea of open space is a significant theme in this book. Many of the cases discussed are examples of open spaces, as well as public ones. Open space has a double meaning – the term refers to parts of a city that remain free from urban development and buildings, but this book highlights that other kinds of openness are important too. A truly open space is one that is inviting, accessible and flexible – in other words, one that exhibits potentiality – and there is evidence that events can help encourage these qualities. However, many commercial events staged in open spaces represent enclosures; they physically close open spaces, but they also close them symbolically to certain users and uses. Because many urban parks are now used for commercial events so regularly, it is debateable whether we should still see them as open spaces. Regular commercial events mean people are excluded physically, financially and symbolically from urban parks and even when people can access these events, they are subjected to strict behavioural codes. In its new guise as a venue for ticketed events Jenkins (2013a) feels 'Hyde Park is no more open to all than the Ritz Hotel'.

Alongside the application of ideas about loose and open spaces, the main conceptual contribution of this book is the way it progresses understanding of the urbanisation of events and the eventisation of space. Eventisation can be located within the broader notion of urban festivalisation (Chapter 3) but represents a more focused process which comprises the dual processes of eventalisation and eventification. Eventalisation involves the production and revitalisation of public space via the use of events, whereas eventification refers to the way events commodify public spaces; and/or contribute to their commercialisation, privatisation and securitisation. These terms have been developed, used and applied by other authors (Jakob, 2013; Pløger, 2010, Spracklen et al., 2013). However, this book has clarified, organised and synthesised these ideas into a coherent conceptual framework that can be deployed, tested and challenged by other researchers.

The city as venue

It is also worth reflecting more widely on the significance of the trends noted in this book. In the twenty-first century the modern distinction between event venues and urban public space has been eroded. Our public spaces are becoming more like venues in terms of their function, but also in terms of their regulation, management and design. Events have been taken out of traditional venues into public spaces but they have brought their regulatory systems with them. Hagemann (2010) notes how the football stadium has become a 'spatial prototype' – its regulatory conditions are now projected into city spaces more widely. In other words, the way cities are regulated is becoming more like the way venues are regulated. Our city centres are not only being used as event venues, and experienced as event venues, they are being managed like event venues – with restrictions imposed on where we can go and what we can do in 'public' spaces. This is most visibly manifested when official events are actually staged – but it extends spatially and temporally beyond these events into the everyday life of the city. The way our cities are slowly morphing into event venues is not just about management, there is a design element too. City centres are now configured as spaces that can stage official events. The landscaping of parks, the configuration of streets and the lay-out of squares is increasingly undertaken with events in mind.

Limitations and recommendations for future research

In drawing the conclusions outlined above, some of the limitations of this book need to be acknowledged. These fall into two main categories: the scope of the book and the methods employed. This book deliberately focuses on events staged in parks, streets, squares, but this means other types of public spaces are neglected e.g. waterfronts, greenways and various 'second tier' public spaces identified in Chapter 2. The orientation of the case studies in the later chapters means that parks are given more attention than streets and squares. In many ways parks are representative of public spaces generally, but this focus obviously skews the book towards some of their particular issues and characteristics. Similarly, although the book covers a wide range of event cases in multiple cities, the focus is mainly prominent spaces in global and capital cities and it is not clear whether many of the trends noted are also applicable to lower profile spaces in smaller cities. The book focuses on large, developed world cities, mainly in the UK, but also in Canada, Australia and the US. More research is required on cities in the global south that are also beginning to deploy events in urban policy.

There are also several methodological limitations. A range of techniques were employed to gather evidence for this book including observation work (attending events and meetings about events, plus observing key spaces), detailed scrutiny of secondary sources, as well as more traditional primary research. This provided a general overview of key issues, as well as detailed consideration of a small number of case studies. However, there is clearly a need to try and explore the issues raised in more detail using more nuanced methods. In particular, more robust research is required to examine the social interactions that occur during events, and the ways that social media affect these interactions. As public spaces and events are phenomena partly created in the moment through the spontaneous practices of participants, detailed phenomenological analyses would be insightful. The discussion of the temporal dimensions of events and their effects also high-lights the potential value of longitudinal research which tracks urban change over extended periods. Finally, although this book employs a basic form of discourse analysis involving 'scrutiny of rhetoric and turns of phrase' to uncover narratives and the framing of issues (Lees, 2004: 102), it is suggested that future research adopts a more sophisticated mode of discourse analysis.

Final comments

Events in the City has examined events in a critical manner and it is hoped that the book becomes part of a wider sets of texts dedicated to critical events studies and the geography of events. The book tries to assess controversial issues in a balanced and fair way. The criticisms included are predominantly concerned with the way commercially oriented events are staged in public spaces; and whether this is appropriate given the very important role these spaces play in urban life. They should not be read as criticisms of events in general or commercial events in particular.

How worried should we be that our public spaces are increasingly used as event venues? It seems churlish to condemn events which provide a great deal of enjoyment and which challenge established uses of urban space. Events make many public spaces more interesting and there is obviously a danger of over-exaggerating the 'threat' they pose. Nevertheless, it is prudent to be wary of the trend to use public spaces as venues. So far, opposition has come from an alliance of the conservative right (worried about inappropriate development) and the anti-corporate left (worried about privatisation/commercialisation). But as events infiltrate a wider range of spaces in a greater number of cities we might see more resistance from the silent majority.

The trend of using public spaces for events seems likely to continue for several reasons. Cities are increasingly obsessed with image and a lack of finance in an age of austerity means municipal governments are desperately seeking ways to generate revenue from public assets. The trend is also set to continue because turning urban spaces into venues is part of wider processes affecting our cities. It is emerging as a key component of the experience economy: one which allows both products and cities to be staged.

References

Addley, E. (2014). Tickled pink. Ulster gears up for Giro d'Italia. *The Guardian*, 6th May, 2014, p. 3.

Agamben, G. (2005). *The State of Exception*. Chicago: Chicago University Press.

Amin, A. and Thrift, N. (2002). *Cities: Reimagining the Urban*. Cambridge: Polity Press.

Anwar, S. and Sohail, M. (2004). Festival tourism in the United Arab Emirates: first-time versus repeat visitor perceptions. *Journal of Vacation Marketing*, 10(2), pp. 16–170.

Askwith, R. (2014). *Running Free: A Runner's Journey Back to Nature*. London: Vintage.

Aslet, C. (1999). *Greenwich Millennium: The 2000-Year Story of Greenwich*. London: Fourth Estate.

Atkinson, D. and Laurier, E. (1998). A sanitised city? Social exclusion at Bristol's 1996 International Festival of the Sea. *Geoforum*, 29(2), pp. 199–206.

Banerjee, T. (2001). The future of public space: beyond invented streets and reinvented places. *Journal of the American Planning Association*, 67(1), pp. 9–24.

Barbican (2013). Beyond Barbican Summer 2013. Available at: http://www.barbican.org.uk/beyond/ (last accessed 1st June 2015).

Batty, M. (2002). Thinking about cities as spatial events. *Environment and Planning B: Planning and Design*, 29(1), pp. 1–2.

Bauman, Z. (1998). On glocalization: or globalization for some, localization for some others. *Thesis Eleven*, 54(1), pp. 37–49.

Bauman, Z. (2000). *Liquid Modernity*. Cambridge: Polity Press.

Beard, M. (2014). Waterslide in Waterloo? £2m to transform London's streets. *Evening Standard*, 24th March 2014, p. 9.

Bélanger, A. (2000). Sport venues and the spectacularization of urban spaces in North America: the case of the Molson Centre in Montreal. *International Review for the Sociology of Sport*, 35(3), pp. 378–397.

Belghazi, T. (2006). Festivalization of urban space in Morocco. *Critique: Critical Middle Eastern Studies*, 15(1), pp. 97–107.

Bell, C. and Lyall, J. (2002). *The Accelerated Sublime: Landscape, Tourism, and Identity*. Westport, CT: Greenwood Publishing Group.

Benford, R. and Snow, D. (2000). Framing processes and social movements: an overview and assessment. *Annual Review of Sociology*, 26(1), pp. 611–639.

Bishop, P. and Williams, L. (2012). *The Temporary City*. Abingdon: Routledge.

Blackheath Society (2014). *Executive Summary - Impact of OnBlackheath Event, Sept 2014*. Available at: http://www.blackheath.org/documents/OnBlackheathReport-Summarywith Comments.pdf (last accessed 1st June 2015).

Blackhurst, C. (2015). Business interview. John Reid, Live Nation. *Evening Standard*, 6th July 2015, p. 44.

Boffey, D. (2014). Would you pay park tax to keep the grass cut, crime down – and your house price up? *The Observer*, 17th August 2014, p. 19.

Bold, J. (2000). *Greenwich. An Architectural History of the Royal Hospital for Seamen and the Queen's House*. London: English Heritage.

Bone, I. (2014). If you tolerate this . . . OnBlackheath. Blog entry. 16th April 2014. https://ianbone.wordpress.com/ (last accessed 1st June 2015).

Boyer, C. (1992). Cities for sale: merchandising history of the South Street Seaport. In M. Sorkin. (Ed.) *Variations on a Theme Park*. New York: Hill and Wang, pp. 181–204.

Boykoff, J. and Fussey, P. (2014). London's shadow legacies: security and activism at the 2012 Olympics. *Contemporary Social Science*, 9(2), pp. 253–270.

Boyle, M. (1997). Civic boosterism in the politics of local economic development– 'institutional positions' and 'strategic orientations' in the consumption of hallmark events. *Environment and Planning A*, 29(11), pp. 1975–1997.

BPTW (2013). *Kensington Gardens and Perks Field, London W8. Planning Statement.* Available at: http://www.rbkc.gov.uk/planningandbuildingcontrol.aspx (last accessed 1st June 2015).

Brandalism (2015). *About.* Available at http://www.brandalism.org.uk/the-project (last accessed 1st June 2015).

Brewer, J. (1997). *The Pleasures of the Imagination: English Culture in the Eighteenth Century*. London: Harper Collins.

Brighenti, A. M. (2010). On territorology: towards a general science of territory. *Theory, Culture and Society*, 27(1), pp. 52–72.

British Equestrian Federation (2013). Letter to Nathan Barrett (RBKC). 15th January 2013. Available at: http://www.rbkc.gov.uk/planningandbuildingcontrol.aspx (last accessed 1st June 2015).

Brown, G. and Smith, A. (2012). London 2012: Olympic venues and the spectator experience. *Olympic Review*, 85, pp. 61–63.

Brown, G., Chalip, L., Jago, L. and Mules, T. (2002). The Sydney Olympics and Brand Australia. In N. Morgan, A. Pritchard, and R. Pride (Eds.) *Destination Branding: Creating the Unique Destination Proposition*. Oxford: Butterworth-Heinemann, pp. 163–185.

Burgess, J., Harrison, C. and Limb, M. (1988). People, parks and the urban green: a study of popular meanings and values for open spaces in the city. *Urban Studies*, 25(6), pp. 455–473.

Cairns, G. (2014). The hybridization of sight in the hybrid architecture of sport: the effects of television on stadia and spectatorship. *Sport in Society*, (ahead-of-print), pp. 1–16.

Campbell Reith (2011). *Environmental Impact Statement Volume 1 Chapter 2 Proposed Development*. Part of Planning Application 11/1765/F Formation of a new equestrian centre. Available at: http://www.royalgreenwich.gov.uk/info/200074/planning (last accessed 1st June 2015).

Canadian Broadcasting Corporation (2010). Hastings Park masterplan adopted. Available at: http://www.cbc.ca/news/canada/british-columbia/hastings-park-master-plan-adopted-1.916203#socialcomments (last accessed 1st June 2015).

Carey, P. (2013). Letter to *Evening Standard*, 18th September, 2013, p. 47.

Carmona, M. (2010). Contemporary public space, part two: classification. *Journal of Urban Design*, 15(2), pp. 157–173.

Carter, T. (2006). Introduction. The sport of cities, spectacle and the economy of appearances. *City and Society*, 18(2), pp. 151–158.

Chalip, L., Green, B. and Hill, B. (2003). Effects of sport event media on destination image and intention to visit. *Journal of Sport Management*, 17, pp. 214–234.

Change.org (2013). Please help protect Kensington Gardens from commercial development! Available at: https://www.change.org/p/please-help-protect-kensington-gardens-from-commercial-development (last accessed 1st June 2015).

Chatterton, P. and Unsworth, R. (2004). Making space for culture(s) in Boomtown. Some alternative futures for development, ownership and participation in Leeds city centre. *Local Economy*, 19(4), pp. 361–379.

Chiesura, A. (2004). The role of urban parks for the sustainable city. *Landscape and Urban Planning*, 68(1), pp. 129–138.

City of Vancouver (2013). Map of master plan areas for development. Available at: http://vancouver.ca/home-property-development/map-of-master-plan-park-areas-for-development.aspx (last accessed 1st June 2015)

City of Westminster (2012). Planning and City Development Committee 10 May 2012. *Report of Strategic Director Built Environment. Subject of Report: Hyde Park.* Available at: https://www.westminster.gov.uk/planning (last accessed 1st June 2015).

City of Westminster (undated a). Guidelines for the planning of events in the City of Westminster. Available at: https://www.westminster.gov.uk/events (last accessed 1st June 2015).

City of Westminster (undated b). *Victoria Embankment Gardens*. Available at: https://www.westminster.gov.uk/sites/default/files/uploads/workspace/assets/publications/Victoria-Embankment-Gardens-1295952233.pdf. (last accessed 1st June 2015).

Coleman, R. (2003). Images from a neoliberal city: the state, surveillance and social control. *Critical Criminology*, 12, pp. 21–42.

Colomb, C. (2012). *Staging the New Berlin: Place Marketing and the Politics of Urban Reinvention Post-1989*. Abingdon: Routledge.

Conway, H. (1991). *People's Parks. The Design and Development of Public Parks in Britain*. Cambridge: Cambridge University Press.

Cook, P. (2015). Letter to *Evening Standard*, 15th July 2015, p. 49.

Cowan, R. (2005). *The Dictionary of Urbanism*. Tisbury: Streetwise Press.

Cuckson, P. (2009). What happens if Greenwich park does not get planning permission? Blog, 9th December 2009. Available at http://www.insidethegames.biz/articles/8369/pippa-cuckson-what-happens-if-greenwich-park-does-not-get-planning-permission (last accessed 1st June 2015).

The Daily Telegraph (2009). Climate Change camp formed at Blackheath. *The Daily Telegraph (online)*, 27th August 2009. Available at: http://www.telegraph.co.uk/news/earth/environment/climatechange/6094838/Climate-Change-camp-formed-at-Black-Heath.html (last accessed 1st June 2015).

Dashper, K. (2012). The Olympic experience from a distance: the case of the equestrian events at the 2008 Games. In R. Shipway and A. Fyall (Eds.) *International Sports Events: Impacts, Experiences and Identities*. Abingdon: Routledge, pp. 141–153.

Davis, R. and Marvin, G. (2004). *Venice, the Tourist Maze: a Cultural Critique of the World's Most Touristed City*. Oakland, CA: Univ of California Press.

Dear, G. (2013). Letter to *The Greenwich Mercury*, January 19th 2013, p. 11.

Debord, G. (1984). *Society of the Spectacle*. Detroit: Black & Red.

Degen, M. (2003). Fighting for the global catwalk: formalizing public life in Castlefield (Manchester) and diluting public life in el Raval (Barcelona). *International Journal of Urban and Regional Research*, 27(4), pp. 867–880.

Deleuze, G. and Guattari, F. (1987*). A Thousand Plateaus. Capitalism and Schizophrenia.* Minnesota: University of Minnesota Press.

Denters, B. and Mossberger, K. (2006). Building blocks for a methodology for comparative urban political research. *Urban Affairs Review*, 41(4), pp. 550–571.

Department of Communities and Local Government (2007). *Outdoor advertisements and signs: a guide for advertisers,* June 2007. London: DCLG.

Deroy, X. and Clegg, S. (2012). Contesting the Champs-Elysées. *Journal of Change Management*, 12(3), pp. 355–373.

Dickens, C. (1836, 1996). *Sketches by Boz.* London: Penguin.

Dovey, K. and Polakit, K. (2007). Urban slippage: smooth and striated streetscapes in Bangkok. In K. Franck and Q. Stevens (Eds.) *Loose Space: Possibility and Diversity in Urban Life.* Abingdon: Routledge, pp. 113–131.

Duman, A. (2012). Legacy as permanent branding. In H. Powell and I. Marrero-Guillermon (Eds.) *The Art of Dissent: Adventures in London's Olympic State.* London: Marshgate Press, pp. 56–64.

Edensor, T. and Kothari, U. (2004). Sweetening colonialism: a Mauritian themed resort. In D. Median Lasansky and B. McClaren (Eds.) *Architecture and Tourism: Perception, Performance and Place.* Oxford: Berg, pp. 189–205.

Edizel, O., Evans, G. and Dong, H. (2014). Dressing up London. In V. Grginov (Ed.) *Handbook of the London 2012 Olympic and Paralympic Games, Volume 2.* Abingdon: Routledge, pp. 19–35.

Edwards, S. (2014). Former Royal Parks head of events launches new business. Event Magazine. Available at: http://www.eventmagazine.co.uk/former-royal-parks-head-events-launches-new-business/business/article/1227167 (last accessed 1st June 2015).

Ehrenreich, B. (2007). *Dancing in the Streets: A History of Collective Joy.* London: Granta.

Eick, V. (2010). A neoliberal sports event? FIFA from the Estadio Nacional to the fan mile. *City*, 14(3), pp. 278–297.

Ercan, M. (2010). Less public than before. Public space improvement in Newcastle City Centre. In A. Madanipour (Ed.) *Whose Public Space?* Abingdon: Routledge, pp. 21–50.

Featherstone, M. (1991). The body in consumer culture. In M. Featherstone, M. Hepworth, and B. Turner (Eds.) *The Body: Social Process and Cultural Theory.* London: Sage, pp. 170–196.

Flecha, A., Lott, W., Lee, T., Moital, M. and Edwards, J. (2010). Sustainability of events in urban historic centers: the case of Ouro Preto, Brazil. *Tourism and Hospitality Planning and Development*, 7(2), pp. 131–143.

Flusty, S. (1997). Building paranoia. In N. Ellin (Ed.) *Architecture of Fear.* New York: Princeton Architectural Press, pp. 47–59.

Foley, M. and McPherson, G. (2007). Glasgow's Winter Festival: can cultural leadership serve the common good? *Managing Leisure*, 12(2–3), pp. 143–156.

Foley, M., McGillivray, D., and McPherson, G. (2012). *Event Policy: From Theory to Strategy.* Abingdon: Routledge.

Franck, K. A. and Stevens, Q. (2007). Tying down loose space. In K. Franck and Q. Stevens (Eds.) *Loose Space: Possibility and Diversity in Urban Life.* Abingdon: Routledge, pp. 1–34.

Frew, M. and McGillivray, D. (2008). Exploring hyper-experiences: performing the fan at Germany 2006. *Journal of Sport and Tourism*, 13(3), pp. 181–198.

Frew, M. and McGillivray, D. (2014). From Fan Parks to Live Sites: mega events and the territorialisation of urban space. *Urban Studies*, ahead of print.

Games Monitor (2015). About Games Monitor. Available at: http://www.gamesmonitor. org.uk/about (last accessed 1st June 2015).

Garvin, A. (2011). *Public Parks: The Key to Livable Communities.* New York: WW Norton.

Gehl, J. (1987). *Life Between Buildings.* New York: Van Nostrand Reinhold.

Germain, A. and Rose, D. (2000). *Montréal: The Quest for a Metropolis*. Chichester: John Wiley & Sons.

Gibson, C. and Homan, S. (2004). Urban redevelopment, live music and public space: cultural performance and the re-making of Marrickville. *International Journal of Cultural Policy*, 10(1), pp. 67–84.

Giddings, B., Charlton, J. and Horne, M. (2011). Public squares in European city centres. *Urban Design International*, 16(3), pp. 202–212.

Giulianotti, R. (2011). Sport mega events, urban football carnivals and securitised commodification. The case of the English Premier League. *Urban Studies*, 48(15), pp. 3293–3310.

Global Champions Tour (2014). London Mayor Boris Johnson welcomes the return of Longines Global Champions Tour. Available at: http://www.globalchampionstour.com/events/2014/london/news/1141/london-mayor-boris-johnson-welcomes-the-return-of-longines-global-champions-tour/ (last accessed 1st June 2015).

Gormley, A. (2009). *One & Other, Fourth Plinth Commission, Trafalgar Square, London*. Available at: http://www.antonygormley.com/show/item-view/id/2277 (last accessed 1st June 2015).

Graham, S. and Marvin, S. (2001). *Splintering Urbanism: Networked Infrastructures, Technological Mobilities and the Urban Condition*. Abingdon: Routledge.

Greater London Authority (2014). Fees for the use of Trafalgar Square and Parliament Square Garden 2014/2015. Available at: https://www.london.gov.uk/priorities/arts-culture/trafalgar-square/managing-trafalgar-square/booking-trafalgar-square (last accessed 1st June 2015).

Green, B., Costa, C. and Fitzgerald, M. (2003). Marketing the host city: analyzing exposure generated by a sport event. *International Journal of Sports Marketing and Sponsorship*, 4(4), pp. 335–52.

Greenwich Council (2006). *Greenwich Unitary Development Plan*. Adopted 20th July 2006. London: Greenwich Council.

Greenwich Council (2011). *Decision Notice for Planning Application 11/1765/F. 4th November, 2011*. Available at: http://www.royalgreenwich.gov.uk/info/200074/planning (last accessed 1st June 2015).

Greenwich Forum (2013). *General Discussions*. Available at: http://forum.greenwich.co.uk/ (last accessed 1st June 2015).

Hagemann, A. (2010). From the stadium to the fan zone: host cities in a state of emergency. *Soccer & Society*, 11(6), pp. 723–736.

Harcup, T. (2000). Re-imaging a post-industrial city: the Leeds St Valentine's Fair as a civic spectacle. *City*, 4(2), pp.215–231.

Haringey Borough Council (2013). *Finsbury Park Outdoor Events Policy Review. Consultation Report*. Available at: http://www.minutes.haringey.gov.uk/documents/s49192/Haringey%20Outdoor%20Events%20Policy%20-%20APPENDIX%20C.pdf. (last accessed 1st June 2015).

Harvey, D. (1989). *The Condition of Postmodernity*. Oxford: Blackwell.

Hayes, G. and Horne, J. (2011). Sustainable development, shock and awe? London 2012 and civil society. *Sociology*, 45(5), pp. 749–764.

Heathcote, E. (2012). Legacy or Lunacy? *The Financial Times (online)*, 20th January 2012. Available at: http://www.ft.com/cms/s/2/0e46376c-4071-11e1-8fcd-00144feab49a.html (last accessed 1st June 2015).

Henderson, J., Foo, K., Lim, H. and Yip, S. (2010). Sports events and tourism: the Singapore formula one grand prix. *International Journal of Event and Festival Management*, 1(1), pp. 60–73.

Hobsbawm, E. (1983). Mass-producing traditions: Europe, 1870–1914. In E. Hobsbawm and T. Ranger. (Ed.) *The Invention of Tradition*. Cambridge: Cambridge University Press, pp. 263–308.

Horne, J. and Whannel, G. (2012). *Understanding the Olympics*. Abingdon: Routledge.

Hughes, G. (1999). Urban revitalization: the use of festive time strategies. *Leisure Studies*, 18(2), pp. 119–135.

Hyde, M. (2012). Olympics 2012: in Greenwich, it's country o'clock. *The Guardian*, 31st July 2012, p. 6.

Ingle, S. (2015). Greg Rutherford defies cold weather to win Manchester City Games title. *The Guardian (online)*, 9th May 2015. Available at: http://www.theguardian.com/sport/2015/may/09/athletics-greg-rutherford-dina-asher-smith-manchester-city-games (last accessed 1st June 2015).

Inglis, S. (2014). *Played in London. Charting the Heritage of a City at Play*. London: English Heritage.

Innes, G., Morton., S. Hyde Peters, Z., Buttery, C., and Pulstow, R (2013). Letter to *Evening Standard*, 18th September 2013, p. 47.

Inroy, N. (2000). Urban regeneration and public space: the story of an urban park. *Space and Polity*, 4(1), pp. 23–40.

Iveson, K. (2012). Branded cities: outdoor advertising, urban governance, and the outdoor media landscape. *Antipode*, 44(1), pp. 151–174.

Jacobs, J. (1961). *The Death and Life of Great American Cities*. London: Vintage.

Jakob, D. (2013). The eventification of place: urban development and experience consumption in Berlin and New York City. *European Urban and Regional Studies*, 20(4), pp. 447–459.

Jamieson, K. (2004). Edinburgh. The festival gaze and its boundaries. *Space and Culture*, 7(1), pp. 64–75.

Jefferson, E. (1970). *The Woolwich Story, 1890–1965*. London: Woolwich & District Antiquarian Society.

Jenkins, S. (2012). The craving for massive live events is ruining our cities. *The Guardian*, 18th July 2012, p. 27.

Jenkins, S. (2013a). Our open spaces aren't commodities – give us them back. *Evening Standard*, 2nd July 2013, p. 14.

Jenkins, S. (2013b). We play second fiddle to Boris's sports stunts. *Evening Standard*, 17th September 2013, p. 14.

Johansson, M. and Kociatkiewicz, J. (2011). City festivals: creativity and control in staged urban experiences. *European Urban and Regional Studies*, 18(4), pp. 392–405.

Kamvasinou, K. (2006). Vague parks: the politics of late twentieth-century urban landscapes. *Architectural Research Quarterly*, 10(3–4), pp. 255–262.

Karageorghis, C. (2014). Run to the Beat: sport and music for the masses. *Sport in Society*, 17(3), pp. 433–447.

Kennelly, J. and Watt, P. (2011). Sanitizing public space in Olympic host cities: the spatial experiences of marginalized youth in 2010 Vancouver and 2012 London. *Sociology*, 45(5), pp. 765–781.

Klauser, F. (2012). Interpretative flexibility of the event-city: security, branding and urban entrepreneurialism at the European Football Championships 2008. *International Journal of Urban and Regional Research*, 36(5), pp. 1039–1052.

Klauser, F. (2013). Spatialities of security and surveillance: managing spaces, separations and circulations at sport mega events. *Geoforum*, 49, pp. 289–298.

Klingmann, A. (2007). *Brandscapes: Architecture in the Experience Economy*. Cambridge, MA: MIT Press.

Koch, R. and Latham, A. (2012). Rethinking urban public space: accounts from a junction in West London. *Transactions of the Institute of British Geographers*, 37(4), pp. 515–529.

Kolamo, S. and Vuolteenaho, J. (2013). The interplay of mediascapes and cityscapes in a sports mega-event. The power dynamics of place branding in the 2010 FIFA World Cup in South Africa. *International Communication Gazette*, 75(5–6), pp. 502–520.

Lamond, I. and Spracklen, K. (Eds.) (2015). *Protests as Events: Politics, Activism and Leisure*. Oxford: Rowman & Littlefield.

Law, L. (2002). Defying disappearance: cosmopolitan public spaces in Hong Kong. *Urban Studies*, 39(9), pp. 1625–1645.

Lee, S. (2012). The slow death of the Edinburgh Fringe. *The Guardian (online)*, 30th July 2012. Available at: http://www.theguardian.com/culture/2012/jul/30/stewart-lee-slow-death-edinburgh-fringe (last accessed 1st June 2015).

Lees, L. (2004). Urban geography: discourse analysis and urban research. *Progress in Human Geography*, 28(1), pp. 101–107.

Leese, R. (2015). The view from Manchester. *The Observer*, 17th May 2015.

Lefebvre, H. (1991). *The Production of Space*. Oxford: Blackwell.

Lehtovuori, P. (2010). *Experience and Conflict: The Production of Urban Space*. Farnham: Ashgate.

Lejlimdawwal (2014). *Notte Bianca, Valletta*. Available at: http://lejlimdawwal.org/about-us/ (last accessed 1st March 2015).

Lloyd, K. and Auld, C. (2003). Leisure, public space and quality of life in the urban environment. *Urban Policy and Research*, 21(4), pp. 339–356.

London 2012 (2004). *Candidate File. Part 1: Olympic Games Concept and Legacy*. Available at: http://webarchive.nationalarchives.gov.uk/20070305103412/http:/www.london2012.com/news/publications/candidate-file.php (last accessed 1st June 2015).

London Borough of Greenwich (2011). *Borough of Greenwich Ward Profiles*. Available at: http://www.royalgreenwich.gov.uk/downloads/200088/statistics_and_census_information (last accessed 1st June 2015).

London Borough of Lewisham (2015). *Blackheath Events Policy 2011–2016*. December 2011 (amended January 2015). London: Lewisham.

London Development Agency (2009). *London Tourism Action Plan 2009–2013*. London: LDA.

Love, M. (2014). Running Free review. *The Guardian (online)*, 28th February 2014. Available at: http://www.theguardian.com/lifeandstyle/the-running-blog/2014/feb/28/running-free-richard-askwith-review-martin-love (last accessed 1st June 2015).

Low, S. and Smith, N. (2006). Preface. In. S. Low and N. Smith (Eds.) *The Politics of Public Space*. New York: Routledge, p.vii.

Lowes, M. (2002). *Indy Dreams and Urban Nightmares: Speed Merchants, Spectacle, and the Struggle over Public Space in the World-Class City*. Toronto: University of Toronto Press.

Lowes, M. (2004). Neoliberal power politics and the controversial siting of the Australian Grand Prix motorsport event in an urban park. *Loisir et Société/Society and Leisure*, 27(1), pp. 69–88.

Lydall, R. (2013). Riders on the lawn. Showjumpers to compete in William and Kate's Garden. *Evening Standard*, 8th February 2013, p. 3.

Lynch, K. (1972). *What Time is this Place?* Cambridge, MA: MIT Press.

Madden, D. (2010). Revisiting the end of public space: assembling the public in an urban park. *City & Community*, 9(2), pp. 187–207.

Maritime Greenwich (2011). Written evidence submitted by Maritime Greenwich World Heritage Site to the Culture, Media and Sport Committee Report: Funding of the arts and heritage. Available at: http://www.publications.parliament.uk/pa/cm201011/cmselect/ cmcumeds/464/464vw98.htm (last accessed 1st June 2015).

Marling, G., Jensen, O. and Kiib, H. (2009). The experience city: planning of hybrid cultural projects. *European Planning Studies*, 17(6), pp. 863–885.

Marrero-Guillermon, I. (2012). Olympic state of exception. In H. Powell and I. Marrero-Guillermon (Eds.) *The Art of Dissent: Adventures in London's Olympic State*. London: Marshgate Press. pp. 20–29.

Martin, I. (2014). This 'urban vibrancy' is really social cleansing. *The Guardian (online)*, 19th January 2014. Available at: http://www.theguardian.com/commentisfree/2014/ jan/19/urban-vibrancy-social-cleansing-gentrification?commentpage=1 (last accessed 1st June 2015).

Massey, D. (2005). *For Space*. London: Sage.

Massey, N. (2011). Plans for equestrian centre in Shooters Hill, Plumstead, likened to horse concentration camp. *News Shopper*, 14th September 2011. Available at: http:// www.newsshopper.co.uk/news/9248409.Plans_for_equestrian_centre_likened_to__ horse_concentration_camp_/ (last accessed 1st June 2015).

McKinnie, M. (2007). *City Stages: Theatre and Urban Space in a Global City*. Toronto: University of Toronto Press.

McLaren, R. (2012). 2012 London Olympics: dispute resolution in a commercial context. *Business Law International*, 13(2), pp. 123–142.

McManus, P. (2004). Writing the palimpsest, again; Rozelle Bay and the Sydney 2000 Olympic Games. *Urban Policy and Research*, 22(2), pp. 157–167.

McQuire, S. (2010). Rethinking media events: large screens, public space broadcasting and beyond. *New Media & Society*, 12(4), pp. 567–582.

Merx, S. (2011). Public Pie. Performing public space. *Performance Research*, 16(2), pp. 132–137.

Mikunda, C. (2004). *Brand Lands, Hot Spots & Cool Spaces*. London: Kogan Page.

Misener, L. and Mason, D. (2009). Fostering community development through sporting events strategies: An examination of urban regime perceptions. *Journal of Sport Management*, 23(6), pp. 770–794.

Mitchell, D. (2015). Corporate sponsorship is everywhere so why see red over Coca-Cola? *The Guardian (online)*, 25th January 2015. Available at: http://www.theguardian.com/ commentisfree/2015/jan/25/corporate-sponsorship-everywhere-why-red-coca-cola-london-eye (last accessed 1st June 2015).

Montgomery, C. (2013). *Happy City: Transforming Our Lives Through Urban Design*. London: Penguin.

Montgomery, J. (1995). Urban vitality and the culture of cities. *Planning Practice and Research*, 10(2), pp. 101–199.

Montgomery, J. (1998). Making a city: urbanity, vitality and urban design. *Journal of Urban Design*, 3(1), pp. 93–116.

Morgan, M. (2008). What makes a good festival? Understanding the event experience. *Event Management*, 12(2), pp. 81–93.

Moss, S. (2012a). London 2012: contrasting views from equestrian £60m picture postcard. *The Observer*, 29th July 2012, p. 16 .

Moss, S. (2012b). She's the regal one: Phillips makes long awaited Olympic debut. *The Guardian*, 30th July 2012, pp. 4–5.

Moss, S. (2012c). Zara delivers a royal performance to match the hype. *The Guardian*, 31st July 2012, pp. 8–9.

National Fairground Archive (2015). *Historic Fairs*. Available at: http://www.nfa.dept. shef.ac.uk/history/charter/index.html (last accessed 1st June 2015).

Nevarez, J. (2007). Central Park: the aesthetics of urban order. In K. Franck. and Q. Stevens (Eds.) *Loose Space: Possibility and Diversity in Urban Life*. Abingdon: Routledge, pp. 154–170.

Newman, O. (1996). *Creating Defensible Space*. Washington: U.S. Department of Housing and Urban Development.

NOGOE (2012). *NOGOE and its Purpose*. Available at: http://www.webarchive.org.uk/ ukwa/target/23167095/collection/4325386/source/collection (last accessed 1st June 2015).

ONBlackheath (2014a). *Event Management Plan*. 1st September 2014. Available at: https://www.lewisham.gov.uk/inmyarea/neighbourhoods/blackheath/Documents/ OnBlackheath%202014%20Event%20Management%20Plan_ABRIDGED_v2.pdf (last accessed 1st June 2015).

ONBlackheath (2014b). *ONBlackheath*. Available at: http://www.onblackheath.com/ onblackheath-2014/ (last accessed 1st June 2015).

Osborn, G. and Smith, A. (2015). Olympic Brandscapes. *London 2012 a*nd the seeping commercialisation of public space. In G. Poynter and V. Viehoff (Eds.) *The London Olympics and Urban Development: The Mega-Event City*. Abingdon: Routledge.

Owen, K. (2002). The Sydney 2000 Olympics and urban entrepreneurialism: local variations in urban governance. *Australian Geographical Studies*, 40(3), pp. 323–336.

Palmer, D. and Whelan, C. (2007). Policing in the 'communal spaces' of major event venues. *Police Practice and Research*, 8(5), pp. 401–414.

Panja, T. (2014). Brazil World Cup city balks at funding fan area during matches. *Bloomberg*, 17th February 2014. Available at: http://www.bloomberg.com/news/ articles/2014-02-17/brazil-world-cup-city-balks-at-funding-fan-area-during-matches (last accessed 1st June 2015).

Papastergiadis, N., McQuire, S., Gu, X., Barikin, A., Gibson, R., Yue, A., Jung, S., Cmielewski, C., Roh, S. and Jones, M. (2013). Mega Screens for Mega Cities. *Theory, Culture & Society* 30(7/8), pp. 325–341.

Pappalepore, I., Maitland, R., and Smith, A. (2014). Prosuming creative urban areas. Evidence from East London. *Annals of Tourism Research*, 44, pp. 227–240.

Parkrun Greenwich (2015). The course. Available at: http://www.parkrun.org.uk/ greenwich/course/ (last accessed 1st June 2015).

Parr, N. (2013). Letter to *Evening Standard*, 18th September 2013, p. 47.

Pine, B. and Gilmore, J. (1999). *The Experience Economy: Work is Theatre & Every Business a Stage*. Boston, MA: Harvard Business Press.

Pløger, J. (2010). Presence-experiences. On the eventalisation of urban space. *Environment and Planning D: Society and Space*, 28, pp. 848–866.

Polanyi, K. (1946). *Origins of our Time: The Great Transformation*. London: Victor Gollancz.

Potters Fields Park Management Trust (undated). Guide to holding events. Available at: http://pottersfields.co.uk/events/hiring-info/ (last accessed 1st June 2015).

Power, M. (2010). Bogotá's Ciclovia could teach Boris Johnson how to run a car-free capital. *The Guardian (online)*, 16th June 2010. Available at: http://www.theguardian. com/environment/green-living-blog/2010/jun/16/cycling-ethical-living (last accessed 1st June 2015).

Prytherch, D. and Maiques, J. (2009). City profile: Valencia. *Cities*, 26(2), pp. 103–115.

Pugalis, L. (2009). The culture and economics of urban public space design: public and professional perceptions. *Urban Design International*, 14(4), pp. 215–230.

Pyyhtinen, O. (2007). Event dynamics: the eventalization of society in the sociology of Georg Simmel. *Distinktion: Scandinavian Journal of Social Theory*, 8(2), pp. 111–132.

Quinn, B. (2005). Arts festivals and the city. *Urban Studies*, 42(5–6), pp. 927–943.

Raffestin, C. (2012). Space, territory, and territoriality. *Environment and Planning D*, 30(1), pp. 121–141.

Red Bull (2012). Red Bull City Trial, Manchester. Available at: http://www.redbull.co. uk/cs/Satellite/en_UK/Article/Red-Bull-City-Trial-Manchester-021243253365761 (last accessed 1st June 2015).

Reeve, A. and Simmonds, R. (2001). 'Public realm' as theatre: Bicester village and universal city walk. *Urban Design International*, 6(3), pp. 173–190.

Reid, G. (2007). Showcasing Scotland? A case study of the MTV Europe music awards Edinburgh03. *Leisure Studies*, 26(4), pp. 479–494.

Retort Collective (2005). *Afflicted Powers: Capital and Spectacle in a New Age of War*. New York: Verso.

Rhind, N. (1987). *The Heath. A Companion to Blackheath Village & Environs*. London: Burlington Press.

Rhind, N. and Marshall, R. (2013). *Walking the Heath*. London: Blackheath Society.

Richards, G. and Palmer, R. (2010). *Eventful Cities*. Oxford: Elsevier.

Richards, G. and Wilson, J. (2004). The impact of cultural events on city image: Rotterdam, cultural capital of Europe 2001. *Urban Studies*, 41(10), pp. 1931–1951.

Roberts, D. (2010). Durban's future? Rebranding through the production/policing of event-specific spaces at the 2010 World Cup. *Sport in Society*, 13(10), pp. 1486–1497.

Roberts, J. (2001). Spatial governance and working class public spheres: the case of a chartist demonstration at Hyde Park. *Journal of Historical Sociology*, 14(3), pp. 308–336.

Roche, M. (2000). *Mega Events and Modernity: Olympics and Expos in the Growth of Global Culture*. Abingdon: Routledge

Roth, S. and Frank, S. (2000). Festivalization and the media: Weimar, cultural capital of Europe 1999. *International Journal of Cultural Policy*, 6(2), pp. 219–241.

Rowe, D. and Baker, S. A. (2012). The "Fall" of what? FIFA's public viewing areas and their contribution to the quality of public life. *Space and Culture*, 15(4), pp. 395–407.

Royal Borough of Greenwich (2012). *A 2012 Legacy for Royal Greenwich*. London. Greenwich Council.

Royal Borough of Kensington and Chelsea (2013). *Report By Executive Director, Planning and Borough Development APP NO. PP/13/00467 /Q06*, 15th March 2013. Available at: http://www.rbkc.gov.uk/planningandbuildingcontrol.aspx (last accessed 1st June 2015).

Royal Opera House (2015). Woolwich. Available at: http://www.roh.org.uk/about/bp-big-screens/woolwich (last accessed 1st June 2015).

Sack, R. (1986). *Human Territoriality: Its Theory and History*. Cambridge: Cambridge University Press.

Sánchez, F. and Broudehoux, A. (2013). Mega-events and urban regeneration in Rio de Janeiro: planning in a state of emergency. *International Journal of Urban Sustainable Development*, 5(2), pp. 132–153.

Sandel, M. (2012). *What Money Can't Buy: The Moral Limits of Markets*. London: Penguin.

Self, W. (2012). Why I hate London's Trafalgar Square. *The Guardian (online)*, 20th January 2012. Available at: http://www.theguardian.com/travel/2012/jan/20/london-trafalgar-square-will-self (last accessed 1st June 2015).

Sennett, R. (1978). *The Fall of Public Man: On the Social Psychology of Capitalism.* New York: Vintage.

Shaftoe, H. (2008). *Convivial Urban Spaces: Creating Effective Public Places*. London: Earthscan.

Shibli, S. and Coleman, R. (2005). Economic impact and place marketing evaluation: a case study of the World Snooker Championship. *International Journal of Event Management Research*, 1(1), pp. 13–29.

Shipway, R. and Jones, I. (2007). Running away from home: understanding visitor experiences and behaviour at sport tourism events. *International Journal of Tourism Research*, 9(5), pp. 373–383.

Skelton, N. (2013). *Letter to Jonathan Bore (RBKC). 16th January 2013*. Available at: http://www.rbkc.gov.uk/planningandbuildingcontrol.aspx (last accessed 1st June 2015).

Smith, A. (2002). *Reimaging the city: the impact of sport initiatives on tourists' images of urban destinations* (Doctoral dissertation, Sheffield Hallam University/University of Sheffield).

Smith, A. (2005). Conceptualizing city image change: the reimaging of Barcelona. *Tourism Geographies*, 7(4), pp. 398–423.

Smith, A. (2008). Using major events to promote peripheral urban areas: Deptford and the 2007 Tour de France. In J. Ali-Knight et al. (Eds.) *International Perspectives of Festivals and Events*. Oxford: Butterworth-Heinemann/Elsevier, pp. 3–19.

Smith, A. (2012). *Events and Urban Regeneration. The Strategic Use of Events to Revitalise Cities*. Abingdon: Routledge.

Smith, A. (2014). Borrowing public space to stage major events. The Greenwich Park controversy. *Urban Studies* 51(2), pp. 247–263.

Smith, A. and Stevenson, N. (2009). A review of tourism policy for the 2012 Olympic Games. *Cultural Trends*, 18(1), pp. 97–102.

Smith, N. and Low, S. (2006). Introduction: the imperative of public space. In. S. Low and N. Smith (Eds.) *The Politics of Public Space*. New York: Routledge, pp. 1–16.

Sonar (2015). *Sonar International Music Festival*. Available at: http://www.sonarfestival.co.uk/ (last accessed 1st June 2015).

Space Hijackers (2014). *Space Hijackers: Introduction*. Available at: http://www.spacehijackers.org/html/history.html (last accessed 1st June 2015).

Sport (2012). London 2012: the Gold Medallists. Nick Skelton. *Sport*. 7th September 2012, p. 46.

Spracklen, K., Richter, A. and Spracklen, B. (2013). The eventization of leisure and the strange death of alternative Leeds. *City*, 17(2), pp. 164–178.

Stevens, Q. and Shin, H. (2014). Urban festivals and local social space. *Planning Practice and Research*, 29(1), pp. 1–20.

Stevens, Q. (2007). *The Ludic City: Exploring the Potential of Public Spaces*. Abingdon: Routledge.

Sugden, J. (2007). Running Havana: observations on the political economy of sport tourism in Cuba. *Leisure Studies*, 26(2), pp. 235–251.

Tallon, A., Bromley, R., Reynolds, B. and Thomas, C. (2006). Developing leisure and cultural attractions in the regional city centre: a policy perspective. *Environment and Planning C*, 24(3), pp. 351–370.

Taylor, H. (1995). Urban public parks, 1840–1900: design and meaning. *Garden History*, 23(2), pp. 201–221.

TFL (2014). *Future Streets Incubator*. Available at: https://www.tfl.gov.uk/travel-information/improvements-and-projects/future-streets-incubator (last accessed 1st June 2015).

The City of Edinburgh Council (2007). Inspiring Events Strategy. Available at: www.eventsedinburgh.org.uk/files/documents/inspiring-events-strategy.pdf (last accessed 10th September 2015).

The Royal Parks (2013a). *Annual Report and Accounts 2012–2013*. Available at: https://www.gov.uk/government/uploads/system/uploads/attachment_data/file/246635/0372.pdf (last accessed 1st June 2015).

The Royal Parks (2013b). *The Royal Parks Business Plan 2012–13*. Available at: http://www.royalparks.org.uk/about-us/publications/business-plans (last accessed 1st June 2014)

The Royal Parks (2015). *Events Rate Card. January 2015*. Available at: https://www.royalparks.org.uk/__data/.../Events-Rate-Card-2015.pdf (last accessed 1st June 2015).

The Victoria and Albert Museum (2015). *Victorian Circus*. Available at: http://www.vam.ac.uk/content/articles/v/victorian-circus/ (last accessed 1st June 2015).

Thörn, C. (2006). "Dressed for success": Entrepreneurial cities, sports and public space. Linköping Electronic Conference Proceedings, No. 20. Linköping: Linköping University Electronic Press.

Thörn, C. (2011). Soft policies of exclusion: entrepreneurial strategies of ambience and control of public space in Gothenburg, Sweden. *Urban Geography*, 32(7), pp. 989–1008.

Tickle, L. (2011). Music festivals. The sound of escapism. *The Guardian (online)*, 18th July 2011. Available at: http://www.theguardian.com/education/2011/jul/18/music-festivals-research (last accessed 1st June 2015).

TimeOut (2005). *New York*. London: Ebury Press.

Tonkiss, F. (2013). Austerity urbanism and the makeshift city. *City*, 17(3), pp. 312–324.

Tranter, P. and Keefee, T. (2004). Motor racing in Australia's Parliamentary Zone: successful event tourism or the Emperor's new clothes? *Urban Policy and Research*, 22(2), pp. 169–187.

Tranter, P. and Lowes, M. (2009). Life in the fast lane. Environmental, economic and public health outcomes of motorsport spectacles in Australia. *Journal of Sport and Social Issues*, 33(2), pp. 150–168.

Tranter, P. and Warn, J. (2008). Relationships between interest in motor racing and driver attitudes and behaviour amongst mature drivers: an Australian case study. *Accident Analysis & Prevention*, 40(5), pp. 1683–1689.

Van Deusen Jr, R. (2002). Public space design as class warfare: urban design, the right to the city and the production of Clinton Square, Syracuse, NY. *GeoJournal*, 58(2–3), pp. 149–158.

Vanguardia Consulting (2014). *OnBlackheath Music Festival. Noise Assessment and Noise Management Plan. Acoustic Report. August 2014*. Available at: https://www.lewisham.gov.uk/inmyarea/neighbourhoods/blackheath/Documents/Appendix2_NMP_v2%20(2014).pdf (last accessed 1st June 2015).

Wainwright, O. (2015). London's Sky Garden: the more you pay, the worse the view. *The Guardian (online)*, 6th January 2015. Available at: http://www.theguardian.com/artanddesign/architecture-design-blog/2015/jan/06/londons-sky-garden-walkie-talkie-the-more-you-pay-the-worse-the-view (last accessed 1st June 2015).

Waitt, G. (2008). Urban festivals: geographies of hype, helplessness and hope. *Geography Compass*, 2(2), pp. 513–537.

Watson, B. and Ratna, A. (2011). Bollywood in the park: thinking intersectionally about public leisure space. *Leisure/Loisir*, 35(1), pp. 71–86.

Weber-Newth, F. (2014). Landscapes of London 2012: 'adiZones' and the production of (corporate) Olympic space. *Contemporary Social Science*, 9(2), pp. 227–241.

Webster, A. (1902). *Greenwich Park: its History and Associations*. London: Henry Richardson.

Weller, S. (2013). Consuming the city: public fashion festivals and the participatory economies of urban spaces in Melbourne, Australia. *Urban Studies*, 50(14), pp. 2853–2868.

Whose Olympics (2012). *Mapping Your Legacy*. Available at: http://www.whoseolympics.org/ (last accessed 1st June 2015).

Whyte, W. (1988). *City: Rediscovering the Center*. New York: Doubleday.

Williams, B. (2015). Publican Opinion. *TimeOut*, March 10–16. pp. 43–44.

Wilson, K. (1995). Olympians or lemmings? The postmodernist fun run. *Leisure Studies*, 14(3), pp. 174–185.

Wood, D. M. and Abe, K. (2011). The aesthetics of control. Mega events and transformations in Japanese urban order. *Urban Studies*, 48(15), pp. 3241–3257.

Wood, D. M. and Ball, K. (2013). Brandscapes of control? Surveillance, marketing and the co-construction of subjectivity and space in neo-liberal capitalism. *Marketing Theory*, 13(1), pp. 47–67.

Zimbalist, A. (2015). *Circus Maximus: The Economic Gamble Behind Hosting the Olympics and the World Cup*. Washington, DC: Brookings Institution Press.

Žižek, S. (2014). *Event: Philosophy in Transit*. London: Penguin.

Zukin, S. (1995). *The Cultures of Cities*. Oxford: Blackwell.

Index

eBooks
from Taylor & Francis

Helping you to choose the right eBooks for your Library

Add to your library's digital collection today with Taylor & Francis eBooks. We have over 50,000 eBooks in the Humanities, Social Sciences, Behavioural Sciences, Built Environment and Law, from leading imprints, including Routledge, Focal Press and Psychology Press.

Choose from a range of subject packages or create your own!

Benefits for you
- Free MARC records
- COUNTER-compliant usage statistics
- Flexible purchase and pricing options
- All titles DRM-free.

Benefits for your user
- Off-site, anytime access via Athens or referring URL
- Print or copy pages or chapters
- Full content search
- Bookmark, highlight and annotate text
- Access to thousands of pages of quality research at the click of a button.

Free Trials Available
We offer free trials to qualifying academic, corporate and government customers.

eCollections

Choose from over 30 subject eCollections, including:

Archaeology	Language Learning
Architecture	Law
Asian Studies	Literature
Business & Management	Media & Communication
Classical Studies	Middle East Studies
Construction	Music
Creative & Media Arts	Philosophy
Criminology & Criminal Justice	Planning
Economics	Politics
Education	Psychology & Mental Health
Energy	Religion
Engineering	Security
English Language & Linguistics	Social Work
Environment & Sustainability	Sociology
Geography	Sport
Health Studies	Theatre & Performance
History	Tourism, Hospitality & Events

For more information, pricing enquiries or to order a free trial, please contact your local sales team:
www.tandfebooks.com/page/sales

www.tandfebooks.com